The Psychology of
Women at Work

The Psychology of Women at Work

Challenges and Solutions for Our Female Workforce

Volume 2
Obstacles and the
Identity Juggle

Edited by
MICHELE A. PALUDI

Praeger Perspectives

Women's Psychology

Westport, Connecticut
London

Library of Congress Cataloging-in-Publication Data

The psychology of women at work : challenges and solutions for our female workforce / edited by Michele A. Paludi
    p. cm. — (Women's psychology, ISSN 1931-0021)
    Includes bibliographical references and index.
    ISBN 978-0-275-99677-2 ((set) : alk. paper) — ISBN 978-0-275-99679-6 ((vol. 1) : alk. paper) — ISBN 978-0-275-99681-9 ((vol. 2) : alk. paper) —
ISBN 978-0-275-99683-3 ((vol. 3) : alk. paper)
    1. Women—Employment—Psychological aspects. 2. Work and family.
3. Women—Job stress. 4. Women—Psychology. I. Paludi, Michele Antoinette.
    HD6053.P75 2008
    158.7082—dc22   2008004119

British Library Cataloguing in Publication Data is available.

Library of Congress Catalog Card Number: 2008004119
ISBN: 978-0-275-99677-2 (set)
        978-0-275-99679-6 (vol. 1)
        978-0-275-99681-9 (vol. 2)
        978-0-275-99683-3 (vol. 3)
ISSN: 1931-0021

First published in 2008

Praeger Publishers, 88 Post Road West, Westport, CT 06881
An imprint of Greenwood Publishing Group, Inc.
www.praeger.com

Printed in the United States of America

∞™

The paper used in this book complies with the Permanent Paper Standard issued by the National Information Standards Organization (Z39.48–1984).

10 9 8 7 6 5 4 3 2 1

For Antoinette and Michael Paludi, who encouraged me
to define what women's work is for myself

Contents

Acknowledgments

I thank Debbie Carvalko at Praeger for her encouragement and support throughout the writing of these three volumes. It is an honor to work with her. I also thank the graduate students in my human resources classes for their comments about the changing nature of work for women. I am confident that they will make a difference in the lives of the next generation of women employees and their families. I am grateful to Carrie Turco and Sharon Butler for their comments on earlier versions of the introduction.

The following family, friends, and colleagues have been invaluable during the preparation of these three volumes. Thank you to Rosalie Paludi, Lucille Paludi, Presha Neidermeyer, and Paula Lundberg Love. I especially acknowledge Carmen Paludi, Jr., for his friendship and sage advice. Together we continue to make the dreams of our grandparents on Weaver Street into realities.

Finally, I wish to thank William Norton Dember, my advisor and mentor in graduate school, who, like my parents, told me to seek my own career path and be tough-minded and kindhearted at the same time. I started drafting these books after I last saw Bill in May 2006, when we discussed my career since graduate school (it had been 26 years since I received my PhD). He reminded me that I came to work with him as a graduate student at the University of Cincinnati because I was interested in the psychology of women's work and achievement motivation. Moreover, he inquired why I hadn't written or edited a book in that field during the course of my career. These three volumes are in response to Bill's question. Bill died in September 2006. These books are in tribute to him as a psychologist, mentor, professor, colleague, and friend.

Introduction

Because I am a woman, I must make unusual efforts to succeed.
If I fail, no one will say, "She doesn't have what it takes."
They will say, "Women don't have what it takes."

—Clare Boothe Luce

Clare Boothe Luce's sentiment was once again highlighted during the preparation of these three volumes of *The Psychology of Women at Work: Challenges and Solutions for Our Female Workforce*, when Senator Hillary Rodham Clinton announced her candidacy for the presidency of the United States. Throughout the initial part of Senator Clinton's candidacy, comments about a woman president received media attention. Polls from CNN.com (July 24, 2007) and YouTube (January 21, 2007; March 5, 2007) reported the following quotations:

> "Hillary Clinton needs to wear a dress or skirt now and then. Her always making public appearances in pants gives a sense she is trying to 'fit in' with the boys, which is never going to be the case."
>
> "Hillary is cute. Those are her qualifications for prez."
>
> "It'll be nice to have a woman president but you know white America won't let her."
>
> "Women, above all, should reject hillary. Missus clinton is the biggest misogynist of all."
>
> "hillary clinton running must be a joke! A woman for president! Ha! Now that['])s a joke."

Elizabeth Edwards, whose husband, John Edwards, also declared his candidacy for president, joined the chorus in criticizing Hillary Clinton. Elizabeth Edwards stated the following:

> She [Hillary Clinton] and I are from the same generation. We both went to law school and married other lawyers, but after that we made other

choices. I think my choices have made me happier. I think I'm more joy-
ful than she is.

Elizabeth Edwards also stated, "Sometimes you feel you have to
behave as a man and not talk about women's issues."

Mrs. Edwards's comments prompted a comparison of the two
women—one perceived as "feminine" and the other "masculine."
Responses from a CNN.com poll (July 24, 2007) included the following:
"It would be awesome if Hillary was more like Elizabeth. But Hillary
lacks the compassion and realness Elizabeth possesses."

Tucker Carlson, host of MSNBC's *Tucker*, asked a guest, "I mean,
let's take this critique [by Elizabeth Edwards] seriously—is Hillary
Clinton too manly to be president?"

This is in direct contrast to the view that many people had of Con-
gresswoman Patricia Schroeder, who, when she dropped out of running for U.S. president in 1984, cried. This raised the question of
whether a woman was too "emotional" to be president. Schroeder
(1998) wrote, "Crying is almost a ritual that male politicians must do
to prove they are compassionate, but women are supposed to wear
iron britches."

In 1870, when Victoria Woodhull, the first woman to run for president, declared her candidacy, the *New York Herald* commented: "She is
rather in advance of her time. The public mind is not yet educated to the
pitch of universal woman's [sic] rights" ("Woman's Idea of Government," 1870, p. 6). In 2008 we are still hearing arguments that the United
States is not ready for a woman president—a view expressed not only to
Victoria Woodhull but also to other women candidates for president
before Hillary Clinton: Margaret Chase Smith (in 1964), Shirley Chisolm
(in 1972), Patricia Schroeder (in 1984), Elizabeth Dole (in 2000), and Carolyn Moseley Braun (in 2004). Similar comments were directed toward
Geraldine Ferraro, the first woman to be placed on a national presidential ticket (as Walter Mondale's vice president in 1984). Ferraro was
criticized for wearing short-sleeved dresses while campaigning because
her arms wobbled when she waved (considered not "feminine").

"The emotional, sexual, and psychological stereotyping of females
begins when the doctor says, 'It's a girl,'" Shirley Chisholm once noted.
Gender-role stereotypes about "appropriate" and "inappropriate"
occupations for women still abound. Gender stereotyping is a psychological process that illustrates a structured set of beliefs about the personal attributes of females and males (Ashmore & DelBoca, 1981;
Doyle & Paludi, 1997; Fiske & Stevens, 1993). When asked to describe a
woman, for example, individuals commonly cite "caring," "nurturing,"
"sensitive," and "passive." When asked to name a woman's occupation, individuals cite "nurse," "elementary school teacher," or "social
worker," but not "president of the United States."

I have frequently used the following riddle when students and trainees indicate that they believe that they themselves do not hold gender-role stereotypes about occupations:

> One afternoon, a man and his son go for a drive through the countryside. After an hour or so they get into a terrible car crash. The father dies instantly. The son is taken by a helicopter to the nearest hospital, where a prominent surgeon is called to help save the boy's life. Immediately on entering the operating room and looking at the boy, the surgeon exclaims, "I can't possibly operate on this boy ... he's my son." How can this be?

The responses I have received to this question have ranged from "The father didn't really die—he sustained only minor injuries and could perform the surgery" to "It was the boy's stepfather who died, and his biological father was the surgeon" to "The boy's adoptive father is the surgeon, and his biological father was with him in the car." Individuals rarely solve this riddle: The surgeon is the boy's mother. When the answer is revealed, these individuals are angry with themselves that they initially stated that they hold no occupational stereotypes for women and men. Individuals also usually "mark" an occupation if they believe that the gender of the person performing the job is atypical. Thus, they say "male nurse," "female physician," "female professor," and "male model" (Paludi, Paludi, & DeFour, 2004). Markings alert listeners or readers to something atypical for the occupation—that it is held by an individual of the sex other than the one with which it is traditionally associated.

An awareness of the contents of occupational stereotypes related to gender begins in the preschool years and is well developed by first grade (Betz, in press; Gottfredson, 1981; Heyman & Legare, 2004; Hughes & Seta, 2003; Sczesny, 2003). Among 6-year-olds, there is research evidence of gender stereotypes in the kinds of occupations that children consider for future employment. Girls commonly choose the occupations of nurse, teacher, or flight attendant. Boys, on the other hand, select police officer, truck driver, architect, or pilot. Children's ranges of occupations are difficult to change once they are set (Betz, in press; Eccles, Wigfield, & Schiefele, 1999).

Levy, Sadovsky, and Troseth (2000) reported that a stereotypic view of the world reinforces many of the common gender-role stereotypes and is a factor in prompting young boys' interest in more than twice as many occupations as that of young girls. Girls thus restrict their occupational aspirations. In addition, girls have a more limited concept than boys do of the career possibilities available to them in math- and computer-related occupations (Burger et al., 2007; Creamer & Laughlin, 2005; Naua, Epperson, & Kahn, 1998; White & White, 2006). Girls focus on occupations that are associated with less status, less satisfaction, and less pay than the occupations considered by boys (Heyman, 2000; Richardson & Sandoval (2007).

Siegel and Reis (1998) reported that although teachers perceived gifted girls as working harder and doing better work than gifted boys, these teachers gave higher grades to the boys. Similarly, Fennema and colleagues (1996) found that teachers perceived that boys are better than gifted girls at math and science. Kerr, Colangelo, and Gaeth (1988) reported that gifted girls are concerned about the negative effects of being gifted on their peers' attitudes toward them. The researchers found that, by the sophomore year of college, most gifted women changed their majors to less intellectually challenging ones. Furthermore, Kerr, Colangelo, and Gaeth found that, by their senior year, these gifted women reduced the level of their career goals.

Brody (1977) reported a decline in self-esteem among girls but not boys in elementary, middle, and high school. For example, 55% of elementary school girls agreed with the following statement: "I am good at a lot of things." This percentage declined to 29% in middle school and 23% in high school. The American Association of University Women (AAUW) (1992) reported that girls who pursued math and science courses and participated in sports maintained their self-esteem from elementary school through high school.

Hall and Sandler (1982) and Allan and Madden (2006) argued that, for girls and women, the educational system is a "chilly climate." Girls and women are discouraged from classroom participation, are sexually harassed by teachers as well as peers, receive a lack of mentoring, and are advised by guidance counselors to lower their expectations for a career (AAUW, 2001; Paludi, Martin, & Paludi, 2007; Richardson & Sandoval, 2007).

As can be seen from this brief review, an important manifestation of gender-role stereotyping is a progressive decrease in girls' and women's career aspirations (Betz, 2007; Farmer, 1997). "The test for whether or not you can hold a job should not be the arrangement of your chromosomes," Bella Abzug once protested.

Lacampagne, Campbell, Herzig, Damarin, and Vogt (2007) reported that gender differences are significant in math-related careers and in career aspirations. For example, of students who took the SAT in 2005, 5% of boys and 1% of girls reported planning to major in computer science. In addition, 10% of boys and 2% of girls were planning to major in engineering (College Board, 2005).

Career education programs continue to be gender-segregated; 90% of women in training programs are in traditionally female fields—for example, office technology and health care (AAUW, 2002). More than 90% of teachers (preschool, elementary, and special education), secretaries, child-care workers, waitress, hairdressers, speech therapists, occupational therapists, dental hygienists, and teacher's aides are women (U.S. Department of Labor, 2003). Betz (in press) reported that women remain underrepresented in technical and scientific fields as well as in managerial positions in education, government, business, and the military.

In a recent study conducted by Catalyst (2007), gender-role stereotyping was linked to women's participation as leaders in business. According to this report, "Gender stereotyping, one of the key barriers to women's advancement in corporate leadership, leaves women with limited, conflicting and often unfavorable options no matter how they choose to lead."

Catalyst found that women constitute more than 50% of management and professional occupations but are only 15.6% of Fortune 500 corporate officers and 14.6% of Fortune 500 board directors. Ilene Lang, president of Catalyst, comments on this as follows:

> When companies fail to acknowledge and address the impact of gender stereotypic bias, they lose out on top female talent.... Ultimately, it's not women's leadership styles that need to change. Only when organizations take action to address the impact of gender stereotyping will they be able to capitalize on the "full deck" of talent.

Women earn less than 20% of the bachelor's degrees in fields such as engineering and physics and less than 10% of the graduate degrees in engineering (Betz, 2007). Women represent only about 14% of engineers, 30% of computer systems analysts, and 25% of computer programmers (U.S. Department of Labor, 2003, 2005). Women account for 8% of physicists and astronomers, 7% of air traffic controllers, 5% of truck drivers, 4% of pilots, 5% of firefighters, and 2% of carpenters and electricians (Betz, 2007).

Equally important, women are paid less for full-time employment than men are; women make only 77% as much as men do when both are employed full-time (U.S. Department of Labor, 2005). This income disparity is greater for Black, Asian, Native American, and Hispanic women than for White women, and for middle-age and older women than for younger women.

"We haven't come a long way," noted Elizabeth Janeway, "we've come a short way. If we hadn't come a short way, no one would be calling us baby."

These realities of the psychology of women at work require an in-depth look at not only the barriers to women's success but also the strategies for empowering women at the individual, organizational, legal, and societal levels. These three volumes provide an overview of the scholarly research on the issues related to women and work.

Volume 1, "Career Liberation, History, and the New Millennium," provides an overview of research on comparisons of men and women in gender-relative (i.e., stereotypical masculine and feminine) communication styles, women as bosses, women as entrepreneurs, personality factors that impact women in the workplace, feminist competing values leadership, career preparation programs in high school, and sexual harassment.

Volume 2, "Obstacles and the Identity Juggle," offers reviews on the double standard for women in the workplace; sexual harassment; women and leadership; the glass ceiling; pay inequalities; incivility toward women in the workplace; women in the sciences, technology, engineering, and math; and the economics of women in the workplace.

Volume 3, "Self, Family, and Social Affects," discusses women and self-esteem, the impact of work on women's physical health, mental health issues for women in the workforce (especially women who have experienced discrimination), women's relationships with male co-workers, and religion and women at work.

In addition to the scholarly reviews of research on the psychology of women at work, I have included women's personal accounts of their career development, especially their experiences in the labor force. A variety of careers is represented in these personal accounts—attorney, human resource manager, college president, chiropractor, and psychologist—as well as students who are pursuing careers. For many years researchers have defined for women what success is, what work is, and what achievement striving should be. These definitions have typically contained masculine biases (Paludi & Fankell-Hauser, 1986). Thus, these personal accounts of women's experiences recognize that women differ in the strength of their striving for achievement and in the roles that elicit their striving, taking into account the effects of family, friends, role models, and partners. It is the goal of these volumes that these personal accounts stimulate additional research, legislation, and advocacy on behalf of female students and employees so that a woman running for the United States presidency will be accepted and encouraged.

REFERENCES

Allan, E., & Madden, M. (2006). Chilly classrooms for female undergraduate students: A question of method? *Journal of Higher Education, 77,* 684–711.

American Association of University Women (AAUW). (1992). *The AAUW report: How schools shortchange girls.* Washington, DC: Author.

American Association of University Women (AAUW). (2001). *Hostile hallways: Bullying, teasing, and sexual harassment in school.* Washington, DC: AAUW Educational Foundation.

American Association of University Women (AAUW). (2002). *Title IX at 30: Report card on gender equity.* Washington, DC: Author.

Ashmore, R., & DelBoca, F. (1981). Conceptual approaches to stereotypes and stereotyping. In D. Hamilton (Ed.), *Cognitive processes in stereotyping and intergroup behavior*. Hillsdale, NJ: Erlbaum.

Betz, N. (2007). Women's career development. In F. L. Denmark & M. Paludi (Eds.), *Psychology of women: A handbook of issues and theories* (2nd ed.). Westport, CT: Greenwood Press, pp. 717–752.

Brody, J. E. (1997, November 4). Girls and puberty: The crisis years. *The New York Times*, p. B8.

Burger, C., Abbott, G., Tobias, S., Koch, J., Vogt, C., & Sosa, T. (2007). Gender equity in science, engineering and technology. In S. Klein (Ed.), *Handbook for achieving gender equity through education* (pp. 255–279). Mahwah, NJ: Erlbaum.

Catalyst. (2007). *The double-bind dilemma for women in leadership: Damned if you do, doomed if you don't*. New York: Author.

College Board. (2005). *2005 College-bound seniors: Total group profile report*. Available online at www.college-board.com

Creamer, E., & Laughlin, A. (2005). Self-authorship and women's career decision making. *Journal of College Student Development, 46*, 13–27.

Doyle, J., & Paludi, M. (1997). *Sex and gender: The human experience*. New York: McGraw-Hill.

Eccles, J., Wigfield, A., & Schiefele, U. (1999). Motivation to succeed. In N. Eisenberg (Ed.), *Handbook of child psychology: Vol. 3. Social, emotional and personality development* (pp. 1017–1095). New York: Wiley.

Farmer, H. S. (1976). What inhibits achievement and career motivation in women? *Counseling Psychologist, 6*, 12–14.

Farmer, H. S. (1997). *Diversity and women's career development*. Thousand Oaks, CA: Sage.

Fennema, E., Carpenter, T. P., Franke, M. L., Levi, L., Jacobs, V., & Empson, S. (1996). A longitudinal study of learning to use children's thinking in mathematics education. *Journal for Research in Mathematics Education, 27*, 403–434.

Fiske, S., & Stevens, L. (1993). What's so special about sex? Gender stereotyping and discrimination. In S. Oskamp & M. Costanzo (Eds.), *Gender issues in contemporary society*. Newbury Park, CA: Sage.

Gottfredson, L. S. (1981). Circumscription and compromise: A development theory of occupational aspirations. *Journal of Counseling Psychology, 28*, 545–579.

Hall, R., & Sandler, B. (1982). *The classroom climate: A chilly one for women*. Washington, DC: Project on the Status and Education of Women.

Heyman, J. (2000). *The widening gap*. New York: Basic Books.

Heyman, G., & Legare, C. (2004). Children's beliefs about gender differences in academic social domains. *Sex Roles, 50*, 227–239.

Hughes, F., & Seta, C. (2003). Gender stereotypes: Children's perceptions of future compensatory behavior following violations of gender roles. *Sex Roles, 49*, 685–691.

Kerr, B., Colangelo, N., & Gaeth, J. (1988). Gifted adolescents' attitudes toward their giftedness. *Gifted Child Quarterly, 32*, 245–247.

Lacampagne, C., Campbell, P., Herzig, A., Damarin, S., & Vogt, C. (2007). Gender equity in mathematics. In S. Klein (Ed.), *Handbook for achieving gender equity through education* (pp. 235–253). Mahwah, NJ: Erlbaum.

Levy, G., Sadovsky, A., & Troseth, G. (2000). Aspects of young children's perceptions of gender-typed occupations. *Sex Roles, 42,* 993–1006.

Naua, M., Epperson, D., & Kahn, J. (1998). A multiple-groups analysis of predictors of higher level career aspirations among women in mathematics, science and engineering majors. *Journal of Counseling Psychology, 45,* 483–496.

Paludi, M., & Fankell-Hauser, J. (1986). An idiographic approach to the study of women's achievement strivings. *Psychology of Women Quarterly, 10,* 89–100.

Paludi, M., Martin, J., & Paludi, C. (2007). Sexual harassment: The hidden gender equity problem. In S. Klein (Ed.), *Handbook for achieving gender equity through education* (pp. 215–229). Mahwah, NJ: Erlbaum.

Paludi, M., Paludi, C., & DeFour, D. (2004). Introduction: *Plus ca change, plus c'est la meme chose* (The more things change, the more they stay the same). In M. Paludi (Ed.), *Praeger guide to the psychology of gender* (pp. xi–xxxi). Westport, CT: Praeger.

Richardson, B., & Sandoval, P. (2007). Impact of education on gender equity in employment and its outcomes. In S. Klein (Ed.), *Handbook for achieving gender equity through education* (pp. 43–58). Mahwah, NJ: Erlbaum.

Schroeder, P. (1998). *24 Years of housework ... and the place is still a mess: My life in politics.* Kansas City, MO: Andrews McMeel.

Sczesny, S. (2003). A closer look beneath the surface: Various facets of the think-manager-think-male stereotype. *Sex Roles, 49,* 353–363.

Siegel, D., & Reis, S. M., (1998). Gender differences in teacher and student perceptions of gifted students' ability and effort. *Gifted Children Quarterly, 42,* 39–47.

U.S. Department of Labor, Bureau of Labor Statistics. (2003). *Facts on women workers.* Washington, DC: U.S. Government Printing Office.

U.S. Department of Labor, Bureau of Labor Statistics. (2005). *Women in the labor force: A data book.* Washington, DC: U.S. Government Printing Office.

White, M., & White, G. (2006). Implicit and explicit occupational gender stereotypes. *Sex Roles, 55,* 259–266.

Woman's idea of government. (1870). *New York Herald,* p. 6.

Chapter 1

Explaining Too Few Women in STEM Careers: A Psychosocial Perspective

Bianca L. Bernstein
Nancy Felipe Russo

The explosion of research on gender differences and similarities (Eagly & Wood, 1999; Hyde, 2005, 2007), stereotyping processes (Steele, 1997; Prentice & Miller, 2006; Steele, Spencer, & Aronson, 2002), and new forms of discrimination in the workplace (Cortina, 2008) provides a context for understanding the work and careers of women in a range of employment sectors and leadership roles. Nine out of 10 women can be expected to work outside the home during their adult lives, but the distribution of women continues to be skewed toward positions of lower pay, responsibility, and prestige (U.S. Department of Labor, 2007). Among the science and health professions, for example, 91% of registered nurses and 83% of social workers are women, compared to 32% of physicians and surgeons, 34% of chemists and materials scientists, 27% of computer scientists, 12% of civil engineers, and 7% of engineering managers (Bureau of Labor Statistics, 2007).

The realities of gender stereotyping, pernicious barriers to advancement, and subtle as well as not-so-subtle forms of discrimination continue to mark the experience of women's work (Benokraitis, 1997; Catalyst, 2007). We argue here that academic careers in science and engineering reflect these forces in particularly stark relief and that understanding academic career outcomes as a result of interactions between intra-psychic and environmental variables can substantially explain the severe underrepresentation of women in these high-stakes, nationally important fields.

Each new national report confirms that the underrepresentation of women in academic science, technology, engineering, and mathematics (STEM) careers persists and that women are still the exception in many science and engineering departments (e.g., Committee on Maximizing the Potential of Women in Academic Science and Engineering [CMPWASE] et al., 2006; National Research Council, 2001; National Science Foundation (NSF), 2004, 2007). The scarcity of women in academic departments of the physical sciences, mathematics, computer sciences, and engineering is more pronounced than in virtually every other employment sector for scientists and engineers or academic discipline for individuals with PhDs.

The underrepresentation of women in academic STEM fields is found at multiple levels and is reflected in who is recruited and hired, gets promoted to higher ranks, receives rewards and recognition, and becomes appointed to academic leadership positions. The picture is particularly dismal at senior levels. Women comprise less than 5% of full professorships at top 50 departments in some fields (math and statistics, electrical, civil, mechanical, and chemical engineering), (Nelson, 2005). In 2000, women held only 2% and 4.6%, respectively, of department head positions in engineering and math and physical science departments at research extensive universities (Niemeier & Gonzales, 2004).

Attributing the small numbers of women in academic science careers to lack of availability of women through prior pipeline leaks is no longer adequate. Recent years have seen steady increases in numbers of women with undergraduate degrees in STEM fields, with some fields like biology now reaching parity (NSF, 2007). Significantly more women are entering graduate programs in science and engineering, although the attrition rates for women from STEM PhD programs are higher than for men in these fields (Anderson-Rowland, Bernstein, & Russo, 2007a, 2007b; Bernstein & Russo, 2007; Danecke, 2005). The proportion of women earning research doctorates among U.S. citizens has hit an historic high (51%) (Hoffer, Hess, Welch, & Williams, 2007). Yet, the ratio of women earning PhDs in a field to the proportion of full professors at top 50 departments is around 4:1 or worse (biology, chemistry, physical science, math and statistics, civil, chemical engineering) (Nelson, 2005). And, there is growing evidence that even women who have the appropriate credentials and experience for entering STEM careers leave their positions significantly more often than men. For example, one study estimated 6-year attrition in the information technology workforce at 40% for women compared to 25% for men (Stephan & Levin, 2005).

Why pay special heed to the persistent phenomenon of male-dominated departments in academic science and engineering? The answers are varied and compelling. From the perspective of national economic, scientific, and security interests, the failure to retain women scientists and create environments that nurture talented women's success represents a serious erosion of intellectual capital. The loss of women from science research careers and the academy has even more impact locally and nationally when each woman is viewed as the embodiment of "knowledge value" (Bozeman, Dietz, & Gaughan, 2001), that is, "a walking set of knowledge, skills, technical know-how and, just as important, a set of sustained network communications, often dense in pattern and international in scope" (Dietz, Chompalov, Bozeman, Lane, & Park, 2000). As Dietz and his colleagues (2000) have suggested, the migration [or loss] of knowledge value produced by the job change [or attrition] of a scientist or engineer has a profound impact on scientific discovery, technological innovation, and economic development. Yet little is known about what leads to the post-appointment attrition of "survivors"—women who have successfully earned PhDs and completed postdocs, overcome obstacles, and obtained academic positions.

When women are scarce in academic science and engineering positions, students are deprived of their vital educational and motivational contributions. There is no more robust finding than the importance of successful women and minority faculty who serve as role models and mentors for future generations of women and minority scientists (Fort, 2005; Nettles & Millett, 2006). Although access to such role models and mentors is important for all academic fields and professions, they are in short supply in STEM fields. Further, gender and ethnic diversity in these fields advances the agendas of innovation, discovery, and use-inspired research well beyond what can be accomplished by people with less diverse perspectives, interests, and worldviews.

From an equity and social justice standpoint, the power and prestige associated with science careers is a fundamental reason to address the underrepresentation of women in STEM fields. As Fox (2001) summarized so aptly, science is a prototype of a professional claim to "authoritative knowledge," defines what billions of world citizens take for granted, and provides the power base for controlling the future. The academic profession occupies a particularly privileged position among careers in that "its members train and allocate the people of all professions" (Hermanowicz, 2003). The profile and quality of the future science and technology workforce depend on the expertise and effectiveness of diverse role models, teachers, and mentors.

There is no dispute, then, about the level of continued underrepresentation of women among STEM faculty, especially at senior levels, or about the importance of the problem in terms of loss of intellectual capital and knowledge value, shortage of vital role models and mentors, and social justice concerns. The numbers of women with degrees in the sciences and engineering are increasing, so the availability of women for faculty positions is now less of an issue (albeit far from resolved) than before. However, we place new attention on the issue of why qualified women do not enter or why they actually leave faculty careers in science and engineering. We ask how we can better explain the meager numbers of eligible women who enter, stay, and are promoted in academic science and engineering careers.

We use a psychosocial perspective to illuminate the complex factors that lead women to continue in or eschew academic life. We propose that the key to understanding career persistence and outcomes from a psychosocial perspective is the individual's perception about fit with the work environment, her success in negotiating disjunctions to improve fit, and the choices she makes as a result. In applying this paradigm, we focus on two drivers of career persistence in science—research productivity and personal satisfaction—and we draw on the literatures of social, vocational, and counseling psychology, as well as the sociology of science.

CAREERS, CHOICE, AND CONSTRUCTION

We begin with the view that careers are individual *constructions* that are dynamic in nature and nonlinear and idiosyncratic in form. Vocational psychologist Mark Savickas (2004) described it this way: "Careers do not unfold; they are constructed as individuals make choices that express their self concepts and substantiate their goals in the social reality of work" (p. 43). From a constructivist perspective, careers represent subjective processes by which individuals derive or impose personal meanings on their memories, experiences, and aspirations.

Career construction theory (Savickas, 2004) is congruent with anthropologist Mary Catherine Bateson's (1989) description of women's lives (and careers) as personal compositions: "Each of us has worked by improvisation, discovering the shape of our creation along the way, rather than pursuing a vision already defined" (p. 1). Bateson observed that the model of a successful life as one of early decision and commitments to education and a certain career path with a single trajectory on an ascending ladder may be particularly outmoded, inappropriate, and even harmful for women (and men) who experience instead discontinuities, disruptions, and new opportunities.

Findings congruent with this view come from a study by the Manhattan-based Center for Worklife Policy (Hewlitt, Luce, Shiller, & Southwell, 2005), The study reported that more than a third of highly qualified women were found to have left their careers for a time and almost 60% took "scenic routes" such as reduced-hour or flexible work options to accommodate child or elder care. The evidence that women in science and engineering actively seek nonlinear pathways is compelling. Using a life-course approach to large datasets, Xie and Shauman (2003) concluded that, for women, "career processes are fluid and dynamic, with exit, entry, and reentry all being real possibilities at any given point in a career" (p. 209).

The realities of women's lives stand in stark contrast to the masculine script that portrays a successful life as linear, singularly purposeful, and narrowly focused on career progression. This script, which continues to dominate the world of the academic sciences, is out of step with the more contemporary conception of a career as a "highway" with many on- and off-ramps (Hewlitt et al., 2005). We view women as active agents who assess their options and make choices in keeping with their values and preferences in navigating, avoiding, or leaving STEM careers. Therefore, understanding the psychosocial processes by which individual women make choices to persist in, exit from, or take a detour from their prior career choice may help us better explain the "brain drain" of talented women from academic environments and scientific fields.

One way to understand the choices people make as they encounter opportunities, surprises, or obstacles is by considering the role of future-oriented notions of the self. Control theory (Carver & Scheier, 1982), for example, predicts that when people experience a discrepancy between their current selves and ideal selves, they are motivated to make changes that reduce the discrepancy. The concept of "possible selves" (Markus & Nurius, 1986) refers to the imagined future selves that "represent individuals' ideas of what they might become, what they would like to become, and what they are afraid of becoming" (p. 954). These cognitive components of hopes, fears, goals, and threats function as incentives and motivators for future behavior and contribute to how the individual evaluates and interprets herself in the present. Understood as personalized representations of important life goals (Ruvolo & Markus, 1992), thinking about a lost possible self is related to regrets and distress (King & Hicks, 2007), and making changes in the present may be linked to avoiding anticipated future regrets.

The construct of possible selves has been studied in the context of identity development and early career choice (career possible selves), particularly as applied to young women considering math and science. In Gottfredson's (1981, 1996, 2004) model of the career development process, his fourth and last step is related to early career choice. This step involves compromise by having to select a career that is a best or "good enough" middle ground between the individual's aspirations and avoidance of feared futures. Scholars are beginning to examine the implications of possible selves for later stages of career development, and what happens when individuals experience external threats (such as getting poor grades or being denied admission to a preferred program) to the viability of their desired career possible selves (e.g., Pizzolato, 2007).

We believe that the construct of possible selves has considerable potential in explaining the changes in direction that women in science and engineering make after they have completed advanced degrees and postdocs, embarked on their careers, and attained faculty positions. When eliciting possible self-narratives, researchers ask participants to imagine their "best possible life" or their "happily ever after" (King & Hicks, 2007). The Cinderella imagery notwithstanding, one can expect that many women might combine elements of brilliant careers and happy families in their visions of their ideal futures. However, as we elaborate below, the large majority of women in science have no role models, mentors, or guidance for crafting this ideal nor confidence that they can accomplish it. Instead, their negative experiences may reinforce their "feared possible selves" that lead to choices that prevent anticipated regrets (King & Hicks, 2007). We propose that a dynamic model of possible selves that illuminates women's constructions of ideal future selves in both career *and* personal realms would provide a useful framework for conceptualizing the choices STEM women make, remake, and alter as they encounter each new challenge in their career paths. We have found no studies in this area but believe it is a promising avenue of investigation.

An agentic view holds that women create lives and careers in a progressive and often nonlinear fashion by deriving meaning, making choices, and taking action in relation to their environments and experiences to achieve their desired life goals. However, as noted above and elaborated below, the large majority of women aspiring to STEM careers find themselves in highly competitive, male-dominated environments, with few female role models, mentors, or guidance for how to craft their ideals for their careers and personal lives, and declining confidence in their ability to attain them.

Thus, women's agency must be considered in the context of the choices that are open to them, that is, in the context of environments in which the choices are made. From an environmental "deficit model" perspective (Sonnert & Holton, 1996), the focus is on the elements of institutional and disciplinary culture that limit women's opportunities and introduce obstacles that reduce success, satisfaction, and retention. These barriers include ambiguous and gendered expectations, inadequate access to resources, discriminatory practices, isolation, and a focus on individualistic achievement. We use research productivity and career satisfaction as organizing concepts for how women make their choices with respect to persisting in academic science environments.

WOMEN AND PRODUCTIVITY IN ACADEMIC SCIENCE AND ENGINEERING ENVIRONMENTS

Lotte Bailyn (2003) links the definitions of academic success in science and engineering fields directly to the gendered nature of these disciplines and institutions: "The academy is anchored in assumptions about competence and success that have led to practices and norms constructed around the life experiences of men, and around a vision of masculinity as the normal, universal requirement of university life" (p. 143). The productivity that counts is *research* productivity. Indicators vary slightly by discipline, but in general, salary, rank, external funding, quantity of publications and patents, and scholarly awards comprise the traditional notions of career success in the academic sciences. Research productivity (primarily measured by number of publications, number of citations, and level of external grant funding) remains a central value in the academic sciences and continues to serve as the primary measuring stick for tenure and advancement.

It is important to note that an individual's products are subjected to the evaluations of others in the academy and do not automatically translate into achievement until they are recognized and valued as appropriate and meeting explicit and often implicit standards. There is a complex web of internal (institutional) and external (professional) gatekeepers whose subjective judgments determine the granting of status and prestige required for advancement in the academic environment. As Fox (2005) has argued, understanding what is recognized as productivity by gatekeepers is critical to the understanding and advancement of women's status in the sciences and engineering because productivity functions both as a partial cause and an effect of that status.

These gatekeepers—including tenured faculty, department chairs, deans, and upper administrators; journal reviewers and editors; study section members and granting agency staff; scientific and professional societies' program and awards committees, among others—often have ambiguous, conflicting, and unrealistic expectations and demands. Sometimes what "counts" as productive is not clear until the tenure decision. For example, teaching may be lauded, and service on committees may result in expressions of strong gratitude and appreciation from one's department chair. A woman may take on a teaching overload in response to departmental requests, serve as a member of numerous graduate student committees, and provide key leadership on a host of committees at the behest of the chair and higher administration. But in STEM disciplines in many universities, although this form of productivity is valuable to the institution, it is generally invisible and unrewarded at evaluation time. All these contributions will not "count" unless she first has a sufficient number of publications in the "right" journals and external funding for her research. Further, there is no one number of publications to shoot for—that depends on what others have done in one's department or peer institutions (the fact that others may have more resources or be less productive in other ways is not relevant to the equation).

The consistently high levels of research productivity that are expected at the top-tier universities require intense mental focus and the dedication of most waking hours to research, publication, and grant proposal preparation. The key activities that are essential for recognition and validation of scientific productivity—gathering data, making presentations at conferences, publishing in peer-reviewed journals, and obtaining grants—are particularly taxing for women who are parents. One study found that almost half of the University of California faculty women surveyed, compared to a quarter of the faculty men, reported that doing field work or field research away from home, attending and giving papers at conferences, and writing and publishing placed stress on their parenting (Mason, Stacy, Goulden, Hoffman, & Frasch, 2005).

The competitive environment combines with ambiguous and shifting standards of evaluation to provide a highly stressful context for pursuing a career, and the degree of stress may be heightened by the particular context in which the faculty member works. All young STEM faculty must learn to assess their environments, identify hidden or implicit weights among evaluation criteria, and weigh and negotiate among multiple expectations and demands at work and at home as they carve out their career paths. The hierarchical nature of science and the gendered nature of these expectations and demands mean that women in STEM fields have a more complex task that has been cited as contributing to the low proportions of women in the sciences (Fox, 2001; Corley, 2005).

The specific context and environment where an individual scientist or engineer works frame the preferences, commitments, and choices she makes. Thus, it is useful to consider differences in the within-science environments where academic scientists and engineers are employed. Hermanowicz (1998, 2003, 2007) has described three types of university physics departments and the corresponding aspirations of their faculty members: *elite* (most highly ranked in the National Research Council studies) where the greatest emphasis is placed on research productivity; *pluralist* (major public universities) where research is important but teaching and service are valued as well; and *communitarian* (usually lower ranked institutions) where teaching and service are emphasized more than research productivity. It should be noted that among science and engineering fields, there is a hierarchy of prestige as well:

> [Physicists] are regarded as having a kind of genius that sets them apart from ordinary mortals. Physics is taken as society's science *par excellence....* Because demigods are part of the direct professional parentage of those who enter the field of physics, the mythification of careers may be especially prominent in this field." (Hermanowicz, 2003, p. 50–51)

Through interviews with physics faculty from each institution type, Hermanowicz (1998, 2003, 2007) traces the meanings they attach to their work, their satisfactions, and their self-doubts. According to Hermanowicz (2003), elite physics faculty aspire to be among the very best nationally and internationally and "appear in regular need of reassurance about their [professional] self-worth" (p. 55) and research standing compared to other eminent scientists. Communitarians emphasize teaching and service and consider their responsiveness to their institutions and local communities to be a shared responsibility of highest importance. They are more likely to frame their concerns within nonwork spheres and may question the value, meaning, and usefulness of research. Scientists in these settings who have been productive in their research express self-doubts about adequate achievement in relation to their scholarly aspirations. Pluralists contribute their unique talents and motivations to a mix of faculty who together meet the teaching loads and research and service needs of the local community and state; their concerns reflect their unique priorities.

The top research universities described by Hermanowicz are fertile grounds for scientific advancement and discovery for top performers according to the traditional models of research productivity. These elite environments provide a rich mix of intellectual stimulation, resources, and recognition for elite faculty (Hermanowicz, 2003) and constitute the targets of aspiration for most people who enter doctoral programs in STEM fields. People who choose science over other careers are more often motivated by passion for the field, their specific focus of interest, and their hopes for making a significant contribution to the field than are people who choose other professional fields, who are more often motivated by extrinsic professional rewards (Stephan, 2007). As Austin (2002) has noted, aspiring faculty begin their graduate programs "with enthusiasm and idealism about engaging in meaningful work" (p. 106) and sustain their hopefulness as they enter the academy (Trower, Austin, & Sorcinelli, 2001). Fort (2005) uses the term "inextinguishable commitment to science" (p. 167) to describe the strong motivation that characterizes women who enter these fields.

As women and men pursue their education and careers, however, they begin to consider multiple priorities in their lives and must consider the extent to which they will balance their continuing passion for science and meaningful work with their commitment to other priorities. For women, especially, this consideration appears to deepen in graduate school (Bernstein & Russo, 2007). It is during this time the perceived incompatibility between meeting the demands of academic culture with fulfilling other life goals (such as family formation or community service) may account for the choice that many talented PhD-level women make to pursue positions outside of research universities.

Women faculty's preferences and patterns of employment are congruent with this conceptualization. Female scientists are significantly less likely than men to set their sights on a position in the top research universities, select their research topics on the basis of scientific curiosity alone, and believe they will be a leading researcher (Corley, 2005). Women comprise less than a quarter of full-time faculty at public research universities but almost half of the total full-time faculty at public two-year colleges. Almost three out of four female faculty members are non-tenure-track instructors (West & Curtis, 2006). Further, the preponderance of academic mothers is concentrated in comprehensive universities and four-year colleges (Mason & Goulden, 2004), career environments that allow a broader range of activities and commitment to both professional and personal roles (Hermanowicz, 2003, 2007).

The interview findings of Hermanowicz, a sociologist of science, warrant multi-method replication as they hold promise for partially explaining why women scientists and engineers may choose to work outside of elite research universities. In these latter environments where the definition of success, tenurability, and advancement is narrowly focused on high levels of research productivity, it is reasonable to expect that multiple-role, multiple-commitment women (and men) would be fewer in number. The stressful overlap of the tenure clock and the biological clock of childbearing exacerbate the conflict of commitments that talented women face in elite universities and fields that have a constricted set of expectations and norms for achievement for tenure and promotion.

SATISFACTION AMONG STEM ACADEMIC WOMEN

Job satisfaction has been studied in an array of occupations and continues to be identified as a key factor in predicting retention and intention to stay in a position (Glomb, Richman, Hulin, Drasgow, Schneider, & Fitzgerald, 1997; Higgins & Thomas, 2001; Sourdif, 2004). The association between women's satisfaction and their persistence in universities has prompted many universities to conduct climate surveys in tracking the mood of faculty and the impact of attempted interventions.

A repeated finding in annual surveys of junior faculty at multiple universities through the Harvard University COACHE program (Collaborative on Academic Careers in Higher Education) is that junior women faculty are significantly less satisfied with their department and institution than men (e.g., Trower & Bleak, 2004). Clearly, tangible rewards and recognition for accomplishments are associated with satisfaction. However, it is important to recognize the central role of collegiality and positive relationships in determining women's satisfaction in their immediate academic environment. In fact, women faculty job satisfaction is related more to their perceptions of relational supports and collegial and inclusive work environments than to the academic resources they receive (Bilimoria, Perry, Liang, Stoller, Higgins, & Taylor, 2006; Cross & Madsen, 1997).

Women place more value on collegiality and positive interactions, opportunities to collaborate and interact professionally with senior colleagues, and female representation on the faculty than do men (Bar-bezat, 1992; Trower & Bleak, 2004). Women are often uncomfortable with the prevailing culture of combative conversational styles, the climate of individualism and fierce competition, the preference for curiosity-driven rather than use-inspired research, and apparent invisibility of and lack of recognition for their contributions. An interesting question for further study is whether men and women differ in the degree to which they perceive these characteristics of science environments as uncomfortable and incompatible with collegiality. One is reminded of the ease with which many men can move from tense and adversarial business negotiations to tee times without difficulty.

People who are severely outnumbered by others in their environments often experience the adverse effects of being tokens (Kanter, 1977). As numerical minorities in physical science, mathematics, computer science, and engineering departments, women may experience a heightened pressure to conform, greater exclusion from group activities and conversations, expectations that they represent "all women," and more discrimination. Effects of tokenism are consistent with the findings of Trower and Bleak (2004) that women reported less satisfaction with their perceived fit in the department along with perceiving more pressure than their male colleagues to conform to colleagues in the department with respect to personal behavior, dress, and political views.

In the natural sciences and engineering, where women faculty are the exception, the women's experience that they don't belong is reinforced at every turn (American Association of University Professors [AAUP], 2000). The concomitant disappointments, along with disruptions and conflicts, reduce job satisfaction (Reybold, 2005), and this association is strongest among those who are motivated primarily by passion and the ideals of science. The consequences of being "the only" extend beyond personal discomfort to actual interference with recognized productivity. Isolated women often lack the interpersonal contacts, which are sources of information, mentors, and role models for learning policies, getting resources and social support, learning of research opportunities, or receiving the feedback necessary to be successful (Smith, 2005).

The forms of exclusion potentially most harmful for women and minority faculty are those that interfere with their acquiring the "tacit knowledge" of success patterns. Women faculty who are not part of the after-hours drinking group, basketball pick-up game, or faculty club buffet line may miss learning about how to get what they deserve. In a context with ambiguous, unarticulated, and shifting standards, knowing the differences between "soft" and "hard" money, what journals are "A list" versus "B list," between power and authority in a hierarchy, and who the real decision maker is with respect to lab space (some examples from Rankin, Nielsen, & Stanley, 2007) can make or break the pre-tenure years. Although there are surely many contributing factors, even at an elite institution such as MIT women scientists were found to have received less salary, space, awards, resources, and response to outside offers, despite professional accomplishments equal to those of their male colleagues (Committee on Women Faculty, 1999).

Among the strategies that have been suggested to combat isolation, exclusion, and their effects, two are especially promising. The first is to deliberately employ and co-locate multiple women in a department or research group through cluster or cohort hiring. There is strong evidence that as the proportion of women begins to be more equitable with men within the organizational unit, in-group/out-group distinctions break down, and the climate, collaboration, and ways of working become more satisfying and encouraging to women, as well as enhance their productivity. The other strategy is facilitating new bonds and communication between women and other individuals and groups that would not otherwise connect. Enhancing these "weak links" as named by Rankin and her associates (2007) can catalyze large and small institutional changes and help compensate for the exclusion and lack of vital information that isolated women experience in their home units. Both strategies can be undertaken if the university commitment to improving conditions for women faculty is strong and there is a cadre of "organizational catalysts" (Sturm, 2007).

BARRIERS GONE UNDERGROUND

For decades now, researchers have catalogued the characteristics of academic and work environments for scientists and engineers that women report as particularly repelling, discouraging, exclusionary, or obstructionist. Some of the more egregious legal, political, and social obstacles that excluded women from laboratories and benches have been reduced. Equal opportunity laws, articulation of discriminatory actions in hiring, prominent court cases, and the rise of strong advocacy groups have served to lower many of the structural barriers to women's entry in STEM programs and positions. It is more difficult now for search committees to invite only white males to an interview, and quid pro quo sexual harassment generally results in punitive actions against the aggressor. Nevertheless, despite the regulatory improvements in the 1970s and 1980s, later studies found almost three out of every four career women with PhDs in science or engineering reported that they experienced discrimination (Holton & Sonnert, 1996; Sonnert, 1995), and women, significantly more often than men, have continued to report being discriminated against on the basis of gender (Corley, 2005). The finding that female natural scientists report more sexual harassment and a more negative department climate than social scientists (Settles, Cortina, Malley, & Stewart, 2006) is partially expected because of differences in the proportions of women in each but should also provide caution in generalizing across all scientific fields.

In a study of tenure-track and tenured faculty women in the natural sciences, engineering, and social sciences at one university, women scientists who reported more sexual harassment and gender discrimination experiences also reported having less influence in their departments and being less satisfied with their jobs (Settles et al., 2006). In contrast, women science faculty who perceived their departments as having a positive climate (more collaboration and cooperation, respect, and collegiality) reported higher levels of job satisfaction and productivity; effective leadership by the chairperson was positively related to felt influence (Settles et al.).

The more egregious forms of discrimination that were visible and could be documented have now been replaced by more subtle and hidden forms of marginalization and discouragement of women in the sciences rooted in gendered stereotypes, perceptions, and assumptions (Rapoport, Bailyn, Fletcher, & Pruitt, 2002). The 2005 *Beyond Bias and Barriers* report calls attention to the elements of the current "meritocracy" that are particularly deleterious to women: The abilities and commitment of all women in science and engineering are continuously challenged, and while assertiveness and single-mindedness are valued and celebrated, women are penalized for demonstrating them. Subtle, unconscious, and unintentional discrimination interferes with women's success and promotion in science (Committee on Women Faculty, 1999).

For women faculty in STEM, the under-the-radar discrimination manifests itself as an extreme form of the "damned if you do, doomed if you don't" double-bind for women (Catalyst, 2007). Being viewed as having "feminine" traits (e.g., being gentle, warm, and helpful) can lead to perceptions of incompetence and devaluation (Cuddy, Fiske, & Glick, 2004); having "masculine" traits (e.g., being forceful and assertive; having a strong personality and leadership ability) can lead to disliking and sanctions, with "uppity women" at even higher risk for sexual harassment (Berdahl, 2007).

The often imperceptible stereotyping that results in exclusion from influential committees, lack of feedback or advice from colleagues, and the necessity for self-promotion, can be the most harmful because it is difficult to document and challenge. Virginia Valian (1998, 2000, 2007) has catalogued how gender schema are enacted, including identifying men as rising stars more often than women, early grooming and advocacy for the careers of men, and assigning more weight to the accomplishments and productions of men. She also describes how male decision makers make selections according to similarity to self. A large body of literature has documented a broad impact of this in-group favoritism effect: People give their in-group members more positive evaluations, make more positive attributions for their behavior, give them more rewards, and find them more persuasive compared to out-group members (Brewer & Brown, 1998). As Faye Crosby (2007) has pointed out, "Often, those in positions of power (men) may not be as interested in keeping women out of good jobs as they are in bringing other men into their in-group. Discrimination in favor of men has the same effect as discrimination against women" (p. 50).

It is important to note that benevolent stereotyping (where, for example, colleagues or a department chair assumes that a mother does not want to attend conferences) interferes with women's career advancement as well. Similarly, professional neglect is not benign—the "null environment" (Betz, 1989; Freeman, 1979), which neither encourages nor discourages women, contributes to their sense of invisibility and not mattering. As Nancy Betz (1989) has argued, a null educational environment "is inherently discriminatory against women because external societal environments are different for men and women with respect to the amount of encouragement they receive for nontraditional career aspirations and achievements" (p. 136).

The complex relationship between gender stereotyping and productivity is illustrated in a series of studies by Vescio and her colleagues (Vescio, Gervais, Snyder, & Hoover, 2005) that found powerful men who stereotype women in a weakness-focused manner (i.e., women are illogical and weak) in a male-dominated domain give fewer valued resources and more praise to subordinate women. That is, women mentored by men holding stronger gender stereotypes were likely to receive more verbal praise, but fewer professional resources and opportunities, than their male peers. Their findings revealed how the same event may lead to different responses on the part of women and men. When given devalued positions by a supervisor, both men and women felt angry, but this anger predicted better performance among men and lower performance among women. Thus, the argument "there's no discrimination—he's equally mean to everyone" rests on an inadequate analysis of the gendered effects of negative feedback (Steinberg, True, & Russo, in press).

Perceptions of exclusion are strongly linked with lower job satisfaction and well-being for women and minorities (Barak & Levin, 2002). The effects may be cumulative; that is, early discouragement among junior women faculty who experience social isolation and embedded hints that they do not belong may set the stage for subsequent disillusionment and intentions to leave (Boice, 1993; Xie & Shauman, 2003). At MIT, it was tenured women in the sciences who were more likely to feel marginalized and excluded from significant roles. Perceptions of marginalization increased as women progressed through their careers at MIT, and this pattern repeated itself in successive generations of women faculty (Committee on Women Faculty, 1999).

A tendency not to perceive gender injustice in society as personally relevant contributes to the slow pace of change toward gender equality in the workplace. The "denial of personal disadvantage" (Crosby, Pufall, Snyder, O'Connell, & Whalen, 1989) refers to the failure to recognize that we as individuals face the same employment disadvantages as women in general. Crosby and her colleagues (1989) summarize emotional and cognitive mechanisms that help account for the denial of women's disadvantage on the part of both women and men, including self-protective cognitions. Because people have difficulty in perceiving discrimination when data are presented on a case-by-case basis, it is important to identify with an oppressed group for discrimination to be perceived. Crosby and colleagues (1989) underscore that all people, whether gender-biased or not, have difficulty in perceiving gender bias in individual cases and that for both men and women information is needed in aggregate form before discriminatory patterns can be revealed. They conclude that the need for social reform should not be measured by how concerned people are with their personal situation— people do not have a well-developed sense of their personal disadvantage. Their advice: "Do not trust your own impressions any more than you trust the impressions of the women in your organization. Women may be motivated to deny their own disadvantage; but nobody ... should trust conclusions based on unaggregated figures. Only by bringing all the data together can one see patterns" (p. 97). The subtlety of these patterns, the confidential personnel practices of universities, and the diffusion of authority and oversight increase the likelihood that they will neither be detected as gendered nor targeted for action.

Even when women and their employers recognize that they may be disadvantaged in some way, it is altogether too easy to ascribe the differences to special circumstances rather than to discrimination (Crosby, 1984). The experience of being "the only" in an environment, such as being the only woman and the only Latina in a department, makes it all the more difficult to name the etiologies of some difficulties. The accumulation of slight disadvantages and micro-aggressions (Bernstein & Russo, 2007; National Academies, 2006; Sonnert & Holton, 1995; Valian, 1998) for an individual woman, especially in environments with masculine norms and where women are outnumbered by men, erodes women's career satisfaction and impedes their productivity and advancement.

Psychologists are tracing the intrapersonal mechanisms by which subtle sexism and unconscious bias interfere with productivity. The seminal research on stereotype threat by Claude Steele and colleagues (Steele, 1997; Steele & Aronson, 1995; Steele, Spencer, & Aronson, 2002) has led to recognition that situational cues (such as a colleague's portraying a task as a measure of ability rather than skills that can be learned or referring to gender) can trigger women's concerns about being judged via gender stereotypes; these worries in turn can negatively affect their performance in math and science and lower self-confidence (Johns, Schmader, & Martens, 2005).

Recent research on identity threat (Murphy, Steele, & Gross, 2007) suggests that one response of women and minorities to situational cues that trigger discomfort (e.g., a woman being outnumbered by men in a group) is allocation of more attention toward those cues. This redirection of attention and focus away from the tasks at hand may lead to a diminution of performance. In a study (Salvatore & Shelton, 2007) of responses by Black volunteers to subtle racism (unfair but ambiguous hiring decisions; e.g., candidate with superior resume rejected without reason) versus overt racism (reason for hiring decision is that the candidate belonged to too many minority organizations), Black participants performed more poorly on a cognitive task under the ambiguous condition when compared with the overt condition. The authors speculate that Black participants were applying their cognitive resources to diagnose the vague unfairness and that this cognitive burden interfered with a competing task. They reason that it is the constant and subtle micro-aggressions that actually interfere most with the cognitive processing necessary for optimum task performance, rather than the overt acts of discrimination that are more easily recognized and cognitively processed.

Discouragement and discrimination, whether acute or accumulated, are particularly damaging for women who feel they have no good alternatives to withdrawing or leaving the institution altogether. The case of the women scientists at MIT is notable for the risk they took and exemplary in illustrating the power of mounting a group effort: Driven all their professional lives to achieve at the highest possible level, to many it seemed they were putting a lifetime of hard work and good behavior at risk. They feared being seen as radical troublemakers, as complainers. But the feeling of an injustice, the anger that accumulates from this recognition, and the strong desire to change things for themselves and for future generations of women propelled them forward (Committee on Faculty Women, 1999, p. 7).

WOMEN ... AND MEN ... WANT MORE

There is growing evidence that the majority of both men and women in the new and emerging generations of professionals seek more balanced lives, place heavier emphasis than ever before on their personal lives outside of work and careers, and wish to apply their talents and abilities through multiple roles (Barnett & Hyde, 2001; Gilbert, 2002). In a study of career changers among "30-something" young adults (Wise & Millward, 2005), both men and women, with or without children, valued employment that allowed time for personal lives. With regard to the academic setting, a recent survey of 7,000 early career faculty were found to report even more dissatisfaction than the previous year's cohort with the imbalance between their professional and personal time; women continued to express significantly more dissatisfaction than men with respect to work/life balance and institutional support for having and raising children (COACHE, 2007). In a study of over 1,500 women in the chemical industry (Fassinger & Giordan, 2007), 63% reported balancing work and family responsibilities among the top two work-related stressors.

Hewlitt and Luce describes a rise in the phenomenon of "extreme working" (2006), where excessively demanding careers exact a high toll from their members. In a series of studies by the Center for Work-Life Policy (Hewlitt & Luce, 2006), most women were found to decide against "extreme" jobs, and among the 20% of extreme job holders who are women, 80% of them do not want to work with the pressure or long hours more than a year, compared with 58% of the men.

Research-intensive universities—particularly in the sciences and engineering as described by Hermanowicz (1998, 2003, 2007)—represent the epitome of extreme working organizations and what Coser and Coser (1974) termed "greedy institutions." In contrast to the increased desire for more balance in work and other life roles on the part of new and aspiring faculty members, the expectations of faculty in research universities are increasing. Research universities, in a perpetual cycle of efforts to strengthen rankings and external support, set ever higher standards for judging the faculty for excellence in multiple academic roles. While perhaps effective in boosting effort in the short run, over time stressed and exhausted individuals experience diminished creativity and become at high risk for burning out. Cathy Trower (2007) of COACHE concludes from hundreds of interviews with talented junior faculty that the anxiety of junior faculty goes way beyond the usual worry about establishing their research programs; rather, the stress derives more from "the lack of resources, time, and support to be an excellent scholar *and* an outstanding teacher *and* a stellar colleague and campus citizen, all at once" (COACHE, 2007).

But the expectation for faculty to excel at multiple roles within the academy is only a part of the picture. There is a strong albeit sometimes implicit expectation that faculty give their work roles their highest priority. There is little tolerance for decrements in research productivity or performance that result from the responsibilities that stem from competing professional or personal roles. Bailyn (2006) notes that the lack of clear boundaries between work and family in academic lives adds to the ease with which work crowds out family:

> The academic career ... is paradoxical. Despite its advantages of independence and flexibility, it is psychologically difficult. The lack of ability

to limit work, the tendency to compare oneself primarily to the exceptional giants in one's field, and the high incidence of overload make it particularly difficult for academics to find a satisfactory integration of work with private life.... It is the unbounded nature of the academic career that is the heart of the problem. (p. 61)

Commitments to work and family are viewed as essential for healthy adult development (Erikson, 1968; Levinson, 1978; Vaillant, 1977). However, it is still more acceptable for men to assert these commitments without assuming their concomitant responsibilities, such as routine tasks of domestic work, chauffeuring children to after-school programs, and making medical visits (Perna, 2005).

Faculty men are more likely than faculty women to have spouses who pick up the responsibilities for house, home, and family. The finding that two of every three University of California faculty mothers compared with half of University of California faculty fathers reported slowing down their careers for parenting (Mason et al., 2005), likely reflects this imbalance of responsibilities. The differential in the pace of career progression may reflect the fact that women scientists may be more likely than men scientists to have a spouse with a demanding career that leaves little time for sharing domestic responsibilities. For example, one study found that in physics, more than two-thirds of women physicists had spouses who were scientists compared to 17% of men physicists (MacNeil & Sher, 1999). As Hewlitt stated poignantly (2007), "Only cosseted white males—many of whom have at-home wives and come from upper middle class backgrounds—can easily conjure up the 65-hour work-weeks that are increasingly needed for advancement in today's competitive professional environments."

Gendered stereotypes related to motherhood magnify the detrimental effects of allocating time to family responsibilities for women. As one blogger put it, "The brilliant young mother appears stressed out and underproductive. The brilliant young father, no longer the obnoxious young nerd he might have seemed when he was hired, now seems all the more human and charming for his (discrete) family responsibilities" (Stansell, 2007). When working women become mothers, they become perceived as more warm but less competent (a trade-off not experienced by men), which puts them at a disadvantage in fields where competence is highly valued (Cuddy et al., 2004). Indeed, discrimination against working mothers, characterized as the "maternal wall," has emerged as the new frontier in the struggle for women's equality in employment (Biernat, Crosby, & Williams, 2004; Steinberg et al., in press).

For some women scientists, the answer is to avoid having children. Two out of three faculty women in research extensive universities do not become mothers (Mason & Goulden, 2004). Sonnert and Holton

(1995) found that among married women scientists who decided against having children, three out of four reported career considerations compared with fewer than half of the men.

Academic careers in science and engineering require more time devoted to work than positions in industry and government (Hoffer & Grigorian, 2005). Women in academic careers, particularly those with children at home, are the most busy, spending more than 100 hours per week in professional, caregiving, and household responsibilities, while faculty without children at home report spending 85 hours a week on these responsibilities (Mason et al., 2005). As Bernstein and Russo (2007) calculated it, "If Mason's faculty women sleep eight hours per night, they are left with an average of one hour and forty minutes per day to choose among exercise, spending time with partners or friends, leisure reading, or other worthy pursuits" (p. 106).

Too many conflicting demands on one's time raises stress levels and can undermine health and productivity. Time restrictions are stressful, but the psychological impact of multiple role demands can be more fully understood by considering the centrality of the respective roles that are presenting conflicts of commitment for the individual. One woman, quoted by Handelsman, Cantor, Carnes, Denton, Fine, Grosz, Hinshaw, Marrett, Rosser, Shalala, and Sheridan (2005), described the conflict well:

> I feel like my career is a constant gamble to strike the right balance between three things: (i) how much I must commit myself to my career in order to get tenured/remain a competitive scientist/earn enough clinical revenue; (ii) how much time and effort I give to my husband/household to stay married; and (iii) how much time and effort I give to my children to guide their growth and development.

There is considerable evidence that married women's participation rates in science and engineering are becoming increasingly similar to men's (Goldin, 2004). However, the evidence is also compelling that having children, particularly within 5 years after the award of a doctorate, hampers professional advancement for women faculty (Mason & Goulden, 2004). Faculty who are mothers and assume child-care responsibilities reduce their involvement with some productivity-related activities such as having lunch with colleagues, putting in extra hours, and going to conferences (Preston, 2004). In one study, tenure-track faculty men with children at home reported spending 41% more time on research than did the tenure-track faculty women with children in the home. The importance of time management is highlighted in interviews with scientists who are also mothers (Cole & Zuckerman, 1987): These women make especially "disciplined allocations" of time and attention to work and children, but little else.

Interventions that have been found to be effective in reducing the conflicts between work and family responsibilities in other employment sectors, such as introducing shorter work schedules (Anttila, Natti, & Vaisanen, 2005), are incompatible with the norms of science and research universities. Although COACHE surveys indicate that women and men view institutional policies and practices to support research and career success as important, opinions on policy effectiveness vary. Among women and men who viewed policies as "fairly important," those related to assistance in obtaining grants and child care were rated as least effective (COACHE, 2007).

Largely through the efforts of teams working with the support of the NSF ADVANCE program, significant progress has been made in crafting an array of benefits that constitute "family-friendly policies" at universities. These benefits have included automatic tenure-clock extensions for new parents, part-time and modified duties options for pretenure faculty with special family or personal health circumstances, dual career hiring assistance, and paid leaves for graduate students for pregnancy and childbirth.

PROMISING PATHWAYS

Recent developments to improve the representation of women in the sciences and engineering have focused largely on flexible work schedules, improved mentoring, and management training to address bias and equity in hiring and evaluation. There is much to be learned about other best practices from the strategic initiatives launched at the 28 institutions that have received major NSF ADVANCE grants for Institutional Transformation projects in these areas.

A significant shift is occurring in science away from the celebration of the individual genius; teamwork now characterizes much of science (Wuchty, Jones, & Uzzi, 2007). Research collaborations among scientists around a theme of interest, as opposed to the more traditional grouping by narrow topic, discipline, or methodology, are characteristic of the large interdisciplinary and multidisciplinary research ventures now being supported by federal sponsors. These projects operate through research centers, training programs like IGERTs (NSF grants for Integrative Graduate Education and Research Traineeships), and the multi-institutional projects geared toward "big science" questions. In many science and engineering fields, about 4 in 10 faculty members are affiliated with research centers in universities (Corley & Gaughan, 2005).

Some scholars have suggested that these types of research groups are more likely to attract and favor women, but there has been little empirical attention directed at verifying or refuting this supposition (Rhoten & Pfirman, 2007). Following the psychosocial model proposed here that a person's perception of fit between one's own preferences and commitments with the environment is related to satisfaction, the critical difference for women might be in the configuration, membership, and organization of the research group rather than by the research content. For example, research groups, whether in centers or in departments, that are characterized by more collaborative, collegial, and less individualistically competitive interactions may be more successful in attracting and retaining women.

Some evidence is available that this may be the case. For example, Etzkowitz and colleagues identified "relational departments" as those with collegial and cooperative atmospheres that facilitate innovation, networking, and safety for taking risks (Etzkowitz, Kemelgor, & Uzzi, 2000). Their interviews with scientists identified several tenured women faculty who left prestigious, competitive, and hierarchical departments where they struggled for recognition and status to more relational departments to heal the isolation and anxiety they experienced.

There is evidence as well that the presence of and ready access to other women are beneficial. Hiring a critical mass of women from the start helps to inhibit patterns of gender segregation (Smith-Doerr, 2004), especially when the women have similar interests and frequent contact (Etzkowitz, Kemelgor, & Uzzi, 2000). The success of several initiatives that have purposefully recruited clusters of faculty women and students (e.g., at Carleton College in the sciences, Wilson, 2006; and Tufts University in engineering, Abriola & Davies, 2006) point to the power of focused strategies to build a critical mass of women role models, mentors, and colleagues. In our judgment, a valid test of whether women are more attracted to, satisfied with, or benefit from participation in collaborative efforts cannot occur until women have comparable exposure and access to these new forms of working and until the mechanisms of collaborative efforts are better understood.

Researchers have focused recently on describing the conditions that appear to enhance research productivity among women. The potential for women's greater satisfaction with their careers in collaborative environments notwithstanding, the increasing evidence that collaborations, team science, and networked organizations enhance research productivity and advancement for participants suggests that these settings for faculty work might be particularly advantageous for women. Two variables associated with collaborations are viewed as critical for research productivity: access to information and resources, and time for research. The finding that women with young children and women who do not engage in research collaborations with other scientists are less research productive than both men and women who do collaborate (e.g., Kyvik & Teigen, 1996) supports this view. Similarly, the majority of married women in science are married to other scientists; the additional access to mainstream networks of information, funding, and resources for research may contribute to the higher productivity of married scientists over single ones (Astin & Milem, 1997; Creamer, 1999).

Citation frequency, often used as a proxy for research quality and as an indicator of impact of the researcher on a field, is an important element in the gatekeepers' evaluations of a scholar's research productivity. There is evidence that in addition to patents obtained, research that is cited frequently is more likely to have been produced by teams than individual researchers (Wuchty, Jones, & Uzzi, 2007). It is important to note that the statistical association can be explained partially by the phenomenon that more members of a team can disseminate findings more widely and cite a particular publication more often than can a sole author. Similarly, co-authoring a publication with one or more highly regarded or highly cited scholars is likely to result in higher citation rates. Further, as Wuchty and colleagues (2007) have pointed out, it is possible that papers with multiple authors require less time by each contributor than does a solo publication, hence participating in team research allows more articles to be produced with higher citation counts for the body of work.

The persistent differences in research productivity between men and women faculty (Cole & Zuckerman, 1984) continue to reflect the accumulated disadvantages (Cole & Singer, 1991) associated with less integration into professional networks, less access to research assistants, collaborators, professional contacts, and other resources, as well as less time available for research because of caretaking responsibilities that many women experience. It may be that participating in collaborative research teams with prominent scholars is a good strategy to maximize the number of well-placed publications and corresponding citation rates, key indicators for definitions of productivity for tenure and promotion. Viewed in this way, women's access to and inclusion in research groups and the extent to which women are mentored and their contributions are valued will influence their actual productivity and their satisfaction.

The possibility of bias in attribution for credit given the context of gender stereotypes of women as dependent and more suited for "helping" roles must also be considered. Just joining a team is insufficient and may even impede a woman's advancement if patterns of exclusion, marginalization, isolation, and subtle sexism continue unabated, attribution for collaborative efforts are denigrated, and collaboration is viewed as evidence for an inability to develop as an independent researcher.

An alternative way to understand the conditions under which women are productive, recognized, and content with their work lives is to compare organizational environments that are hierarchical with those that are flatter and have more permeable boundaries. Smith-

Doerr's (2004) important work traced the experiences and pathways of women with PhDs in the life sciences who entered academia or bio-tech companies from 1992 to 1996. In Smith-Doerr's analysis, the biotech companies are prototypical examples of "networked organiza-tions," where collaboration, cooperation, teamwork, role flexibility, and open communication are essential to proposing, developing, and delivering the products of the network, not of a single investigator or research lab. In contrast, the levels of hierarchy and bureaucratic rules common in male-dominated organizations increase "the power and salience of informal hidden modes of operation" (Smith-Doerr) that characterize subtle sexism. In a dramatic illustration of the tan-gible benefits to women of more fundible work settings, Smith-Doerr found that female scientists were eight times more likely to be supervisors in networked biotech firms than in hierarchical biotech organizations.

The unit of analysis for performance evaluation remains one of the unchallenged sources of implicit sexism. The salience of individualistic forms of achievement and competition for status in universities is embodied in hiring the one "best" candidate, appointing one "x" and one "y" to a key committee, and comparing faculty by decimal points on teaching evaluations, numbers of publications in the "right" jour-nals, and order of authorship. In a tantalizing suggestion about tenure, for example, Smith-Doerr (2004) asks her reader to "imagine if team tenure were an option, in which three or four academics would be evaluated on their collective productivity" (p. 151). We would invoke a similar challenge in asking, "What if administrators were evaluated not on how many women they hired but rather on the basis of their success in coaching women and minority faculty to tenure and full pro-motion?" In some academic settings, departments may recognize that the research productivity of their research-focused faculty is only possi-ble because of the productive contributions of other faculty that take up the slack in meeting the teaching, mentoring, and service needs of the unit, and wish to recognize and reward all members of the "team." Ironically, upper administration's focus on the individual may lead to overturning recommendations for promotion and tenure based on fail-ure to recognize the full range of productivity of the faculty member— and ultimately undermine the overall productivity of the unit.

Evidence for the advantages that networked organizations in indus-try provide women suggests that new organizational forms may hold significant potential for enhancing the satisfaction and productivity of women faculty. Networks broaden the number of people for interaction and enhance the collaborative connections among them. The elabora-tion of professional networks is a central component of success that NSF ADVANCE institutions name (Stewart, Malley, & LaVaque-Manty, 2007), and one that internal groups and organizations, like a faculty women's association, a local AWIS chapter (Association for Women in Science), or the women faculty in several departments can develop.

CONCLUSIONS

We have argued that the persistently low numbers of women in many science and engineering positions, particularly on the faculty of research universities, can be attributed largely to the clash between what STEM departments and universities offer and demand and what talented women (and more and more junior faculty men) want and deserve. University administrators as well as faculties have been slow to recognize and respond to what even some industry sectors have made central to their planning. Building an organizational culture that promotes and honors both the career satisfaction and personal goals of the individual along with the needs of the institution is becoming a necessary condition for attracting and retaining the most talented workforce. Bailyn (2006) noted that these matters pertain to all professionals now, not just to women:

> The assumption that work roles can engage the exclusive commitment of those who occupy them is no longer tenable. Nor can the difficulties of pursuing complex careers any longer be seen as individual dilemmas, to be solved in isolation. The issues transcend individual boundaries. They involve the very core of organizational processes and demand dramatic revision in a number of key underlying assumptions of organizational life. (pp. xvi–xvii)

We have gone beyond the time when gender stereotyping and discrimination were merely lamentable. We have a body of law that makes overt discrimination, sexual harassment, and hostile working environments illegal. However, overt discrimination, documentable in courts of law, has mutated into more subtle forms of discrimination—with their damage just as potent. The hierarchical structures of decision making, the purveyors of departmental rankings, the striving for inclusion in the disciplinary elite, the ambiguous and shifting standards of evaluation, and the adherence to an individualistic, linear, reductionist, and limited definition of productivity contribute to the circumplex that characterizes today's research universities and that makes them such inhospitable and unforgiving environments in which to work.

Research universities continue to be slow to consider the very real transformation that is occurring in the American psyche, and therefore among students and aspiring and current faculty. Talented people, whether women or men, scientists or artists, students or professionals, have choices about how to construct or re-construct their lives.

Scientists and engineers, already elite by virtue of their educational and professional achievements, are typically not hindered by doubts about what they can achieve if they set their sights in a given direction. They have the advantage of attractive options and the luxury to base their actions and choices more on what they *want* for their lives.

As professional men and women shape their lives and careers today, they are more likely than their parents to consider careers and places of work that provide flexibility, allow a blend of productive work with a satisfying personal and family life, and encourage creativity, collaboration, and connection. They seek environments that provide active support for professional success, demonstrate concern for the individual, and celebrate improvisation and change. Women who are talented and accomplished scientists and engineers make choices that help them progress toward their desired possible selves: productive, satisfied, and meaningfully connected to colleagues, family, and society. It is the challenge for universities to become the environments of choice for these women.

ACKNOWLEDGMENTS

This material is based upon work supported by the National Science Foundation under Grant No. REC-0634519 to Bianca L. Bernstein. Nancy Felipe Russo is a co-investigator.

Any opinions, findings, and conclusions or recommendations expressed in this material are those of the authors and do not necessarily reflect the views of the National Science Foundation.

REFERENCES

Abriola, L. M., & Davies, M. W. (2006). *Attracting and retaining women in engineering: The Tufts experience.* Cornell Higher Education Research Institute Policy Research Conference. Doctoral Education and the Faculty of the Future. Ithaca, NY. October 8–9, 2006. http://www.ilr.cornell.edu/cheri/conf/chericonf2006/Abriola.pdf.

American Association of University Professors (2006). *AAUP faculty gender equity indicators 2006.* Retrieved November 6, 2007, from http://www.aaup.org/AAUP/pubsres/research/geneq2006.htm.

Anderson-Rowland, M. R., Bernstein, B. L., & Russo, N. F. (2007a). Encouragers and discouragers for domestic and international women in doctoral programs in engineering and computer science. Proceedings of the American Society for Engineering Education (ASEE) 2007 Annual Conference, Honolulu, Hawaii, June 2007. Available from http://www.asee.org/acPapers/AC%202007Full2403.pdf.

Anderson-Rowland, M., Bernstein, B. L., & Russo, N. F. (2007b). The doctoral program experience in engineering and computer science: Is it the same for women and men? Proceedings of the Women in Engineering Programs and Advocates Network (WEPAN) 2007 Annual Conference, Orlando, Florida, June 2007. Available from http://www.x-cd.com/wepan07/WEPAN2007_0055.pdf.

Anttila, T., Natti, J., & Vaisanen, M. (2005). The experiments of reduced working hours in Finland: Impact on work-family interaction and the importance of the sociocultural setting. *Community, Work, and Family, 8*, 187–209.

Astin, H., & Milem, J. (1997). The status of academic couples in U.S. institutions. In M. A. Ferber & J. W. Loeb (Eds.), *Academic couples: Problems and promises* (pp. 128–155). Urbana, IL: University of Illinois Press.

Austin, A. E. (2002). Preparing the next generation of faculty. *The Journal of Higher Education, 73*(1), 94–122.

Bailyn, L. (2003). Academic careers and gender equity: Lessons learned from MIT. *Gender, Work and Organizations, 10*(2), 137–153.

Bailyn, L. (2006). *Breaking the mold: Redesigning work for productive and satisfying lives* (2nd ed.) New York: Cornell University Press.

Barak, M., & Levin, A. (2002). Outside of the corporate mainstream and excluded from the work community: A study of diversity, job satisfaction and well-being. *Community, Work and Family, 5*, 133–157.

Barbezat, D. A. (1992). The market for new Ph.D. economists. *Journal of Economic Education*, Summer, 262–275.

Barnett, R. C., & Hyde, J. S. (2001). Women, men, work, and family: An expansionist theory. *American Psychologist, 56*, 781–796.

Bateson, M. C. (1989). *Composing a life: Life as a work in progress—the improvisations of five extraordinary women.* New York: Plume.

Benokraitis, N. V. (Ed.). (1997). *Subtle sexism: Current practice and prospects for change.* Thousand Oaks, CA: Sage Publications.

Berdahl, J. (2007). The sexual harassment of uppity women. *Journal of Applied Psychology, 92*, 425–437.

Bernstein, B. L., & Russo, N. F. (2007). Career paths and family in the academy: Progress and challenges. In M. A. Paludi & P. E. Neidermeyer (Eds.), *Work, life, and family imbalance: How to level the playing field.* Westport, CT: Praeger.

Betz, N. E. (1989). Implications of the null environment hypothesis for women's career development and for counseling psychology. *The Counseling Psychologist, 17*, 136–144.

Biernat, M., Crosby, F. J., & Williams, J. C. (2004). The maternal wall: Research and policy perspectives on discrimination against mothers. *Journal of Social Issues, 60* (special issue).

Bilimoria, D., Perry, S. R., Liang, X., Stoller, E. P., Higgins, P., & Taylor, C. (2006). How do female and male faculty members construct job satisfaction? The roles of perceived institutional leadership and mentoring and their mediating processes. *The Journal of Technology Transfer, 31*, 355–365.

Boice, R. (1993). Primal origins and later correctives for mid-career disillusionment. *New Directions for Teaching and Learning, 55*, 33–41.

Bozeman, B., Dietz, J. S., & Gaughan, M. (2001). Scientific and technical human capital: An alternative approach to R&D evaluation. *International Journal of Technology Management, 22*(8), 716–740.

Brewer, M. B., & Brown, R. J. (1998). Intergroup relations. In D. T. Gilbert, S. T. Fiske, & G. Lindzey (Eds.), *Handbook of social psychology* (4th ed., pp. 554–594). New York: McGraw Hill.

Brown, S., & Lent, R. (2004). *Career development and counseling: Putting theory and research to work.* New York: Wiley.

Bureau of Labor Statistics (2007). *Women in the labor force: A databook* (2007 Edition); Table 11. Employed persons by detailed occupation and sex, 2006 annual averages. Available from http://www.bls.gov/cps/wlf-table11-2007.pdf

Callister, R. R. (2006). The impact of gender and department climate on job satisfaction and intentions to quit for faculty in science and engineering fields. *Journal of Technology Transfer, 31*, 367–375.

Carver, C. S., & Scheier, M. F. (1982). Control theory: A useful conceptual framework for personality-social, clinical, and health psychology. *Psychological Bulletin, 92*, 111–135.

Catalyst (2007). *The double-bind dilemma for women in leadership: Damned if you do, doomed if you don't.* New York: Catalyst. Available from http://www.catalyst.org.

Collaborative on Academic Careers in Higher Education [COACHE] (2007). *COACHE highlights report 2007.* Cambridge, MA.

Commission on Professionals in Science and Technology (2006). *Professional women and minorities: A total human resources data compendium.* Washington, DC: CPST.

Cole, J. R., & Singer, B. (1991). A theory of limited differences: Explaining the productivity puzzle in science. In H. Zuckerman, J. R. Cole, & J. T. Bruer. *The outer circle: Women in the scientific community* (pp. 277–310). New York: W.W. Norton.

Cole, J. R., & Zuckerman, H. (1984). The productivity puzzle: Persistence and change in patterns of publication among men and women scientists. In M. W. Steinkamp, M. L. Maehr, D. A. Kleiber, & J. G. Nicholls (Eds.), *Advances in motivation and achievement* (pp. 217–258). Greenwich, CT: JAI Press.

Cole, J. R., & Zuckerman, H. (1987). Marriage, motherhood, and research performance in science. *Scientific American, 255*, 119–125.

Committee on Maximizing the Potential of Women in Academic Science and Engineering & Committee on Science, Engineering, and Public Policy, National Academy of Sciences, National Academy of Engineering, and Institute of Medicine (2006). *Beyond bias and barriers: Fulfilling the potential of women in academic science and engineering.* Washington, DC: National Academies Press.

Committee on Professionals in Science and Technology (CPST, 2006). *Four decades of STEM degrees, 1966–2004: "The devil is in the details."* STEM Workforce Data Project: Report No. 6. Washington, DC: CPST.

Committee on Women Faculty in the School of Science at MIT (1999). *A study of the status of women faculty in science at MIT.* Cambridge, MA: Massachusetts Institute of Technology. Available from http://web.mit.edu/fnl/women/women.pdf.

Corley, E. A. (2005). How do career strategies, gender, and work environment affect faculty productivity levels in university-based science centers? *Review of Policy Research, 22*(5), 637–655.

Corley, E. A., & Gaughan, M. (2005). Scientists' participation in university research centers: What are the gender differences? *Journal of Technology Transfer, 20*(4), 371–381.

Cortina, L. M. (2008). Unseen injustice: Incivility as modern discrimination in organizations. *Academy of Management Review, 33*, 55–75.

Coser, R. L., & Coser, L. A. (1974). The housewife and her greedy family. In L. A. Coser (Ed.), *Greedy institutions* (pp. 89–100). New York: Free Press.

Creamer, E. (1999). Knowledge production, publication productivity, and intimate academic partnerships. *Journal of Higher Education, 70,* 261–277.

Crosby, F. (1984). The denial of personal discrimination. *American Behavioral Scientist, 27,* 371–386.

Crosby, F. (2007). Sex discrimination at work. In J. E. Chrisler (Ed.), *Lectures in the psychology of women* (4th ed.). New York: McGraw-Hill.

Crosby, F. J., Pufall, A., Snyder, R., O'Connell, M., & Whalen, P. (1989). The denial of personal disadvantage among you, me, and all the other ostriches. In M. Crawford & M. Gentry (Eds.), *Gender and thought: Psychological perspectives* (pp. 79–99). New York: Springer-Verlag.

Cross, S. E., & Madsen, L. (1997). Models of the self: Self-construals and gender. *Psychological Bulletin, 122,* 5–37.

Cuddy, A.J.C., Fiske, S. T., & Glick, P. (2004). When professionals become mothers, warmth doesn't cut the ice. *Journal of Social Issues, 60,* 701–718.

Danecke, D. D. (2005). PhD completion project: Preliminary results from baseline data. *Council of Graduate Schools Communicator, 38*(9), 1–8.

Dietz, J. S., Chompalov, I., Bozeman, B., Lane, E. O., & Park, J. (2000). Using the curriculum vita to study the career paths of scientists and engineers: An exploratory assessment. *Scientometrics, 49*(3), 419–442.

Dipboye, R. L., & Halverson, S. K. (2004). Subtle (and not so subtle) discrimination in organizations. In R. W. Griffin & A. M. O'Leary-Kelly (Eds.), *The dark side of organizational behavior* (pp. 131–158). San Francisco: Jossey-Bass.

Eagly, A. H., & Wood, W. (1999). The origins of sex differences in human behavior: Evolved dispositions versus social roles. *American Psychologist, 54,* 408–423.

Erikson, E. (1968). *Identity: Youth and crisis.* New York: Horton.

Etzkowitz, H., Kemelgor, C., & Uzzi, B. (2000). *Athena unbound: The advancement of women in science and technology.* Cambridge: Cambridge University Press.

Fassinger, R., & Giordan, J. (2007). *It's elemental: Enhancing career success for women in the chemical industry.* Arlington, VA: National Science Foundation. Available from http://www.education.umd.edu/EDCP/enhance_site.

Fort, D. C. (Ed.) (2005). *A hand up: Women mentoring women in science.* Washington, DC: The Association for Women in Science.

Fox, M. F. (2001). Women, science, and academia: Graduate education and careers. *Gender and Society, 15,* 654–666.

Fox, M. F. (2005). Gender, family characteristics, and publication productivity among scientists. *Social Studies of Science, 35*(1), 131–150.

Fox, M. F., & Colatrella, C. (2006). Participation, performance, and advancement of women in academic science and engineering: What is at issue and why. *Journal of Technology Transfer, 31,* 377–386.

Freeman, J. (1979). How to discriminate against women without really trying. In J. Freeman (Ed.), *Women: A feminist perspective* (2nd ed., pp. 194–208). Palo Alto, CA: Mayfield.

Gilbert, L. A. (2002). *Changing roles of work and family.* Paper presented at the meeting of the American Psychological Association, Chicago, August.

Gilbert, L. A., & Kearney, L. K. (2006). Sex, gender, and dual earner families. In W. B. Walsh & M. J. Heppner (Eds.), *Handbook of career counseling with women* (2nd ed., pp. 193–218). Mahwah, NJ: Lawrence Erlbaum.

Glomb, T. M., Richman, W. L., Hulin, C. L., Drasgow, F., Schneider, K. T., & Fitzgerald, L. F. (1997). Ambient sexual harassment: An integrated model of antecedents and consequences. *Organizational Behavior and Human Decision Processes, 71,* 309–328.

Goldin, C. (2004). The long road to the fast track: Career and family. *National Bureau of Economic Research Working Paper 10331.* Available from http://www.nber.org/papers/w-10331.

Gottfredson, L. S. (1981). Circumscription and compromise: A developmental theory of occupational aspirations. *Journal of Counseling Psychology, 28,* 545–579.

Gottfredson, L. (1996). Gottfredson's theory of circumscription and compromise. In D. Brown, L. Brooks, & Associates (Eds.), *Career choice and development* (pp. 179–232). San Francisco: Jossey-Bass.

Gottfredson, L. S. (2004). Applying Gottfredson's theory of circumscription and compromise in career guidance and counseling. In S. D. Brown & R. W. Lent (Eds.), *Career development and counseling: Putting theory and research to work* (pp. 71–100). Hoboken, NJ: John Wiley.

Handelsman, J., Cantor, N., Carnes, M., Denton, D., Fine, E., Grosz, B., Hinshaw, V., Marrett, C., Rosser, S., Shalala, D., & Sheridan, J. (2005). More women in science. *Science, 309,* 1190–1191.

Hermanowicz, J. C. (1998). *The stars are not enough: Scientists—their passions and professions.* Chicago: University of Chicago Press.

Hermanowicz, J. C. (2003). Scientists and satisfaction. *Social Studies of Science, 33,* 45–73.

Hermanowicz, J. C. (2007). Argument and outline for the sociology of scientific (and other) careers. *Social Studies of Science, 37,* 625–646.

Heslin, P. A. (2005). Conceptualizing and evaluating career success. *Journal of Organizational Behavior, 26,* 113–136.

Hewlitt, S. A., & Luce, C. B. (2006). Extreme jobs: The dangerous allure of the 70-hour workweek. *Harvard Business Review.*

Hewlitt, S. A., Luce, C. B., Shiller, P., & Southwell, S. (2005). *The hidden brain drain: Off-ramps and on-ramps in women's careers.* Cambridge, MA: Harvard Business Review Research Report. Available from http://harvardbusiness online.hbsp.harvard.edu/email/pdfs/9491p4_rev_Harvard_site.pdf.

Higgins, M. C., & Thomas, D. A. (2001). Constellations and careers: Toward understanding the effects of multiple developmental relationships. *Journal of Organizational Behavior, 22,* 223–247.

Hoffer, T. B., & Grigorian, K. (2005). *All in a week's work: Average work weeks of doctoral scientists and engineers.* InfoBrief NSF 06-302. Arlington, VA: National Science Foundation.

Hoffer, T. B., Hess, M., Welch, Jr., V., & Williams, K. (2007). *Doctorate recipients from United States universities: Summary report 2006.* Chicago: National Opinion Research Center.

Holland, J. L. (1997). *Making vocational choices: A theory of vocational personalities and work environments* (3rd Ed.). Odessa, FL: Psychological Assessment Resources.

Holton, G., & Sonnert, G. (1996). Career patterns of women and men in the sciences. *American Scientist, 84,* 63–71.

Hyde, J. S. (2005). The gender similarities hypothesis. *American Psychologist, 60,* 581–592.

Hyde, J. S. (2007). New directions in the study of gender similarities and differences. *Current Directions in Psychological Science, 16,* 259–263.

Johns, M., Schmader, T., & Martens, A. (2005). Knowing is half the battle: Teaching stereotype threat as a means of improving women's math performance. *Psychological Science, 16,* 175–179.

Kanter, R. M. (1977). *Men and women of the corporation.* New York: Basic Books.

King, L. A., & Hicks, J. A. (2007). Whatever happened to "what might have been"? Regrets, happiness, and maturity. *American Psychologist, 62,* 625–636.

Kyvik, S., & Teigen, M. (1996). Child care, research collaboration, and gender differences in scientific productivity. *Science, Technology, & Human Values, 21,* 54–71.

Levinson, D. J. (1978). *The seasons of a man's life.* New York: Alfred A. Knopf.

MacNeil, L., & Sher, M. (1999). The dual career couple problem. *Physics Today, 52*(7), 32–37.

Markus, H., & Nurius (1986). Possible selves. *American Psychologist, 41,* 954–969.

Mason, M., & Goulden, M. (2004). Do babies matter (Part II)? Closing the baby gap. *Academe, 90*(6), 1–10.

Mason, M., Stacy, A., Goulden, M., Hoffman, C., & Frasch, K. (2005). *Faculty family friendly edge: An initiative for tenure-track faculty at the University of California.* Berkeley, CA: University of California.

Mor Barak, M.E.M., & Levin, A. (2002). Outside of the corporate mainstream and excluded from the work community: A study of diversity, job satisfaction and well-being. *Community, Work & Family, 5*(2), 133–157.

Murphy, M. C., Steele, C. M., & Gross, J. J. (2007). Signaling threat: How situational cues affect women in math, science, and engineering settings. *Psychological Science, 18,* 879–889.

National Academies (2006). *Beyond bias and barriers: Fulfilling the potential of women in academic science and engineering.* Washington, DC: Author.

National Research Council, Committee on Women in Science and Engineering (2001a). *From scarcity to visibility: Gender differences in the careers of doctoral scientists and engineers.* Washington, DC: NRC.

National Research Council, Committee on Women in Science and Engineering (2001b). *Female engineering faculty at U.S. institutions: A data profile.* Available from http://www7.nationalacademies.org/cwse.

National Science Foundation (2004). *Women, minorities, and persons with disabilities in science and engineering: 2004,* NSF 04-317. Arlington, VA: National Science Foundation, Division of Science Resources Statistics.

National Science Foundation (2007). *Women, minorities, and persons with disabilities in science and engineering: 2007,* NSF 07-315. Arlington, VA: National Science Foundation, Division of Science Resources Statistics. Available from http://www.nsf.gov/statistics/wmpd.

Nelson, D. J. (2005). *A national analysis of diversity in science and engineering faculties at research universities.* Norman, OK: University of Oklahoma. Available from http://cheminfo.chem.ou.edu/~djn/diversity/briefings/Diversity%20Report%20Final.pdf.

Nettles, M. T., & Millett, C. M. (2006). *Three magic letters: Getting to the PhD.* Baltimore: The Johns Hopkins University Press.

Niemeier, D. A., & Gonzales, C. (2004). Breaking into the Guild Masters' Club: What we know about women science and engineering department chairs at AAU universities. *National Women's Studies Association Journal, 16*(1), 157–171.

Ostroff, C., Shin, Y., & Kinicki, A. J. (2005). Multiple perspectives of congruence: Relationships between value congruence and employee attitudes. *Journal of Organizational Behavior, 26*, 591–623.

Perna, L. W. (2005). Sex differences in faculty tenure and promotion: The contribution of family ties. *Research in Higher Education, 46*(3), 277–307.

Pizzolato, J. E. (2007). Impossible selves: Investigating students' persistence decisions when their career-possible selves border on impossible. *Journal of Career Development, 33*(3), 201–223.

Prentice, D. A., & Miller, D. T. (2006). Essentializing differences between women and men. *Psychological Science, 17*, 129–135.

Preston, A. E. (2004). *Leaving science: Occupational exit from science careers.* New York: Russell Sage Foundation.

Rankin, P., Nielsen, J., & Stanley, D. M. (2007). Weak links, hot networks, and tacit knowledge – Why advancing women requires networking. In A. J. Stewart, J. E. Malley, & D. LaVaque-Manty (Eds.), *Transforming science and engineering: Advancing academic women* (pp. 31–47). Ann Arbor: University of Michigan Press.

Rapoport, R. L., Bailyn, L., Fletcher, J. K., & Pruitt, B. H. (2002). *Beyond work-family balance: Achieving gender equity and workplace performance.* San Francisco: Jossey-Bass.

Reybold, L. E. (2005). Surrendering the dream: Early career conflict and faculty dissatisfaction thresholds. *Journal of Career Development, 32*(2), 107–121.

Rhoten, D., & Pfirman, S. (2007). Women, science and interdisciplinary ways of working. *Inside Higher Education.* Retrieved on October 22, 2007, from http://www.insidehighered.com/views/2007/10/22/rhoten.

Ruvolo, A. P., & Markus, H. R. (1992). Possible selves and performance: The power of self-relevant imagery. *Social Cognition, 10*, 95–124.

Salvatore, J., & Shelton, J. N. (2007). Cognitive costs of exposure to racial prejudice. *Psychological Science, 18*, 810–815.

Savickas (2004). The theory and practice of career construction. In S. D. Brown & R. W. Lent (Eds.), *Career development and counseling: Putting theory and research to work.* Hobokon, NJ: John Wiley & Sons.

Settles, I. H., Cortina, L. M., Malley, J., & Stewart, A. J. (2006). The climate for women in academic science: The good, the bad, and the changeable. *Psychology of Women Quarterly, 30*, 47–58.

Smith, J. W. (2005). The influences of gender, race, and ethnicity on workplace experiences of institutional and social isolation: An exploratory study of university faculty. *Sociological Spectrum, 25*, 307–334.

Smith-Doerr, L. (2004). *Women's work: Gender equality vs. hierarchy in the life sciences.* Boulder, CO: Lynne Rienner.

Sonnert, G. (1995). Gender equity in the academy: Still an elusive goal. *Issues in Science and Technology, 12*(2), 53–58.

Sonnert, G., & Holton, G. (1995). *Gender differences in science careers.* New Brunswick, NJ: Rutgers University Press.

Sonnert, G., & Holton, G. (1996). Career patterns of women and men in the sciences. *American Scientist, 84*(1), 63–71.

Sourdif, J. (2004). Predictors of nurses' intent to stay at work in a university health center. *Nursing and Health Sciences, 6*, 59–68.

Stansell, C. (2007). Women in academia. The New Republic, Open University, Feb. 23, 2007. Available from http://www.tnr.com/blog/openuniversity?pid=83431.

Steele, C. M. (1997). A threat in the air: How stereotypes shape intellectual identity and performance. *American Psychologist, 52,* 613–629.

Steele, C. M., & Aronson, J. (1995). Stereotype threat and the intellectual test performance of African Americans. *Journal of Personality and Social Psychology, 69,* 797–811.

Steele, C. M., Spencer, S., & Aronson, J. (2002). Contending with group image: The psychology of stereotype and social identity threat. In M. P. Zanna (Ed.), *Advances in experimental social psychology* (Vol. 34, pp. 379–440). San Diego, CA: Academic Press.

Steinberg, J., True, M., & Russo, N. F. (in press). Work and family: Selected issues. In F. L. Denmark & M. A. Paludi (Eds.), *Psychology of women: A handbook of issues and theories* (2nd ed). Westport, CN: Greenwood Press.

Stephan, P. E. (2007). *Early careers for biomedical scientists: Doubling (and troubling) outcomes.* Harvard University/NBER Science and Engineering Workforce Project. Retrieved on January 26, 2007, from http://www.nber.org/~sewp/Early%20Careers%20for%20Biomedical%20Scientists.pdf.

Stephan, P. E., & Levin, S. G. (2005). Leaving careers in IT: Gender differences in retention. *Journal of Technology Transfer, 30,* 383–396.

Stewart, A. J., Malley, J. E., & LaVaque-Manty, D. (2007). *Transforming science and engineering: Advancing academic women.* Ann Arbor, MI: University of Michigan Press.

Sturm, S. (2007). Gender equity as institutional transformation: The pivotal role of "organizational catalysts." In A. J. Stewart, J. E. Malley, & D. LaVaque-Manty (Eds.), *Transforming science and engineering: Advancing academic women.* Ann Arbor, MI: University of Michigan Press.

Trower, C. A., Austin, A. E., & Sorcinelli, M. D. (2001). Paradise lost: How the academy converts enthusiastic recruits into early-career doubters. *American Association for Higher Education Bulletin, 53*(9), 3–6.

Trower, C. A., & Bleak, J. L. (2004). *Study of new scholars, gender: Statistical Report.* Cambridge, MA: Harvard Graduate School of Education.

Trower, C. (2007). *Tenure-track faculty job satisfaction survey highlights report.* Cambridge, MA: The Collaborative on Academic Careers in Higher Education, Harvard Graduate School of Education.

U.S. Department of Labor, Bureau of Labor Statistics (2007). *Employment and earnings.* Washington, DC: Author.

Vaillant, G. E. (1977). *Adaptation to life.* Cambridge, MA: Harvard University Press.

Valian, V. (1998). *Why so slow: Advancement of women.* Boston, MA: MIT Press.

Valian, V. (2000). Sex, schemas, and success: What's keeping women back. In P. Murphy, P. G. Devine, V. Valian, K. D. Harper, T. DeAngelis, Z. R. Dowdy (Eds.), *Prejudice, discrimination and stereotyping.* Guilford, CT: Dushkin/McGraw-Hill.

Valian, V. (2007). Women at the top in science—and elsewhere. In S. J. Ceci & W. W. Williams (Eds.), *Why aren't more women in science? Top researchers debate the evidence.* Washington, DC: American Psychological Association.

Vescio, T. K., Gervais, S. J., Snyder, M., & Hoover, A. (2005). Power and the creation of patronizing environments: The stereotype-based behaviors of the powerful and their effects on female performance in masculine domains. *Journal of Personality and Social Psychology, 88*(4), 658–672.

West, M. S., & Curtis, J. W. (2006). *AAUP faculty gender equity indicators 2006.* Washington, DC: American Association of University Professors. Available from http://www.aaup.org/NR/rdonlyres/63396944-44BE-4ABA-9815-5792D93856F1/0/AAUPGenderEquityIndicators2006.pdf.

Wilson, R. (2006, May 5). A hothouse for female scientists: At Carleton, working closely with professors leads women to careers in science. *Chronicle of Higher Education, 52*(35). http://chronicle.com/weekly/v52/i35/35a01301.htm.

Wise, A. J., & Millward, L. J. (2005). The experiences of voluntary career change in 30-somethings and implications for guidance. *Career Development International, 10,* 400–417.

Wuchty, S., Jones, B. F., & Uzzi, B. (2007). The increasing dominance of teams in production of knowledge. *Science, 316*(5827), 1036–1039.

Xie, Y., & Shauman, K. A. (2003). *Women in science: Career processes and outcomes.* Cambridge, MA: Harvard University Press.

Chapter 2

Women as Leaders: From the Lab to the Real World

Florence L. Denmark
Erika M. Baron
Maria D. Klara
Janet Sigal
Margaret Gibbs
Dorothy Wnuk

Barriers preventing women from becoming leaders in a wide variety of settings have been the focus of research for a number of years. The "glass ceiling" concept (Morrison, White, & Van Velsor, 1987) illustrated the idea that women could succeed in climbing the ladder to leadership positions only so far, until they reached the invisible glass ceiling; that is, the existence of barriers, both direct and subtle, have prevented women from achieving top leadership positions in professions as diverse as academia, the military, and the corporate world. Eagly and Carli (2007) argued that the appropriate metaphor is a labyrinth, not a glass ceiling; rather than a single barrier, women in their attempt to become leaders encounter a series of dead ends, detours, and unusual paths.

Leadership studies in the laboratory examined a variety of theories explaining who becomes a leader, including the "trait approach," which suggested that leaders are born, not made, and have tremendous influence based on their personality characteristics, and charisma (Zaccaro, 2007); the "situational approach," which at first claimed that situational factors outweighed the importance of the attributes of any particular leader, but subsequently changed to the "contingency approach," which focused on the types of leaders who are most effective in specific types of situations (Vroom & Jago, 2007); and "integrative theories" of leadership, which not only examined the contribution of specific characteristics of leaders and the impact of the situation, but expanded the analysis to include factors such as relationships with followers, and the role of the context and culture in determining effectiveness of leaders (Avolio, 2007).

Many of these past and current theories appear to be more explanatory of how men achieve high positions rather than women. For years in business, academia, and the military, the majority of leaders were male, which can account for the research emphasis on men as leaders. More recently, however, women began to be promoted to middle-management positions in a variety of settings, including politics. Although the situation has improved somewhat for potential women leaders, it still appears that the glass ceiling exists with respect to the highest positions; for example, women are underrepresented as chief executive officers (CEOs), on corporate boards, as presidents of universities, as generals and admirals in the Armed Forces, and as president and vice president in the United States. In the past 2 years, the gender imbalance in U.S. politics seems to be changing to some degree. Nancy Pelosi is the first woman Speaker of the House, an extremely powerful political position; there are female senators; and Hillary Rodham Clinton is running for president of the United States.

In this chapter, first we will describe a model or approach to leadership that has considerable applicability to women in various fields. In subsequent sections, we will examine barriers preventing women from achieving leadership positions as well as the conditions that favor women leaders. Brief discussions of conditions in the corporate world, academia, the health professions, and blue-collar occupations, with accompanying barriers and recommendations to eliminate these barriers, will be presented.

LEADERSHIP STYLES

As described by Eagly (2007), Burns (1978) distinguished among three types of leadership styles:

1. *Transformational style*: Leaders adopting this approach are role models, are sensitive to followers' needs, "mentor and empower their subordinates," "creatively innovate," and help organizations achieve their goals. Eagly stated that these leaders have been termed "charismatic leaders."

2. *Transactional style*: Leaders reward subordinates for constructive behavior and criticize them for falling short of organizational goals.

3. *Laissez-faire style*: Leaders adopt a hands-off approach to leading, which generally is ineffective.

Eagly described several studies that indicated that the transformational leadership style was most effective, although the rewarding aspect of the transactional style also was a positive factor. What is particularly pertinent for this chapter is that leadership styles seem to be intertwined with gender role characteristics. Women, on the one hand, in terms of sex-role stereotypes are considered to be "communal," warm, sensitive to other people's feelings and needs, inclusive, and rewarding. These characteristics, according to Eagly, seem to embody the qualities of transformational leadership styles, plus the positive rewarding aspect of transactional styles. Men, on the other hand, are considered to be "agentic," which implies traits of confidence, assertiveness, and toughness, qualities more associated with transactional than transformational styles. Therefore, according to Eagly, women should be more effective leaders than men because women embody the style that has been shown to be effective.

BARRIERS TO LEADERSHIP FOR WOMEN

If the Eagly model, which asserts that transformational leadership is in fact more effective and that women are more likely to adopt this style, is accurate, women should have an easy road to leadership. However, there are a number of factors that prevent women from achieving high positions. One explanation advanced by Eagly and Karau (2002) is that the perceived incongruity between agentic leadership and female gender roles means that women are perceived as ineffective leaders regardless of their actual leadership performance. The authors also argued that even if women are agentic, their behavior is misperceived, and if they are identified accurately as agentic, they will be perceived negatively because their behavior is unfeminine. This paradox is referred to later as the "double bind" (Oakley, 2000, p. 323).

Another viewpoint suggests that stereotyped associations may mediate between actual performance and evaluation of women leaders. Fernandes and Cabral-Cardoso (2003) provided empirical support for this explanation when they found that "man manager" and "manager" constructs are perceived as closer than "female managers" and "manager" in a Portuguese sample. In terms of power, Ridgeway (2001) suggested that one of the major components of gender stereotypes is status. Men are automatically accorded higher status, and when women are placed in high-status positions, there is a perceived incongruity. In fact, women also may feel uncomfortable at higher-status positions because of conflict with traditional gender norms.

In an attempt to further resolve inconsistent findings on women and leadership, Yoder (2001) adopted an integrative approach. She stated that the transformational approach to leadership, which is more consistent with traditional gender stereotypes associated with women than with men, should be effective in what Yoder called "a congenial setting." In this type of situation, empowering subordinates is valued and the product or achieving the goal is not the sole or determining criterion defining effective leadership.

Yoder (2001) also asserted that the issue of women as leaders is inevitably associated with gender and gender stereotypes. She suggested that women can become more effective leaders (and overcome barriers caused by rigid or traditional sex-role stereotyping) through their individual efforts, such as being extremely competent, valuing group as opposed to individual rewards, or adopting some characteristics associated with male leaders (e.g., assertive speech patterns). However, Yoder argued that it is important not to place the burden of becoming an effective leader upon the woman. The organization should play a supportive role by legitimizing and encouraging women leaders and by ensuring that the male/female ratio of employees is not skewed in favor of male employees. Yoder thought that transformational leadership also may be more effective at certain times in the development of companies than at other times.

It is apparent that barriers exist at several different levels. Women internalize cultural and institutional values, and often must fight against feelings of lack of self-worth (Eagly & Carli, 2007). These self-perceptions may prevent women from seeking leadership positions. In addition, current practices may tend to favor agentic leadership, which is a less comfortable style for women to adopt than the transformational style. Most institutions also do not make it easy for women to devote time to their families, while at the same time condemning them if they do not have families.

Some of the barriers to female leadership discussed in this section will become clearer in sections describing leadership within particular fields. Specifically, female leadership in the corporate world, in academia, in the helping professions, and in the blue-collar workforce will be discussed and case vignettes will be provided. This analysis, and further suggestions to be presented subsequently, may be conducive to developing strategies to enhance women's abilities to achieve upper management and administrative positions. Lastly, future recommendations that are pertinent to all women leaders will be discussed, regardless of the specific field of expertise.

FEMALE LEADERSHIP IN THE CORPORATE WORLD

Both Oakley (2000) and Kottke and Agars (2005) report that although women have achieved a significant proportion of middle management positions in business (possible estimates are around 40%), there is a much smaller percentage of women in top CEO management positions, particularly in large and prestigious companies such as the Fortune 500.

Oakley (2000) analyzed some organizational processes and policies that may act as barriers or glass ceilings preventing women from achieving high leadership positions. One important factor preventing women from moving up the corporate ladder is what Oakley termed "lack of line experience" (p. 323). Because many women middle managers are in areas such as human relations, they have not had essential experiences in line jobs (e.g., production, sales, marketing). This lack of line experience often is used as a reason to prevent women from being promoted to higher administration positions in corporations.

Another crucial factor in terms of guiding women's work performance to achieve success and visibility is the lack of constructive performance-related feedback from their supervisors. This feedback is crucial in assisting women to alter their behavior appropriately, according to Oakley. Women also receive lower salaries and benefits than men, and lack organizational support in many cases, which impedes their progress to the top of the management chain.

Kottke and Agars (2005) suggest that another factor, "threat rigidity" (p. 194), represents a strong barrier for women in the corporate world. Men who have been favored in the past feel threatened by the idea that competent women will be competing for scarce jobs as they ascend the corporate ladder. These men have a vested interest in maintaining the status quo, which always has benefited men in these organizations. The authors also state that research has not been performed to illustrate concretely and adequately that hiring and promoting women to top corporate positions will have a positive impact on a company's financial future. Although these studies are difficult to conduct, if advocates simply pressure companies to develop more woman-friendly (or at least gender-neutral) policies and practices because of past discrimination against women, prejudice and bias against women will continue to exist. In fact, as the authors indicated, male employees will see this gender affirmative action policy itself as unfair to men.

Both Oakley (2000) and Kottke and Agars (2005) emphasize the importance of gender issues and sex-role stereotypes in creating additional glass ceiling barriers for women in the corporate world. If women speak and act decisively and assertively, they may be seen as tough enough but unfeminine. This double-bind (Oakley, p. 324) situation is evident in some attacks against Hillary Clinton and other women politicians. Oakley also suggests that qualities seen as associated with femininity have been equated with incompetence by prejudiced people in the past. According to the author, "old boy networks" represent another major barrier preventing women from being promoted. These networks often operate in informal settings that are not available to women, such as golf courses and squash courts. Some companies, including a major accounting firm in New York City, are attempting to eliminate this problem by teaching, on company time, all new employees to learn how to play golf. One other negative factor relates to the issue of tokenism. Being hired as a token is an isolating experience and puts tremendous pressure on the token to outperform her associates. In an academic situation, a Black female chair of a psychology department at a southern university complained to one of the authors (Sigal) that "everything I say or do is associated with Black people in general" at her university.

Oakley claimed that it will be difficult to change the corporate climate to make it more welcoming for women. It may be necessary to address and alter basic gender stereotypes as well as to change corporate practices before a corporation can become woman-friendly.

Kottke and Agars (2005) expanded on the above recommendation by suggesting that, instead of making the corporate world more woman-friendly, the business world should be made more people-friendly by accommodating employees' family needs (e.g., family leave policies, telecommuting, etc.), establishing open communication, providing successful mentoring, and empowering men and women to achieve their highest potential at work.

In conclusion, although women have advanced to middle management positions in various corporations, several barriers still exist and prevent women from achieving high-level executive positions. This situation seems unlikely to change very quickly unless rigid sex-role stereotypes are altered and lose their impact on individuals' attitudes and perceptions. Although many companies may claim that they have developed woman-friendly practices, unless the organization is supportive of women, and the practical advantage of having women in executive positions is demonstrated, women will continue to be frustrated by glass ceiling barriers in the corporate world and may opt out of fighting these barriers to go into other professional fields.

WOMEN LEADERS IN ACADEMIA

In recent years, the number of women who have obtained professional degrees and occupied positions of leadership in academia has increased dramatically. However, individuals attempting to advance in a world that was previously male-dominated have been confronted with obstacles that are similar in nature and scope to those of the female blue-collar worker. The following section explores the history of women in academia, the barriers to leadership for women in academia, the steps toward strengthening the role of women in academia, and lastly, the progress that women have made thus far.

HISTORY OF WOMEN AND EDUCATION

Until the last half of the twentieth century, the majority of women obtained a formal education through high school. This was a time when women's roles were rigidly defined, and the conventional life path involved marrying and bearing children at a young age. Females began to question their traditional places as the United States saw an increase in various societal trends. These trends included expansion of public school systems, an increased desire for female teachers, the growth of other employment opportunities, a proliferation of literature for women, and the development of domestic labor-saving devices that afforded more leisure time. All of these factors served to further women's interest in education and promote realistic opportunities for knowledge acquisition in secondary institutions (Women's History in America, n.d.).

The number of individuals who have enrolled in postsecondary institutions has increased dramatically over the past decades. From 1970 to 2001, women went from being the minority to the majority of the United States' undergraduate population, increasing their representation from 42% to 56%. Female enrollment in degree-granting institutions is expected to rise to 57% by the year 2014. This increase in enrollment reflects the number of older women returning to pursue an education as well as the number of minority women attending degree-granting institutions (National Center for Education Statistics [NCES], n.d.).

Compatible with the rise in female enrollment, women have surpassed men in degree attainment over the past several decades. Among freshman who were enrolled in a college or university in the 1995–1996 school year, a greater percentage of females (66%) than males (59%) had earned a bachelor's degree by the spring of 2001 (Freeman, 2004). In 2002 and 2003, women also earned the majority of master's degrees, 48% of first-professional degrees, and 47% of doctorate degrees. The NCES (n.d.) projects that, between 2002 and 2014, the number of women who earn associate's, bachelor's, master's, doctorate's, and first-professional degrees will increase by 21%, 22%, 39%, 28%, and 35%, respectively.

The number of minority women who have enrolled in institutions of higher education accounts for a significant portion of the overall growth. The NCES tracked enrollment of persons by race/ethnicity from October 1965 to October 1997 and found that the number of Black, non-Hispanic women entering college had increased by approximately 5.3% and the number of Hispanic women had increased by 3.0% (NCES, 1998). Furthermore, women comprised 63% of the African-American undergraduate population enrolled in college in the 1999–2000 school year.

Examining the undergraduate and gradate degrees awarded to minority women reveals a similar pattern. By 2001, African-American women earned two-thirds of the bachelor's and associate's degrees awarded to African-American students. Additionally, 60% of the degrees awarded to Hispanic and American-Indian individuals and 57% of the degrees conferred on Asian individuals were earned by women (Peter & Horn, n.d.). The NCES projects that the number of minority women acquiring first-professional, master's, and doctorate degrees will continue to increase substantially (NCES, n.d.).

The growth in the frequency of women obtaining doctorate and professional level degrees is important in women's attempts to gain ground in academia. These achievements demonstrate that a growing number of women have the educational tools necessary to hold a high-powered position at a top-tier university. This, in addition to the change in national climate toward supporting more gender-equitable perceptions of women and men, has influenced the opportunities for women in academia. However, several barriers continue to exist that have hindered women from obtaining positions of leadership as frequently as their male counterparts.

BARRIERS

Underrepresentation in Academia

Some researchers suggest that women in the professoriate are underrepresented as compared to men because of the fact that they have only recently gained degrees. With predictions that the number of women who obtain professional degrees will continue to increase comes part of the solution that will likely ease the gender disparity problem. Contrary to this is data from the NCES, which indicates that, while the percentage of women who have obtained doctorates has grown significantly, the percentage of women who have achieved tenured status at academic institutions has remained fairly consistent since the 1970s (Mason & Goulden, 2002).

The Glass Ceiling and/or Leaky Pipeline Theory

The glass ceiling theory emphasizes the notion that inherent patterns of gender discrimination in academia inhibit women from advancing to top positions. Data continue to show that advancement in the realm of academia is slower for women than for men, earnings are lower (except at entry level), there is a noticeable underrepresentation of women in positions at top-tier institutions, and fewer academically based national awards and prizes are given to women (Valian, 2005).

Despite the fact that women receive a large proportion of PhDs in a variety of fields, the number of women in biological science, computer science, engineering, and technology fields continues to increase at a much slower rate as compared to women whose expertise lies in social sciences (National Science Foundation, 2000). This phenomenon, termed the "leaky pipeline," suggests that the sciences "selectively leak women"—a trend that is likely the result of entrenched beliefs that women do not have the qualities and/or knowledge necessary to succeed in a male-dominated field (Valian, 2005, p. 207). Research indicates that men in the sciences are more likely to be tenured than woman, even after controls are introduced for years working since obtaining a degree, discipline, and parental status (Long, 2001).

Work and Family Conflict

Another factor that is posited to make advancement in academia difficult for women is the "work versus family" conflict. This phenomenon is thought to force women to have to make decisions that influence their ability to progress in their careers. A woman's choice to have children is a factor that can often delay the desire to continue with and/or complete undergraduate and graduate schooling, both of which are often prerequisites for obtaining a position of leadership at an academic institution. Those women who acquire professional degrees and subsequently have children are often more likely to take time off and/or work part-time— both of which are obstacles that men probably do not have to overcome. If and when women make the decision to stay at home with their children for a predetermined amount of time, this can imply that they are more willing than men to remove themselves from such a career path at a potentially pivotal time (Mason & Goulden, 2002).

Research conducted by Mason and Goulden (2002) examined family formation and its effects on the career lives of both women and men in academia from the time they received their doctorates until 20 years later. The study found that timing of babies mattered most, differentiating between "early babies" (one who joins the household prior to 5 years after his or her parent completes the PhD) and "late babies" (one who joins the household more than 5 years after his or her parent completes the PhD). Overall, there is a consistent and large gap in tenure achievement between women and men who have early babies. In the sciences and engineering there is a 24% gap between men's and women's rates of having achieved tenure 12 to 14 years after receiving a PhD. The same pattern exists in the fields of humanities and social sciences where researchers found a 20% gap in tenure achievement between men and women who have early babies. Remarkably, men across all fields who had early babies achieve tenure at a slightly higher rate than men and women who do not have early babies.

When comparing women with children and women without, the study yielded an interesting finding that women who have late babies and women without children demonstrated similar rates of achieving tenure—both of which were higher than the rate of women with early babies. Overall, women who achieve tenure across the various disciplines are unlikely to have children in the household. Approximately 62% of tenured women in the humanities and 50% of those in the sciences do not have children in the household. Furthermore, tenured women are twice as likely to be single as compared to tenured men (Mason & Goulden, 2002).

Access to Resources

Lack of access to career advice, resources, mentoring, and socialization of women faculty (i.e., being taught negotiation and self-promotion skills) is another variable purported to negatively impact the attainment of leadership positions for women. One woman's experience working as a faculty member at a top-tier institution follows:

> I feel like there's this system that is more likely to take these men under their wings. I've seen it. They take men under their wings, and they give them the inside scoop, and they "mentor them"—tell them what they need to or have to do or put you on this paper, and I just don't see that happening with the women. (Tracy, Singer, & Singer, n.d., slide 4)

Research also shows evidence of bias in hiring and CV reviews, post-doctoral fellowship awards, peer reviews, letters of recommendation, salary determinants, and teaching evaluations (Tracy et al., n.d.). Furthermore, marginalization is more likely to occur as women progress into better paying and higher level positions (Glazer, 1999).

CAREER DEVELOPMENT OF WOMEN IN ACADEMIA

Research exploring the career development of women who progress to hold positions of leadership in academia is sparse. The most notable study conducted by the *Chronicle of Higher Education* (2005) reported nearly 84% of female university presidents had doctorates (PhD, EdD, etc.), 7.2% had obtained professional degrees (JD, MD, PsyD, etc.), and 5.2% held a variety of master's degrees. Furthermore, the women held positions such as provost, chief academic officer, non-academic university vice president, and dean before beginning their presidency. In an effort to expand upon existent research, Madsen (2007) set out to understand the backgrounds, experiences, and perceptions of women university presidents via conducting in-depth, qualitative interviews with 10 U.S. women who served as president at various colleges and/or universities.

Results pertaining to educational history reveal that five women received bachelor degrees in education, four in math, one in science, and one in social science. Seven presidents pursued master's degrees immediately after graduating from university, two started within two to four years, and one took a longer break as a result of child-rearing responsibilities. All presidents pursued higher education, with six receiving their doctorate degrees in education and four in non-educational areas. Throughout their careers, four women worked as teachers in a K–12 setting while another four worked in a postsecondary setting. Positions held just prior to serving as president included provost, vice chancellor of academic affairs, president of administration and finance, vice president of university relations, and a government agency leadership position. A primary finding was the fact that these women took nonlinear career paths and did not intentionally choose positions that would lead to eventual presidential status. Furthermore, none of the subjects expressed feelings of regret for taking an indirect path, citing that the diverse jobs that they held previously allowed them to develop the knowledge and competency imperative for success (Madsen, 2007).

Overall, the educational backgrounds and career paths of the 10 women presidents illustrate a history of drive for continuous learning and development as well as an interest in taking on new and challenging responsibilities. Additionally, ongoing personal and professional development was reported to be facilitated by the diverse jobs that the women held previous to their presidency. It becomes clear that achieving a top position at an institution requires more than just mastery of one's subject matter. It necessitates keen self-monitoring, judicious negotiation skills, the ability to empower oneself and those around her, and the capacity to support and inspire others (Eagly, 2007).

DECREASING GENDER DISPARITY IN ACADEMIA

The most recent movement emphasizes the importance of maximizing gender equity in positions of leadership in academia for several reasons. First, hiring women at a rate equal to that of men encourages underrepresented groups and minority students to achieve higher levels of education and feel confident that they have a promising future in a variety of professional fields.

Equity in the realm of academia also ensures diversity in teaching, scholarship, and research. The varying experiences and interests of women and men are critical in a field where collaborative work is the catalyst for innovation and change. Additionally, "equity creates a stronger and more viable institution via a reputation for fairness. Demonstrations of fairness and concern for fairness build loyalty from within, attract interest from outside, and increase the attractiveness of the institution to underrepresented groups" (Valian, 2005, p. 209). Overall, gender equity in initial opportunities for higher-level positions at academic institutions, in the likelihood of promotion, in salary, and in access to resources, is extremely important.

Collins, Chrisler, and Quina (1998) suggest the following principles for individuals as well as institutions that should guide efforts to improve the status and experience of women in academia. With regard to the individual, it is critical to have contextual knowledge of the institution; develop a master career advancement plan with objectives; build power through making your actions visible; use mentoring to get feedback as well as "unwritten" information; and be active through networking within the academic community.

It is not just the individual who must work toward decreasing gender disparity in the leadership positions at academic institutions. The university or college itself must put significant effort into creating an environment that welcomes and supports qualified females. Several suggested objectives for universities include installing accountability at all levels and across all employees, irrespective of one's status, position, or gender; establishing a routine in terms of hiring as well as evaluative practices (i.e., developing search committees that seek out qualified women); broadening job descriptions to include nontraditional and/or interdisciplinary work; organizing interviews and orientations that portray the university as a welcoming and unbiased environment; and establishing faculty development committees for promotion and tenure that are comprised of both men and women.

Female university presidents are on the rise, and it is clear that an increasing number of academic institutions are creating opportunities for women to advance to positions of leadership. The following section relays personal accounts of women who have ascended the ranks to become well-known fixtures and strong leaders in the academic world.

Judith Rodin

Judith Rodin, former president of University of Pennsylvania, was the first female president of an Ivy League university and served from 1994 to 2004. She is an alumna of the University of Pennsylvania and received her PhD from Columbia University in 1970. While president at Penn, the university rose from 16th place to 4th place in the U.S. News College Ranking. Furthermore, Dr. Rodin is credited with improving the atmosphere of the areas that surround the campus. In her final year as president of the University of Pennsylvania, Dr. Rodin's salary was $986,915, making her the highest paid university president in the country (Wikipedia.org, n.d.).

Ruth Simmons

Ruth Simmons is the 18th president of Brown University and the first African-American president of an Ivy League institution. She graduated from Dillard University in 1967 and received her doctorate in

Romance literature from Harvard University. Prior to her period in office at Brown, Dr. Simmons served as dean at Princeton University from 1983 to 1990 and president of Smith College from 1995 to 2001. In 2001, she was named by *Time* as America's best college president, and in 2002 *Newsweek* selected her as Ms. Woman of the Year (Wikipedia.org, n.d.). In the fiscal year of 2005, Dr. Simmons received $684,709 in total compensation (Kelleher, 2006).

Catharine Drew Gilpin Faust

Dr. Faust was named the first female president of Harvard University and began her term on July 1, 2007. She will be the fourth of the eight Ivy League universities to name a woman as its president. She graduated from Bryn Mawr College and obtained her PhD in American civilization at the University of Pennsylvania in 1975. Upon graduation, she joined the University of Pennsylvania faculty and proceeded to teach American history there for more than two decades. Prior to becoming president of Harvard, Dr. Faust was dean of the Radcliffe Institute for Advanced Study, the smallest of Harvard's schools, which emphasizes the study of women, gender, and society (Finder & Rimer, 2007).

A recent survey conducted by the American Council on Education revealed that the total percentage of female presidents more than doubled from approximately 10% in 1986 to 21% in 2001. However, the majority of those women were at 2-year institutions and liberal arts and women's colleges. Furthermore, the study indicated that private and doctoral-granting institutions continue to have the smallest percentage of women presidents (9%) (O'Connor, 2004). Although, historically, men have dominated the leadership positions of academia, the fact that increasingly more women have been assuming similar, high-powered roles at top-tier institutions speaks to the radical shift that is taking place toward gender equality. However, although improvements have been made, there are still impediments that must be addressed in the journey toward gender parity in academe.

HEALTH AND HELPING PROFESSIONS

One of the authors (Gibbs) remembers the first day she entered her PhD program at Harvard in 1963. There were equal numbers of male and female students, and the chair in addressing the students gave himself a pat on the back for this decision, because he said that we all know that most of the women would drop out of the field to have families! In 1970, women made up just 20% of the graduates from PhD programs in psychology. In 2005, nearly 75% of the entering workforce in doctoral-level psychology were women (Cnkar, 2007). Women have come a long way within psychology, but they still have not achieved leadership positions. Stereotypical roles operate in psychology as in other fields, and women are less likely to have attained leadership positions in academia or the professional association, the American Psychological Association (APA), than men. Although these figures are increasing, only about 25% of the full professors within U.S. graduate institutions of psychology are female. Only 11 of APA's past presidents have been women, and in 2005 women held fewer than 38% of the editor and associate editor roles for APA journals (Cnkar, 2007).

A similar pattern exists in the medical field. Women made up 49% of the first-year medical class in 2005, but in U.S. medical school faculties only one-sixth of the full professorship is female (Association of American Medical Colleges [AAMC], 2007). This figure has increased, but not dramatically in the last few years. Yedidia and Bickel (2001) asked clinical department chairs why there were not more women leaders in academic medicine. The authors received a variety of responses in their open-ended interviews with 34 chairs and two division chiefs. The responses tended to center on the following issues:

- The constraints of traditional gender roles (e.g., women are less likely to have the time since they have more family responsibilities; it is harder for them to move to accept job offers; only superstar women can do it all)
- Sexism in the medical environment (e.g., sexual harassment, lack of respect for women's opinions, old-boy patterns of promotion)
- Lack of mentoring

Yedidia and Bickel proposed interventions ranging from strategies to help individual female faculty find a mentor or confront bias to more institutional change, for example extending the probationary period for tenure or establishing mentoring networks across the university. The authors concluded that institutional change is necessary to combat the problem.

In 2002, the AAMC reviewed the data from past years of faculty surveys and concluded that the waste of talent from not allowing women to work at their full potential was critical. The report concluded that the "long-term success of academic health centers is thus inextricably linked to the development of women leaders" (Bickel et al., 2002, p. 1043). The authors developed recommendations that are relevant not only to the health professions but to various other fields. The recommendations to medical schools included the following:

- Start using departmental reviews as a strategy for evaluating the effectiveness of departmental chairs in developing female faculty. Most advantage and disadvantage for faculty is created at the departmental level, and the chair plays a critical role. Deans can play a stronger role in training and monitoring their chairs.

- A program for general faculty development should be created in institutions so that the professional development needs of women are addressed within this context. For instance, one criterion for evaluating faculty can be their skill in and experience of mentoring junior faculty, including women.

- Institutional practices should be assessed to see which policies favor men's over women's professional development. For instance, the definition of professional success as a number of publications as sole author ignores contributions to local missions and collaborative research. In general, women faculty members' more collaborative, relational work is less visible, and criteria may need to change to recognize and reinforce these activities. In addition, ignoring one's family's needs should not be seen as a sign of commitment to the profession.

- Enhance the effectiveness of search committees in attracting female candidates. Committees should assess for unintended gender bias within their work. In addition, search committees need more than one female member.

- Provide financial support for programs that monitor the representation of women at senior ranks.

As noted, these recommendations are practical and resonate positively with our discussions in other sections of this chapter. These recommendations focus on institutional change rather than on blaming the victim or on cultural change that is difficult to attain. The fact that women have shown gains within the leadership of the corporate world and academic, blue-collar professions as well as health professions indicates that there is an active movement to create more change and bodes well for the future.

LEADERSHIP AND BLUE-COLLAR WOMEN WORKERS

Leadership has many definitions, and there is no clear-cut agreement on a meaning of leadership that covers all circumstances. However, all leadership theories have one element in common, that is, that a leader is one who exerts more influence within a group than does any other member of the group (Denmark, 1977).

Although leadership is important in any subgroup of society, it plays an especially important role in disenfranchised or underrepresented groups, in that leadership is essential in helping these groups gain more power. Through active and positive leadership, the group can work toward empowerment and change. Having a leader is not only essential in mobilizing a group, making it effective and productive, but a leader can also inspire individual members and show people what can be accomplished by example. Martin Luther King Jr. is a prime example of someone who mobilized not only specific groups, but the nation, and who also exemplified what can be done, instilling hope and inspiring others to continue to fight.

The discussion of leadership therefore must be inclusive of women working in blue-collar professions. Blue-collar positions are those filled by members of the working class who perform manual labor. Blue-collar work may be skilled or unskilled, and may involve factory work, building and construction, law enforcement, mechanical work, maintenance or technical installation, and so on.

Although blue-collar women are not considered to be disenfranchised, per se, they do have a different set of concerns as opposed to women in white-collar positions; namely, pressing salary concerns, child care, and working conditions are three primary areas of note for blue-collar working women. Blue-collar positions are paid less than white-collar positions, and thus these positions are more difficult to navigate than those reaping a higher market value. These positions have an inherent lack of flexibility in terms of compensation, days off, and so on. Therefore, women in blue-collar positions frequently have more difficulty with child care, difficulty making enough to put food on the table, and hazardous health conditions on the job. Whereas a white-collar working woman frequently must pay for child care, this may not be possible for blue-collar working women; conditions in a mine are much more hazardous than those in an office. Therefore, when discussing the topics of leadership and women, it is critical to examine the lives and roles of the leaders of female blue-collar working groups.

In 1962, 36% of the workforce were blue-collar "production workers"; in 1992, 26% of the labor force fell into the blue-collar category (DeLong, 1997). Thus, approximately one-fourth of all of the labor force is considered to be blue-collar. Although women represent approximately 46% of the working force (Einhart, 2001), only 10% of working women are employed in blue-collar positions as compared to 43% of working men (Bond et al., 2002).

Women in these roles who want to assume leadership positions face a unique set of challenges. First, many of these positions are considered to be more stereotypically male than are other areas of work. Firefighters, police officers, welders, electricians, plumbers, and so on are male-dominated fields, and women entering these jobs face an array of obstacles. Many of these occupations have long constituted an old boys' club, and breaking into this inner circle is difficult as is remaining in the job because many men make it uncomfortable to do so. This is even more difficult in the case of women who want to assume leadership roles and thus have the duty of supervising men.

In traditionally male-dominated fields, blue-collar women workers do not escape pressure to perform stereotypical women's roles within the context of their work. Frequently women blue-collar workers are expected to perform tasks that are related to their duties at home, or to conduct responsibilities that mimic chores that service and support men. In this framework, women are still called upon to do housework. Tallichet (1995) quotes a female miner who complained that her job consisted of carrying cinder blocks and rock dust behind the male miners, "cleaning up after them." Tallichet points out that women miners who wished to advance in their field have had to maintain a strong and consistent work ethic, with little room for failure or mistakes.

UNIONS

In March 1974, more than 3,000 blue-collar women gathered in Chicago to form the Coalition of Labor Union Women (CLUW) (U.S. Department of Labor, 2000). The agenda included ways to end sex discrimination in wages and hiring and how to elect more female officials to the American Federation of Labor–Congress of Industrial Unions (AFL-CIO). At the time, the CLUW was considered evidence of a new offshoot of the women's liberation movement deemed to be "blue-collar feminism." Feminism became an integral part of the working women's agenda, and in blue-collar positions this took the form of advocating for day care, maternity benefits, equal pay, and other issues important to working women.

Despite many obstacles in the past, many women have organized themselves or joined with men to form unions to fight for equal rights and benefits on behalf of all workers. One of the earliest unions was the Collar Laundry Union of Troy, New York. The Knights of Labor, a national union founded in 1969, is another example. Unions such as the United Auto Workers have made consistent strides in protecting their female workers; it has endorsed equal pay, gender-integrated seniority lists, day care, and the Equal Rights Amendment. However, in the United States, only 7 million out of a total of 58 million working women (11%) belong to unions or professional organizations.

Although union wages have not risen as fast as nonunion wages in recent years, union workers still earn more, on average, than their nonunion counterparts. Estimates of Employer Costs for Employee Compensation, for example, show that, in March 2001, wages and salaries for private industry union workers averaged $18.36 per hour, compared with $14.81 for nonunion workers (Bureau of Labor Statistics, 2001). Similarly, data from the Current Population Survey show that, in 2000, median weekly earnings of full-time wage and salary workers were $691 for workers represented by unions, compared with $542 for nonunion workers (U.S. Department of Labor, 2000). Finally, data from the 1999 National Compensation Survey show that union workers had average hourly earnings of $18.31, compared with $14.76 for nonunion workers (U.S. Department of Labor, 1999).

CASE VIGNETTES

Despite barriers to women in blue-collar occupations, more and more women in the police and fire forces are beginning to take on leadership positions, which were previously exclusively reserved for men. By 2004, there were four female police chiefs of major U.S. cities: Boston, San Francisco, Milwaukee, and Detroit, the first women in each respective city to hold that position.

Cathy Lanier

In May 2007, Cathy Lanier was appointed the new Washington, DC, police chief. A high school dropout and a mother at 15 years old, Lanier has always faced challenging life situations and is someone who has succeeded and pulled herself up in the face of them. After earning her high school equivalency degree, she became a police officer in 1990 and then went on to earn a bachelor's and then a master's degree in management from Johns Hopkins University. Lanier then completed another master's degree in national security from the Naval Postgraduate School. A hard worker, she was promoted up through the ranks, but this was not without cost. Lanier reports being sexually harassed several times on the job, once by her supervisor (CNN, 2007). She stated that during those times she reminded herself of the other women who suffered from similar discrimination and continued to persevere.

Joanne Hayes-White

On Monday July 2, 2004, Joanne Hayes-White was sworn in as San Francisco Fire Department's new chief; she was the first female chief of the city. Additionally, Hayes-White will be a female chief of the largest urban fire department headed by a woman, with Cobb County, Georgia, and the Tacoma, Washington, departments being second and third, respectively (West, 2004). Hayes-White graduated with a business degree from the University of Santa Clara and joined the fire department in 1990. Impressively, by 1993 she was promoted to lieutenant and by 1996 was a captain. In 1998, she was promoted to assistant deputy chief. The San Francisco Fire Department only had its first female firefighter in 1987, after a U.S. District Court Judge ruled that the department had to hire more women and minorities. Currently, in San Francisco approximately 12% of the 230 firefighters are women (West).

In sum, blue-collar industries represent a segment of the population where women are becoming more vocal and are becoming strong and credible leaders. This field, like many others before, is experiencing a transformation where gender stereotypes are being challenged and women are emerging as qualified and competent as their male counterparts. However, there is still much to be done.

RECOMMENDATIONS

Regardless of the progress that women have made in leadership in various occupations and settings, there is still much to be accomplished in the future. As Margaret Chesney stated regarding women and leadership: "The ceiling is breaking—but watch out for falling glass" (Chesney, 2007). Unfortunately, despite progress, there is still a vast amount yet to be achieved and other sets of concerns of which women must be aware. The following are some general recommendations suggested by Margaret Chesney at the 2007 Committee on Women in Psychology Leadership Institute meeting, which are geared toward helping women accomplish success in various fields, deal with discrimination, and become strong leaders.

1. Determine what type of leader you want to be: "Instrumental," i.e., those dedicating their life to their job, or a "Balancer," i.e., those who look for more of a balance in life. Women who seek more balance in their life must make personal choices about how much they can do, and work within those boundaries.

2. Identify what is valued at the workplace. Each work setting is different and a woman should identify not just what is "said" is important, but what the real messages are.

3. Seek mentors. Finding another female leader who will offer practical advice, give support, and show other women the ropes is important. This opens up vast networks and gives much-needed support and encouragement to women who are trying to succeed. Men can be helpful mentors as well, and may offer a different perspective, which can be valuable.

4. Become educated. Taking some form of leadership training or educational classes helps women advance. This will add knowledge and marketability.

5. Support other women. Women should work on keeping the lines of communication open by decreasing a cut-throat atmosphere between women, often found in the workplace. Helping other deserving women to be promoted is one step that can help increase the numbers and successes of female leaders. This also can include helping later career women reenter the workforce.

6. Do not be satisfied with modest gains—expect more. Women should not be satisfied with what they are given. Rather, they should work, not just for medium gains, but for all gains they truly deserve.

Overall, women should band together and actively participate in groups that unite women. Whether this be a union or a group of women within a department, it has been through this action of uniting and supporting that women have made progress in the past and which provides a key to progress in the future.

REFERENCES

Association of American Medical Colleges (2007). Women in U.S. Academic Medicine Statistics and Medical School Benchmarking 2005–2006. Available from http://www.aamc,org/members/wim.statistics/Stats06/start.htm.

Avolio, B. J. (2007). Promoting more integrative strategies for leadership theory-building. *American Psychologist, 62*, 25–33.

Bickel, J., Wara, D., Atkinson, B. F., Cohen, L. S., Dunn, M., Hostler, S., Johnson, T.R.B., Monahan, P., Rubenstein, A. H., Sheldon, G. F., & Stokes, E. (2002). Increasing women's leadership in academic medicine: Report of the AAMC Committee. *Academic Medicine, 77*, 1043–1061.

Bond, J. T., Thompson, C., Galinksy, E., & Prottas, D. (2002). *Highlights of the national study of the changing workforce.* New York: Families and Work Institute.

Bureau of Labor Statistics (2001, January). *National compensation survey: Occupational wages in the United States, 2001,* Bulletin 2552.

Burns, J. M. (1978). *Leadership.* New York: Harper & Row.

Chesney, M. A. (2007, September). *Women in leadership – the ceiling is breaking … but watch out for falling glass.* Paper presented at the meeting of the Committee on Women in Psychology Leadership Institute for Women in Psychology: Qualitative Evaluation of Training Needs, Washington, DC.

Cnkar, A. (2007). The changing gender composition of psychology. *Monitor on Psychology 38*, 46–47.

CNN (2007). *D.C.'s first female police chief not afraid of challenge.* Retrieved on August 12, 2007, from http://www.cnn.com.

Collins, L. H., Chrisler, J. C., & Quina, K. (Eds.) (1998). *Career strategies for women in academe.* Thousand Oaks: Sage.

DeLong, B. J. (1997). *Assessing globalization as a cause of blue-collar wage decline.* Retrieved from http://econ161.berkeley.edu/Politics/Global_Wages.htm.

Denmark, F. L. (1977). Styles of leadership. *Psychology of Women Quarterly, 2,* 99–113.

Eagly, A. H. (2007). Female leadership advantage and disadvantage: Resolving the contradictions. *Psychology of Women Quarterly, 31*, 1–12.

Eagly, A. H., & Carli, L. (2007). *Through the labyrinth: The truth about how women become leaders.* Cambridge, MA: Harvard Business School Press.

Eagly, A. H., & Karau, S. J. (2002). Role congruity theory of prejudice toward female leaders. *Psychological Review, 109*, 573–598.

Einhart, N. (2001). Survival tactic: Recognize your female talent. *Fast Company.* Retrieved on August 10, 2007, from http://www.fastcompany.com.

Fernandes, E., & Cabral-Cardoso, C. (2003). Gender asymmetries and the manager stereotype among management students. *Women in Management Review, 18*, 77–87.

Finder, A., & Rimer, S. (2007, February 9). Harvard plans to name its first female president. *The New York Times.* Retrieved on August 26, 2007, from http://www.nytimes.com/2007/02/09/business/08cnd-harvard.html?ex=1328677200&en=86812ecb327aa651&ei=5088&partner=rssnyt&emc=rss.

Freeman, C. E. (2004). Trends and education equity of girls and women: 2004. *National Center for Education Statistics.* Retrieved on August 10, 2006, from http://nces.ed.gov/programs/quarterly/vol_6/6_4/8_1.asp.

Glazer, J. (1999). *Shattering the myths: Women in academe.* Baltimore, MD: The Peters Hopkins University Press.

Kelleher, K. (2006, September). Simmons' compensation nears $700K. *The Brown Daily Herald.* Retrieved on August 26, 2007, from http://media.www.browndailyherald.com/media/storage/paper472/news/2006/09/06/CampusNews/Simmons.Compensation.Nears.700k-2258413.shtml.

Kottke, J. L., & Agars, M. D. (2005). Understanding the processes that facilitate and hinder efforts to advance women in organizations. *Career Development International, 10,* 190–202.

Long, J. S. (Ed.) (2001). *From scarcity to visibility.* Washington, DC: National Academy Press.

Madsen, S. R. (2007). Women university presidents: Career paths and educational backgrounds. *Academic Leadership, 5*(1), 11–16.

Mason, M. A., & Goulden, M. (2002). Do babies matter: The effect of family formation on the lifelong careers of academic men and women. Retrieved on August 25, 2007, from http://www.aaup.org/publications/Academe/2002/02nd/02ndmas.htm.

Morrison, A. M., White, R. P., Van Velsor, E., & the Center for Creative Leadership (1987). *Breaking the glass ceiling.* Reading, MA: Addison-Wesley.

National Center for Education Statistics (1998). *Digest of education statistics tables and figures.* Retrieved on August 10, 2006, from http://nces.ed.gov/programs/digest/d98/d98t212.asp.

National Center for Education Statistics (n.d.). Degrees conferred: Degrees, by level of degree and sex of recipient. In *Projection of Education Statistics to 2014* (section 4). Retrieved on August 10, 2006, from http://nces.ed.gov/programs/projections/sec_4b.asp.

National Science Foundation Advance Proposal (n.d.). Retrieved on August 25, 2007, from http://www.case.edu/admin/aces.

National Science Foundation (2000). *Women, minorities, and persons with disabilities in science and engineering: 2000.* Appendix, Table 5-24. Arlington, VA: National Science Foundation.

Oakley, J. G. (2000). Gender-based barriers to senior management positions: Understanding the scarcity of female CEOs. *Journal of Business Ethics, 27,* 321–334.

O'Connor, L. (2004, September). Female college, university presidents are on the rise. *The Daily Collegian Online.* Retrieved on August 25, 2007, from http://collegian.psu.edu/archive/2004/09/09-30-04tdc/09-30-04dnews-05.asp.

Peter & Horn (n.d.). Gender differences in participation and completion of undergraduate education and how they have changed over time. *National Center for Education Statistics.* Retrieved on August 10, 2006, from http://nces.ed.gov/das/epubs/2005169/gender_2.asp.

Powell, G. N., & Butterfield, D. A. (2003). Gender, gender identity, and aspirations to top management. *Women in Management Review, 18*, 88–96.

Ridgeway, C. (2001). Gender, status and leadership. *Journal of Social Issues, 57*, 637–655.

Rudman, L. A., & Glick, P. (2001). Prescriptive gender stereotypes and backlash toward agentic women. *Journal of Social Issues, 57*, 743–762.

Tallichet, S. (1995). Gendered relations in the mines and the division of labor underground. *Gender & Society, 9*, 697–711.

Tracy, E. M., Singer, M. I., & Singer, L. T. (n.d.). *Gender issues in the path to academic leadership*. Retrieved on August 15, 2007, from case.edu/admin/aces/documents/Gender_Issues_in_the_Path_to_Academic_Leadership.ppt.

U.S. Department of Labor (1999). National Compensation Survey (NCS).

U.S. Department of Labor (2000). Current Population Survey (CPS).

Valian, V. (2005). Beyond gender schemas: Improving the advancement of women in academia. *Hypatia, 20*(3), 198–213.

Vroom, V. H., & Jago, A. G. (2007). The role of the situation in leadership. *American Psychologist, 62*, 17–24.

West, P. (2004). San Francisco installs female fire chief. Retrieved on August 12, 2007, from http://www.firechief.com.

What presidents think about higher education (2005, November 4). *Chronicles of Higher Education*, pp. A25–A39.

Wikipedia.org (n.d.). "Susan Hockfield," "Judith Rodin," and "Ruth Simmons." Retrieved on August 20, 2007, from wikipedia.org.

Women's History in America (n.d.). Retrieved on September 15, 2006, from http://www.wic.org/misc/history.

Yedidia, M. J., & Bickel, J. (2001). Why aren't there more women leaders in academic medicine? The views of clinical department chairs. *Academic Medicine, 76*, 453–465.

Yoder, J. (2001). Strategies for change: Making leadership work more effectively for women. *Journal of Social Issues, 57*, 815–828.

Zaccaro, S. (2007). Trait-based perspectives of leadership. *American Psychologist, 62*, 6–16.

Chapter 3

My Life as a Woman Psychologist: In My Own Voice

Marilyn P. Safir

I began my psychology graduate studies in the 1960s—an exciting time. I quickly became involved with the budding civil rights movement. A major impetus resulted from my feelings of being discriminated against because I was a woman, and from my interest as a young girl in non-traditional areas. My love of science resulted from encouragement from my father, who, desiring a son, had train sets and trucks awaiting my birth. He happily accepted a daughter, and encouraged me to join him in taking apart and fixing things—including his automobile. He fanned my interest in how things work and was happy to work on science projects with me. My early negative experiences in being a girl resulted from my father's and my mother's overprotection, so that I wished I had a boy's freedom. I remember that around the age of 10, as an avid reader, I thought that if I were a boy, I would be a sailor and see the world. My first experience with actual discrimination occurred in grammar school. I devoted a great deal of time and effort to my science projects in 7th and 8th grade and received scores of 100 on my work and tests, but only received a final grade of 98. When I screwed up the courage to ask why a boy who had lower grades than I did was given 100, my male science teacher informed me that grades (in elementary school!) were important for boys who would go on to college—but not for girls.

By the time I began college in 1955, I had decided to major in biochemistry and become a physician. It was in college that I experienced what I now understand was sexual harassment demonstrating that a woman's place was not in the lab. My reaction was, Anything they can do, I can do better! However, I discovered that I was more interested in interacting with people. Courses in psychology and the social sciences were far more interesting than my biology and chemistry courses and lab work, and my interest in medicine found a new focus in psychiatry. I joined the premed club, only to discover that women were judged by higher standards both to be accepted into the city colleges and to obtain references for medical school because of a limiting quota. If a man had to be in the top 15% of his class to be eligible for a recommendation, a woman had to be in the top 2% of her class. I also joined the psych club—where I was informed that it was more difficult for women to be accepted. Hal Proshansky was the club advisor and he became a mentor. It also began to seem foolish to me to study medicine in order to become a psychiatrist. It made much more sense to major in psychology and continue in graduate studies to become a psychologist. Hal encouraged me and wrote letters of recommendations for me. I applied to graduate schools in the same universities and cities where my premed fiancé was applying to medical school, without examining the programs—even though I was interested in majoring in personality and social psychology. Hal didn't suggest that I pay more attention as I assume it was "obvious" to him that I would follow my partner to be.

Thus I began my studies at Syracuse University in experimental psychology as there was no program in personality and social psychology. I discovered that a program that focused on animal learning using goldfish and rats did not satisfy my interests. Having done well my first semester, I was invited by Edward J. Murray (a student of Neal Miller) to become his research assistant and to move into the clinical psych program. My first-year experimental psychology advisor had suggested what courses I take and advised me to take the advanced elective that Murray taught, as this would give me information on Freud's approach to personality development. This elective, unknown to me, was one that second- and third-year clinical students took. He later told me that he anticipated that I wouldn't be able to keep up and so would drop out of grad school sooner. This was yet another example of sexual harassment. Many psychology programs maintained (officially or unofficially, according to Hal Proshansky) quotas for women in psychology grad school in the 1950s and early 1960s, and women were never more than 10% to 35% of the students during this period. I was acutely aware of this discrimination, even though it was not out in the open.

I joined the civil rights movement as a result of my personal experiences of discrimination because I was a woman (and also having heard of the discrimination my parents experienced as Jews). There were few students from psychology, as our department was very ivory tower. I became an resident advisor for a professor, Warren Hagstrom, in SW who brought a union organizer, Sol Olinsky, to work with us in developing community organization skills that would help us empower community people. I considered transferring to SW because of the more hands-on approach, but decided that these skills could benefit me in my practice of psychology.

I became more and more disillusioned with the discrimination that women experienced within the civil rights movement. The proverbial straw for me was hearing Stochley Carmichael in Canton, Mississippi, in 1966, blame Black women for emasculating Black men, and state that the only place in the movement for women was prone. This took place in a rally attended by Martin Luther King, Jr., Ralph Abernathy, and Jesse Jackson, who overlooked these female discriminatory statements.

At that point Israel beckoned to me—not because I was a Socialist or a Zionist—but because here was a country where women had obtained equality with men. They did manual labor—building roads, draining swamps. They established kibbutzim that destroyed the division of labor created by the traditional patriarchal family. Women even served in the army! I arrived in Israel in 1968 with a new PhD in psychology and the expectation to work in a modern egalitarian society that had dealt with the "woman question" during the 1920s. My first impressions supported my original beliefs. Israeli women moved and spoke in a less feminine fashion than American women. They used less makeup and wore less jewelry. However, in discussions, it became obvious to me that they were far more traditional in family and social roles than my compatriots in the United States. When I raised the issue of equality, both women and men said that I had come 50 years too late and that women themselves decided to retreat to the traditional social roles. As a social scientist this explanation seemed very unlikely. What was most significant was that Israelis believed in the same myths that had brought me to Israel.

To develop awareness of the inequality within Israeli society, Marcia Freedman and I began two consciousness-raising groups in 1970 at the University of Haifa. Many of those who joined with us came from abroad and had also believed that Israel was far more advanced in granting equal rights to women and that both sexes shared power in Israel in contrast to their former homelands. The contrast between our expectations and women's actual situation in Israel resulted in dissonance that produced, through participation in consciousness-raising groups, the impetus for the new movement. We were joined at first by *sabres*—native Israelis—many of whom were children of earlier "Anglo Saxon" immigrants. (By immigrating to Israel, I became an "Anglo Saxon.") The first women to call themselves feminists were university lecturers and students. We decided to work to establish a new women's liberation movement. We began to attract media attention. As a result, Martha Mednick, on sabbatical in Israel in 1972 to study kibbutz women, read about our group and initiated a meeting. She told us about the new feminist scholarship taking hold in the

United States. Mednick planted the idea of women's studies in fertile ground.

It had never occurred to me that researching women was a legitimate focus for psychological research. Martha spent some time telling me about her kibbutz research. I decided to study diaries of women who immigrated at the turn of the century to join communes (Kvutsot and latter Kibbutzim). My earlier suspicions were confirmed. The myths began to crumble. I discovered that the earliest communes grudgingly accepted women, if at all. They often accepted no more than 10% women members. The women were accepted as employees of the men. These women were then expected to do the cooking in huge vats over open fires, bake bread in ovens built of stone, and do laundry in huge vats using lye and stirring them over these open fires, putting themselves at great risk, but still confined to traditional roles. Interestingly, when there were no women in the commune, the men rotated through these jobs. The work was grueling, exhausting, and not satisfying for many of the women. Women were further disadvantaged. Men had studied the Hebrew language for six or seven years for Bar Mitzvah and had the basics for communicating in Hebrew. Also overlooked was the fact that single women were a significant minority in the early waves of immigration. These women decided to deal with their dissatisfaction by forming women-only communes. What I discovered was that women were free to move into traditional male roles. There was no role sharing. Unisex dressing, in masculine fashion, became the norm. Since the Zionist Socialistic values of these early settlers became the ideal for the budding new country, the types of behaviors I noted observing Israeli women, a minimization of external gender differences in the direction of being less feminine, was a carry-over from that early time. This situation no longer exists.

Martha Mednick has been an important mentor in my life. She introduced me to Division 35 in the American Psychological Association (APA), the International Council of Psychologists (ICP), and the Association for Women in Psychology. My first experience in a woman-centered organization was in ICP. I attended my first exciting and heady international ICP conference in Paris in 1975, where I met Anne Steinman. We collaborated on several comparative studies of Israeli and U.S. students on male/female gender roles and developed a very close relationship. I had become a part of the newly developing international network of feminist psychologists.

When I started to receive requests from Israeli colleagues in other fields about existing feminist research in psychology, it became obvious that interdisciplinary communication was lacking. I discovered that feminist scholars worked in isolation and were unaware of each other's work because of the absence of a national network. Women's studies was nonexistent and unknown in Israeli academia.

In discussions with Mednick, it became obvious that lack of interdisciplinary communication was a problem in the United States as well. We continually discussed the need for an international, interdisciplinary congress that focused on scholarship on women. Finally, in 1979, we decided to do something about it. We proposed holding such a congress under the auspices of the APA's Division 35—Psychology of Women Council. We also proposed holding this congress in Israel to create awareness and to create the groundwork to establish women's studies programs at the Israeli universities. A congress seemed to be a way to bring the message of the importance and developing stature of the new scholarship to this isolated place, as well as to create both Israeli and international networks.

Division 35 agreed to be a co-sponsor. We were fortunate, because among the executive committee members were Florence Denmark, president-elect of APA, Carolyn Sherif as the chairperson, and board members Matti Kubrick Gershenfeld, Martha Mednick, and Nancy Felipe Russo, who was the president of the Federation of Organizations of Professional Women, composed of 110 organizations with branches all over the world. Nancy proposed that the Federation become a co-sponsor. Jessie Bernard and Dafna Izraeli invited Sociologists for Women in Society to be another co-sponsor.

That first congress was held at the University of Haifa, which enabled an almost unanimous approval of the opening of the women's studies program of which I was a founder and director for the first 10 years. The Haifa program clearly evolved from the feminist movement of the 1970s, and it continues to combine activism with academic pursuits. It was also the largest women's studies program through the beginning of the 1990s. Approved in the 1982–1983 academic year, it opened in 1983 with 13 courses. The 1993–1994 academic year saw an enrollment in the Introduction to Women's Studies of almost 10% of the freshman class. The students included women and a few men, who came from different backgrounds: Christian and Moslem Arabs, Druze, Jews from Western and Eastern worlds, each different, according to her cultural background and experience, and how this relates to double oppression. Although these issues are taken for granted in the United States and in many European countries, multiculturalism and diversity are matters that have only been considered by Israeli feminists and by women's studies activists in the last 10 years or so.

The women's studies program at Haifa University serves as an efficient bridge between academia and feminist grassroots organizations in the city. This interaction encourages feminist activists to begin their studies or to return to academia. It involves students in the different feminist grassroots organizations.

Another unique project at the University of Haifa that I have been involved in from its inception is named KIDMA, an acronym for The Project for the Advancement and Involvement of Women in Society. This project was created in 1984, and the major aim was to bring Women's Studies topics to women who would not ordinarily be a part of the university community by actually bringing them to the university and by bringing the university into their communities. I served as its academic advisor from 1984 until 1996 when I became the director. KIDMA promotes personal advancement and social contribution. KIDMA aims to provide a supportive environment and to give information to women who do not have any other frameworks for personal and professional advancement. Furthermore, KIDMA is interested in maintaining this place of knowledge and consciousness as a lever for women's involvement and contribution to their communities and for leading social change. The participants in KIDMA projects get a unique opportunity to familiarize themselves with the University of Haifa and to study in an academic environment as well. We have expanded our projects and provide leadership training courses for women students at the university and for community leaders and potential community leaders from the various sectors of Israeli society. We have developed courses for women employees of the Haifa municipality to teach the necessary skills in on-the-job advancement.

KIDMA is my commitment to help bring about positive social change in Israeli society. Haifa, as a mixed city, provides an environment that enables much of this type of activity. An exciting and successful project was developed with the Women's Army corp as we developed training courses to help young officers break "the iron ceiling" and develop skills to crack the macho army systems. Unfortunately, because of the deteriorating economic situation, many of our projects must be put on hold at this time. In Israel in 2007, the situation for us feminists is very complex. We now see a renewed surge of traditionalism and nationalism, stemming from the impossible political situation. The call for unity at times of war has always come at the expense of women, and now, more than ever, we must stand guard to protect the achievements that have been made over the past decades and continue to strive for a better future for us all, men and women. In conclusion, being a "pioneer" in the battle for the advancement of the status of women in general, as well as in academia, has been a wellspring of personal satisfaction, leading to close relationships with feminist colleagues throughout the world and a chance to view the positive changes that are occurring for women in general and in our field in particular.

Having lacked mentors during the beginning stages of my career, I made choices that were not career-savvy. I was fortunate to learn how important these relationships can be through my close contacts with

Martha Mednick, Florence Denmark, Anne Steinman, Jesse Bernard, and Nancy Felipe Russo—just to name a few. Thus, being a mentor to students and early career academics has been very important to me. I hope that I have been successful in providing the support and knowledge for smoother sailing in the workplace.

Chapter 4

Workplace Incivility, Sexual Harassment, and Racial Micro-Aggression: The Interface of Three Literatures

Eros R. DeSouza

Sexual harassment has dominated the literature on interpersonal mistreatment at work. Recently, however, other types of mistreatment have gained attention by researchers, including mild forms of workplace mistreatment, such as incivility (e.g., Cortina, Magley, Williams, & Langhout, 2001) and racial/ethnic micro-aggressions (e.g., Deitch et al., 2003; Sue et al., 2007). Unfortunately, with a few exceptions (e.g., Berdahl & Moore, 2006; Krieger et al., 2006; Lim & Cortina, 2005), these behaviors have been investigated in isolation, as if they occurred in a vacuum. Moreover, research on sexual harassment has focused on the prototypical case of a superior (usually a man) harassing a subordinate (usually a woman) and has neglected the plurality of forms that sexual harassment may take, including same-sex sexual harassment (DeSouza & Solberg, 2004; DeSouza, Solberg, & Cerqueira, 2007). Therefore, the purpose of this chapter is to integrate the separate literatures on incivility, sexual harassment, and racialized incivility and sexual harassment. Specifically, each of these concepts will be defined. Then, empirical studies on frequency rates and consequences on employees' physical and mental health as well as work-related outcomes will be presented. Finally, these central concepts will be integrated and implications will be discussed.

CENTRAL CONCEPTS

Incivility

Workplace incivility is a mild form of workplace mistreatment, which also includes bullying, emotional, physical, and psychological abuse, tyrannical, deviant, and antisocial behavior. Andersson and Pearson (1999) defined workplace incivility as "low-intensity deviant behavior with *ambiguous* (italics added) intent to harm the target, in violation of workplace norms for mutual respect. Uncivil behaviors are characteristically rude and discourteous, displaying a lack of regard for others" (p. 457). Ambiguity or lack of deliberate intent to do harm is a key element of incivility that differentiates it from other types of workplace mistreatment. Because the uncivil behavior is subtle, the perpetrator can easily mask his or her intent to do harm on another person, for example, by suggesting that he or she was just joking around or by using silence as a form of suppression and censorship; such silence may exclude or negate an important aspect of an individual's identity (Ward & Winstanley, 2003). Because incivility is often linked to an employee's ability to do his or her job, it promotes social isolation and withdrawal from one's job and work (Pearson, Andersson, & Wegner, 2001).

There are many potential causes or antecedents of workplace incivility suggested in the literature. According to Andersson and Pearson (1999), incivility is an interpersonal process dependent on person-environment factors that create incivility spirals (e.g., a perceived act of incivility fosters further uncivil acts, forming a spiral of aggression and counter-aggression that permeates the entire organization). Incivility spirals may begin with a perception of interpersonal injustice (e.g., a slight to one's self-identity or social identity) that causes an employee to feel aggrieved, which may result in anger and desire for revenge for the perceived organizational or societal norm that has been violated. Thus, perceived injustice is an important antecedent of incivility (Baron, Neuman, & Geddes, 1999).

Andersson and Pearson (1999) argue that personal factors that predict incivility spirals include propensity to anger, impulsiveness (e.g., lack of self-control), reactivity (e.g., sensitivity to negative events), and rebelliousness (e.g., independence, self-sufficiency, and resistance to peer pressure). Individuals with these personality traits tend to handle the daily hassles of work by engaging in disrespectful or condescending behaviors.

Furthermore, to handle occupational stress, individuals with the above personality traits may use alcohol and/or drugs while at work as coping mechanisms, which, in turn, further incites inappropriate behaviors (Andersson & Pearson, 1999). Although there is empirical evidence to support a "hot temperament" personality type as a predictor of workplace aggression (e.g., Baron et al., 1999; Hepworth & Towler, 2004), more research on the interaction of personality traits and environmental influences is necessary, given the fact that there is also evidence that fails to support a "hot personality" type as a predictor of workplace aggression (e.g., Jennifer, Cowie, & Ananiadou, 2003).

Another antecedent to workplace incivility suggested by Andersson and Pearson (1999) is an organizational culture that creates a climate of informality. Such organizational climate adds ambiguity to the boundary of acceptable behavior. Casualness at work may facilitate breaches of etiquette (e.g., calling someone by a nickname), disrespect, and thoughtless actions (e.g., hazing), which may create incivility spirals that spread throughout everyday interpersonal interactions at work (Pearson, Andersson, & Porath, 2005; Pearson et al., 2001; Pearson & Porath, 2002).

Another factor that may increase incivility is emerging technologies (e.g., e-mail, text messaging), creating cyber-incivility spirals (Pearson, Andersson, & Porath, 2000). Such technologies remove the need for face-to-face interactions as well as bystanders who might otherwise intervene when incivilities occur. Furthermore, these new technologies are often fast-paced and may increase the pressure for more productivity than traditional methods that require face-to-face interactions, possibly contributing to higher levels of stress and misunderstandings (Vickers, 2006). Rather than fighting technology, organizations should use it to personalize communication and lessen stress (e.g., working from home and communicating with colleagues through video-conferencing). Organizations also need to generate and disseminate a new cyber-etiquette, including having clear policies and procedures to protect complainants and punish perpetrators. Related to emerging technologies in the workplace, other antecedents to incivility include an increasingly diverse workforce (e.g., race/ethnicity, culture/nationality, gender, sexual orientation, age, and ability), economic changes (e.g., service-oriented economy), and organizational changes (e.g., down-sizing, outsourcing, and so on) (Hearn & Parkin, 2001; Neuman & Baron, 1998).

Frequency rates and consequences

Pearson et al. (2000) conducted 700 interviews and collected surveys from 775 employees throughout the United States. Pearson et al. found that perpetrators of incivility generally had higher status than their victims and were typically men. Interestingly, men were more likely to be uncivil toward subordinates than toward superiors, whereas women were as likely to behave uncivilly toward their superiors as toward their subordinates. The consequences of incivility included negative effects on victims and organizations, including impaired concentration, reduced organizational commitment and productivity, and increased intentions to quit; in fact, 12% of the sample reported having ultimately quit their jobs. In addition, 75% of the victims reported being dissatisfied with how their organization handled uncivil incidents, suggesting that the organization was tolerant of incivility.

Pearson et al. (2000) concluded that there was scant attention by organizations to address incivility spirals. Some managers even reported that rudeness and disrespect were justified as being beneficial to their organizations. In fact, it has been recently argued that there may be positive outcomes associated with incivility; that is, managers who use a Machiavellian leadership style may use strategic incivility (e.g., implicit threats) as a negative reinforcer to motivate "low maturity" employees to increase their productivity or to leave the organization (Ferris, Zinko, Brouer, Buckley, & Harvey, 2007). In the opinion of this author, a more appropriate response may be to entice "low maturity" employees to increase their productivity through positive reinforcement (e.g., praise).

Cortina, Magley, Williams, and Langhout (2001) investigated the incidence and impact of incivility in a sample of 1,180 public sector employees (88% of whom reported to be White). The authors created the Workplace Incivility Scale (WIS), which has appropriate reliability and validity properties, to assess how often participants experienced incivility (e.g., disrespect, rudeness, and condescension) from superiors or coworkers. Participants also completed several job-related as well as psychological and health measures. The authors found that 71% of the sample reported having experienced at least one uncivil behavior during the previous 5 years, with women experiencing more uncivil acts than men. However, both men and women experienced similar negative effects: Those who experienced more uncivil acts were less satisfied with their employment (including their jobs, supervisors, coworkers, pay and benefits, and promotional opportunities; they also considered quitting) and had greater psychological distress, especially men, than those who experienced less incivility.

The above studies indicate that incivility is widespread. Moreover, incivility has negative outcomes and should not be ignored by organizations, as is frequently the case. Now we turn to another type of interpersonal mistreatment that is not only common, but also illegal in the United States and in many other countries as well (see DeSouza & Solberg, 2003, for a review of international definitions of sexual harassment).

Sexual Harassment

In the United States, sexual harassment is a type of sex discrimination that violates Title VII of the Civil Rights Act of 1964. Since 1980, the Equal Employment Opportunity Commission (EEOC) has defined sexual harassment as follows:

> Unwelcome sexual advances, requests for sexual favors, and other verbal or physical conduct of a sexual nature constitutes sexual harassment when (1) submission to such conduct is made either explicitly or implicitly a term or condition of an individual's employment, (2) submission to or rejection of such conduct by an individual is used as the basis for employment decisions affecting such individuals, or (3) such conduct has the purpose or effect of unreasonably interfering with an individual's work performance or creating an intimidating, hostile, or offensive work environment. (Code of Federal Regulations, 2000, p. 186)

Parts 1 and 2 refer to quid pro quo sexual harassment in which sexual favors are required to keep a job or receive job-related benefits, whereas part 3 refers to a hostile work environment. Additionally, the EEOC (2007a) states the victim and the alleged perpetrator may be of the same sex. The victim does not have to be the direct target, but could be anyone affected by the offensive conduct (e.g., a bystander). Further, the victim of sexual harassment does not have to show that she or he has suffered economic or psychological harm; however, the harassment must be unwelcome.

Although men are also victims of sexual harassment, women are much more likely to be victims than men are. For instance, during 2006 the EEOC (2007a) received 12,025 charges of sexual harassment, of which 15.4% were filed by men.

Psychologically, sexual harassment is defined as unwanted sexually offensive behavior that threatens one's psychological health and well-being (Fitzgerald, Swan, & Magley, 1997). Fitzgerald et al. (1988) developed a behavior-based instrument, the Sexual Experiences Questionnaire (SEQ), to assess sexual harassment by asking respondents if they had experienced a list of unwanted sexual behaviors. The authors reported that the factor structure of the SEQ revealed a tripartite model consisting of gender harassment, unwanted sexual attention, and sexual coercion. Gender harassment refers to sexist behaviors that do not appear to elicit sexual cooperation but rather convey hostile and offensive attitudes toward members of one gender. Unwanted sexual attention refers to sexual behaviors that are unwanted and unreciprocated. Sexual coercion refers to explicit or implicit bribes or threats in order to gain sexual favors. Gender harassment and unwanted sexual attention seem to parallel the legal definition of hostile work environment, whereas sexual coercion seems to parallel the legal definition of quid pro quo. Research indicates that gender harassment is the most common type of sexual harassment, followed by unwanted sexual attention, with sexual coercion being the least common (Pryor & Fitzgerald, 2003).

Also using a behavioral experiences approach, the U.S. Congress commissioned three large-scale studies to determine the prevalence of sexual harassment across representative national samples of federal workers. The findings showed that 42% to 44% of women and 14% to 19% of men reported having experienced at least one potentially sexually harassing behavior during the last 24 months (U.S. Merit Systems Protection Board, 1981, 1988, 1995).

The Department of Defense (DoD) conducted a survey in 1988 to assess sexual harassment among active-duty military personnel. The DoD survey was modeled after the U.S. Merit Systems Protection Board survey. Of the 20,400 participants who completed the survey, 64% of the women and 17% of the men reported having experienced a potentially sexually harassing experience at least once during the last 12 months (Martindale, 1991).

In 1995, the DoD surveyed active-duty military personnel's experiences of unwanted sexual behavior based on adaptations of Fitzgerald et al.'s (1988) SEQ. Of the 28,296 participants who completed the 25-item SEQ-DoD survey, 76% of the women and 37% of the men reported having experienced at least one potentially sexually harassing behavior during the last 12 months (Bastian, Lancaster, & Reyst, 1996).

In 2002, the DoD again surveyed the active-duty military personnel's experiences of unwanted sexual behavior during the last 12 months using a revised 19-item version of the SEQ; however, to be counted as sexual harassment, respondents had to have experienced a sexually harassing behavior at least once and had to have indicated that any of the behaviors experienced constituted sexual harassment (Lipari & Lancaster, 2003). The 1995 SEQ-DoD data were also re-analyzed according to this new procedure. Of the 19,960 participants who returned usable surveys in 2002, there was a significant drop in sexual harassment between 1995 and 2002 for both women (46% vs. 24%, respectively) and men (8% vs. 3%, respectively). Overall, the findings reported by the EEOC (2007a), the U.S. Merit Systems Protection Board (1981, 1988, 1995), and the DoD (Bastian et al., 1996; Lipari & Lancaster, 2003; Martindale, 1991) indicate that women are more likely to be victims of sexual harassment than men are.

Same-sex Sexual Harassment

Of those federal employees who reported at least one potentially sexually harassing experience in the 1980 survey (U.S. Merit Systems Protection Board, 1981), 3% of the women reported having been harassed by one or more women, whereas 22% of the men reported having been harassed by one or more men. In the 1994 survey (the 1987 survey did not examine the gender of the harasser), the numbers remained about the same; only 1% of harassed women reported other women as the harassers, whereas 21% of the men reported other men as the harassers (U.S. Merit Systems Protection Board, 1995).

Dubois, Knapp, Faley, and Kustis (1998) re-analyzed the 1988 DoD survey results. Of those military personnel who reported at least one potentially sexually harassing experience, only 1% of military women reported having experienced same-sex sexual harassment, whereas 35% of military men did. Next, the authors compared the impact of same- and cross-sex sexual harassment on the professional and personal lives of military men and women. They found that the impact of same-sex sexual harassment was much more harmful for men than for women. Dubois et al. concluded that same-sex sexual harassment of men is part of a masculine culture in which harassment is directed at those who violate traditional gender norms.

Bastian et al. (1996) examined the 1995 SEQ-DoD survey results among military personnel who reported at least one potentially sexually harassing experience. They found that 51% of military men reported having been harassed exclusively by other men and another 16% reported having been harassed by both male and female perpetrators. However, only 2% of military women reported having been harassed by other women and another 6% reported having been harassed by both men and women.

Furthermore, Stockdale, Visio, and Batra (1999) re-analyzed the 1995 SEQ-DoD survey results among military personnel who reported at least one potentially sexually harassing experience. The authors found that among those who completed a section that asked them to describe "the most distressing experience," 53% of the men, as compared to 2% of the women, reported that the harasser was of the same sex. Next, Stockdale et al. compared the impact of same- and cross-sex sexual harassment. They found that men who had experienced same-sex sexual harassment rated their experience as more annoying, offensive, disturbing, embarrassing, and upsetting than did men who had experienced cross-sex sexual harassment. Similar to Dubois et al.'s conclusion (1998), Stockdale et al. concluded that same-sex sexual harassment induces "lesser" men to conform to hypermasculine gender role expectations, in which masculinity is related to dominance, whereas femininity is related to weakness and subservience.

The 2002 SEQ-DoD survey results also showed that 51% of military men reported having been harassed exclusively by other men and another 27% reported having been harassed by both men and women (Lipari & Lancaster, 2003). However, only 1% of military women reported having been harassed exclusively by other women, and another 14% reported having been harassed by both men and women.

The above studies suggest that men experience same-sex sexual harassment more often than women do. However, the surveys from the U.S. Merit Systems Protection Board (1981, 1988, 1995) and those from the DoD (Bastian et al., 1996; Lipari & Lancaster, 2003; Martindale, 1991) were originally designed to measure the experiences of women; hence, these surveys may not adequately account for the experiences of men, especially experiences that involve same-sex sexual harassment (Berdahl, Magley, & Waldo, 1996).

Berdahl et al. (1996) suggested that men feel harassed by behavior that challenges current constructions of masculinity as a domain of qualities reserved for men (e.g., dominance, privilege, and success in the workplace), whereas women feel harassed by behavior that reinforces constructions of femininity as subordination in the workplace. Berdahl et al. discovered behaviors that were perceived to be harassing to men that were not identified as such for women (e.g., being harassed for engaging in "non-masculine behavior"). These behaviors were then incorporated into a new instrument called the Sexual Harassment of Men (SHOM) (Waldo, Berdahl, & Fitzgerald, 1998).

Like the SEQ, the SHOM (Waldo et al., 1998) uses a behavioral experiences approach to assess men's experiences with sexual harassment. The SHOM has five subscales: three for gender harassment (lewd comments, enforcement of the traditional masculine gender role, and negative remarks about men), one for unwanted sexual attention, and one for sexual coercion. The SHOM has good internal reliability coefficients across three diverse samples of men (378 men from a large public utility company in the northwest, 209 male faculty and staff from a large midwestern university, and about 420 men from western agribusiness food processing plants).

Waldo et al. (1998) found that, during the past 24 months, between 40% and 53% of these men identified *men* or *mostly men* as the perpetrators of sexually harassing behavior, and these same-sex experiences consisted mostly of lewd comments and endorsement of masculine gender-role behavior. The authors concluded that "male–male sexual harassment is far more common than typically assumed by researchers, popular media, or the general public" (p. 72).

Gender differences in perceptions of sexual harassment

Two meta-analytic studies of gender differences in perceptions of sexual harassment found that the overall mean differences were between .30 and .35, which suggests that women perceive a broader spectrum of behaviors as sexual harassment than do men (Blumenthal, 1998; Rotundo, Nguyen, & Sackett, 2001). Furthermore, two recent studies on perceptions of same-sex sexual harassment indicated that U.S. college women consistently judged hypothetical sexual harassment cases between two women or between two men as being significantly more sexually harassing, needing an investigation, and being punishable than did U.S. college men (DeSouza & Solberg, 2004; DeSouza et al., 2007). College women were also significantly more likely to endorse unwanted sexual behaviors between individuals of the same sex as constituting sexual harassment at work or in educational settings than did college men. The authors suggested that women are more likely to empathize with the victim, regardless of the victim's sex or sexual orientation, because of women's inferior position in society and of their greater personal experience with, and therefore greater knowledge of, the negative consequences of sexual harassment.

Consequences

A recent meta-analysis of 41 empirical studies with a total sample size of almost 70,000 employees, of which 59% completed the SEQ, examined three types of consequences of sexual harassment experiences: job-related, psychological, and health-related (Willness, Steel, & Lee, 2007). The findings showed that sexually harassing experiences had several negative outcomes, including decreased job satisfaction (especially with interpersonal aspects of work, such as with co-workers), lower organizational commitment, work withdrawal (e.g., missing work, neglecting tasks), ill physical and mental health, and symptoms of post-traumatic stress disorder, which suggests that some types of sexual harassment may be considered traumatic events.

The above findings indicate that sexual harassment is a work stressor to employees, which is costly to organizations. Willness et al. (2007) estimated that sexual harassment is costing organizations an average of $22,500 per employee in terms of lost productivity alone. In addition, unlike incivility, sexual harassment is illegal behavior that can cost organizations millions of dollars in litigation and monetary awards; for instance, during 2006, the EEOC (2007b) reported $59.8 million paid in monetary benefits over and above litigation.

Lapierre, Spector, and Leck (2005) conducted a meta-analytic study to compare the effects of sexual versus nonsexual workplace aggression (including incivility) on employees' overall job satisfaction, which is one of the best indicators of employees' attitude toward the quality of their overall work experience. The authors included in their analyses 25 studies on incivility and related constructs, representing a total of 28 independent samples (three of which completed the WIS), and 19 studies on sexual harassment, representing a total of 22 independent samples (12 of which completed the SEQ). Concerning sexual aggression, because there were only two samples that included women as well as men, the authors compared sexual to nonsexual aggression only among women in order to hold victims' gender constant. Hence, gender comparisons were conducted only on nonsexual aggression. The findings showed that both types of workplace aggression negatively affected victims' overall job satisfaction. When the authors compared the two types of workplace aggression (among women only), they found that nonsexual aggression had a stronger negative relationship with overall job satisfaction than did sexual aggression. Further, nonsexual aggression had a stronger negative relationship with overall job satisfaction among women than among men. Such a finding is not in keeping with Cortina et al.'s (2001) study, possibly because Lapierre et al. (2005) used only a single outcome (i.e., job satisfaction), whereas Cortina et al. used several job-related measures, including other measures to assess psychological and health-related outcomes.

The negative consequences of workplace mistreatment (e.g., incivility and sexual harassment) go beyond the direct targets, affecting bystanders' professional, psychological, and physical well-being (e.g., Hoel, Faragher, & Cooper, 2004; Glomb et al., 1997; Miner-Rubino & Cortina, 2004, 2007). Hoel et al. (2004) and Miner-Rubino and Cortina (2007) suggested that the negative consequences on bystanders might be due to a perception that the organization is unjust by being tolerant of workplace mistreatment, fear of becoming the next target of mistreatment, empathy (they vicariously experience what the target is going through), and guilt for not intervening, supporting the victim, or reporting the perpetrator.

Furthermore, ambient (indirect) sexual harassment negatively affects team- and organizational-level outcomes (Raver & Gelfand, 2005). Raver and Gelfand found that team ambient sexual harassment was associated with intragroup conflict, decreased group cohesion, and decreased team productivity, as mediated by group conflict and group cohesion, after controlling for general levels of stress, racial diversity, team size, and team gender ratio. Thus, workplace mistreatment is not just an individual problem, but is related to teams and ultimately organization productivity.

The Escalation: From Incivility to Sexual Harassment

Bernstein (1997) suggested that sexual harassment, especially gender harassment, "is a type of incivility or ... disrespect" (p. 449). However, until recently, the literature on sexual harassment and incivility have not interfaced. In addition, organizations have typically focused on sexual harassment rather than incivility, because the former is illegal but not the latter. This is unfortunate because incivility is an interpersonal process that often facilitates other forms of workplace mistreatment, such as sexual harassment (Andersson & Pearson, 1999). One way to link the two literatures is to examine empirical studies that measured both workplace incivility and sexual harassment.

Richman et al. (1999) conducted a study with 2,492 university employees. There were significant gender differences for overall incivility only among faculty members, with female faculty members (68%)

reporting having experienced more uncivil acts than their male counterparts (52%). Concerning sexual harassment, there were significant
gender differences. Among the faculty, more women (40%) than men
(29%) reported having experienced overall sexual harassment. However, more service men (46%) than service women (27%), as well as
more clerical men (46%) than clerical women (31%), reported having
experienced overall sexual harassment. There were no gender differences among student workers. When consequences of overall incivility
and sexual harassment were examined separately, after controlling for
race, age, and occupation, both men and women who experienced
overall incivility and sexual harassment had worse mental health (i.e.,
depression, anxiety, and hostility) than those who did not experience
incivility or sexual harassment. The association with drinking outcomes
and prescription drug use was mixed. For women, both incivility and
sexual harassment were related to drinking, but only sexual harassment was related to prescription drug use. For men, both incivility and
sexual harassment were related to heavy episodic drinking and prescription drug use.

Lim and Cortina (2005) investigated the relationships and outcomes
of incivility and sexual harassment in two samples of women ($Ns = 833$
and 1,425; 88% and 93% of whom reported to be White, respectively)
employed within a large public sector organization. The authors used
the WIS and SEQ to measure the frequency of incivility and sexual harassment during the past 5 years, respectively. They combined unwanted
sexual attention and sexual coercion items into a sexualized harassment
composite. The findings showed that incivility and sexual harassment
co-occurred. That is, in both samples, gender harassment was strongly
related to both incivility and sexualized harassment. There was also a
moderate relationship between incivility and sexualized harassment,
even after controlling for the correlation between incivility and gender
harassment. Almost all women who experienced gender or sexualized
harassment also experienced incivility, but not vice versa. In fact,
women rarely experienced sexual harassment in isolation (only 1%–3%
did). In addition, confirmatory factor analyses indicated that gender harassment linked incivility to sexualized harassment.

Moreover, Lim and Cortina (2005) found an incremental worsening
of both job outcomes and psychological/health outcomes even after
controlling for behavior frequency, with women who experienced incivility, gender harassment, and sexualized harassment having the worst
outcomes, followed by women who experienced both incivility and
gender harassment. Even women who experienced incivility alone had
significantly worse outcomes than women who never experienced incivility, gender harassment, or sexualized harassment.

Incivility spirals are often associated with sexual harassment. Such
spirals may also trigger further victimization when victims complain

about workplace mistreatment. Cortina and Magley (2003) examined retaliation in the context of interpersonal mistreatment at work that occurred during the past 5 years by using the WIS and SEQ to measure the frequency of both workplace incivility and sexual harassment in a sample of 1,167 public sector employees (88% of whom reported to be White). Of these, 71% experienced some type of interpersonal mistreatment. Among mistreated employees, 27% spoke out about the mistreatment. The authors found that different coping mechanisms triggered different forms of retaliation (i.e., social or work-related), depending on the status (power) of the perpetrator over the victim. As expected, victims of work mistreatment had worse professional, psychological, and physical well-being compared to non-mistreated employees. Interestingly, those who coped with workplace mistreatment by having a "voice," for example, by directly addressing the mistreatment (e.g., confronting the abuser or complaining to a supervisor) or indirectly by seeking social support, generally experienced more social retaliation victimization (e.g., antisocial behaviors like social ostracism and blame), especially when the perpetrators had more power than the victims, than did those who remained silent. This pattern was stronger when the victim sought social support from colleagues. Compared with silent victims, those who directly confronted the perpetrator also experienced more tangible work-related retaliation victimization (e.g., involuntary transfer, demotion, and so on), especially when the perpetrators had more power than the victims.

Cortina and Magley (2003) also found health-related costs associated with enduring mistreatment in silence. That is, those who were frequently mistreated but remained silent had the worst psychological and physical well-being. Conversely, individuals who expressed "voice" and did not experience retaliation had the best psychological and physical well-being. Overall, these findings suggest that re-victimization in the form of retaliation provides additional costs to organizations in terms of decreased employee performance, absenteeism, and turnover.

Racialized Incivility and Sexual Harassment

Uncivil acts may reach a tipping point that spirals into micro-inequalities that comprise the principal component for workplace discrimination by focusing the incivility on someone's gender or race/ethnicity (Rowe, 1990). Thus, the uncivil act may become gendered by being aimed at some aspect of one's masculinity or femininity, or it may become racialized by being aimed at some aspect of one's race/ethnicity, or it may combine both gender and race/ethnicity by becoming racialized gender micro-inequalities. For instance, Haslett and Lipman (1997) reported findings on everyday gender micro-aggressions in a sample of 31 women lawyers, 84% of whom were White. The results showed that 71% of the respondents reported having experienced some form of micro-inequality. Their most disturbing micro-inequalities included exclusion, isolation, and being ignored. Women who experienced micro-inequalities reacted with frustration (35%), stress (23%), anger (17%), withdrawal (12%), avoidance (6%), depression (4%), and open hostility (3%). For women of color, the authors described a double jeopardy that included micro-inequalities based on both their racial/ethnic and gender identities, e.g., "joking around about my Spanish clients and their 'relationship' to me (or we all look alike)" (p. 46).

Deitch et al. (2003) and Sue et al. (2007) define racial micro-aggressions as subtle and ambiguous verbal, behavioral, or environmental indignities directed at people of color. For instance, Deitch et al. reported more everyday racial micro-aggressions (e.g., being ignored or treated as if one did not exist) directed significantly more often against African-American workers than against White workers in a sample of 314 first-line workers (study 1). In addition, African-American workers reported more negative job-specific well-being outcomes than did their White counterparts. Deitch et al. also reported findings from 5,483 Navy personnel (study 2) and from 8,311 Army personnel (study 3) based on re-analyses of the 1995 SEQ-DoD survey dataset. The authors selected survey items that focused on everyday mistreatment (e.g., not being given the right information to do one's job). The findings reflected the same patterns as those evidenced with civilians. Specifically, being African American was associated with mistreatment. In addition, being African American was associated with negative job-specific well-being, negative emotional well-being, as well as negative perceived physical well-being outcomes.

Krieger et al. (2006) found widespread incivility, sexual harassment, and racial discrimination in a sample of 1,202 low-income women and men union workers (24% of whom reported to be White) in the greater Boston area. Specifically, 52% of the workers reported having experienced incivility during the past 12 months, 24% reported having experienced at least one potentially sexually harassing behavior, and 53% reported having experienced racial/ethnic discrimination, with 12% of the sample reporting having experienced all three types of workplace mistreatment. On the one hand, the results showed that White workers were significantly more likely to experience uncivil behavior than workers of color, which is not in keeping with Deitch et al.'s (2003) findings, and gender was not a significant predictor. On the other hand, Krieger et al. found that workers of color significantly experienced more sexual harassment than White workers. Again, gender was not a significant predictor—both women (26%) and men (22%) experienced similar numbers of sexually harassing experiences. However, sexual orientation was a significant predictor. Lesbian, gay, bisexual, and transgendered workers reported having experienced more sexual harassment than heterosexual workers did. In addition, workers of color (58%) experienced significantly more racial discrimination than White workers (37%). Interestingly, compared to men, women were significantly less likely to report having experienced racial discrimination.

The argument that women of color often experience both gender and racial harassment in the workplace, since sexism and racism have been historically and experientially intertwined (Murrell, 1996), is known as the double jeopardy hypothesis. In fact, some researchers suggest that racialized sexual harassment is a central factor in the harassment experience of women of color (e.g., Buchanan, 2005; Welsh, Carr, MacQuarrie, & Huntley, 2006).

Although some studies failed to support the double jeopardy hypothesis (e.g., Krieger et al., 2006), others showed support for racialized sexual harassment in the workplace (e.g., Buchanan & Ormerod, 2002; Cortina, Fitzgerald, & Drasgow, 2002; Mansfield, Koch, Henderson, & Vicary, 1991; Schneider, Hitlan, & Radhakrishnan, 2000; Texeira, 2002; Yoder & Aniakudo, 1995).

Recently, two models of the double jeopardy hypothesis were empirically tested: The additive (main-effect) model was compared with the multiplicative (interaction) model on the incidence of both sexual and racial/ethnic harassment (Berdahl & Moore, 2006). The sample consisted of 238 employees (48% of whom reported to be White) who were recruited from five organizations. Sexual harassment was measured with 19 items that were worded to apply to both men and women, with 14 items measuring traditional sexual harassment on the basis of Fitzgerald et al.'s (1988) typology (gender harassment, unwanted sexual attention, and sexual coercion) and five additional items measuring "not-man-enough harassment," which were previously identified by Berdahl et al. (1996) and Waldo et al. (1998). Ethnic harassment was measured using seven items from the Ethnic Harassment Experiences scale (Schneider et al., 2000). The procedure used to measure both sexual and ethnic harassment consisted of multiplying frequency of harassment (0–4) by negative evaluation of the experience (1–2). Thus, the amount of harassment ranged from 0 (never experienced or experienced such harassment in a neutral or positive way) to 8 (experienced such harassment most of the time and evaluated it very negatively).

Berdahl and Moore (2006) found that when racial/ethnic harassment and sexual harassment were combined to form an overall measure of harassment, women of color experienced significantly more overall harassment compared to men of color, White women, and White men, supporting the double jeopardy hypothesis. When the two models were tested, the findings showed that women experienced significantly more sexual harassment than men, race/ethnicity was not significant, and there was no interaction between sex and race/ethnicity. In addition, people of color experienced significantly more racial/ethnic harassment than did Whites, but women did not experience it more so than men did, and there was no significant interaction between sex and race/ethnicity. Lastly, women experienced more overall harassment than men, and people of color also experienced more overall harassment than did Whites, but there was no interaction between sex and race/ethnicity. These findings support the additive model, suggesting that race/ethnicity does not affect sexual harassment and that sex does not affect racial/ethnic harassment.

CONCLUSIONS

The existing literature reviewed in this chapter suggests that personal slights lead to incivility spirals. Moreover, incivility is a type of interpersonal discrimination (Hebl, Foster, Mannix, & Dovidio, 2002), because it is subtle and easily masked (covert) and is often targeted at women and racial/ethnic minorities. Unfortunately, incivility becomes a systemic organization problem that is often ignored and unpunished by organizations compared to formal (overt) discrimination of the past that is protected by law (Code of Federal Regulations, 2000). According to Dipboye and Coletta (2005), "the subtlety and complexity of [interpersonal] discrimination in today's workplace makes it even more pernicious in some respects than the simple and easily identifiable discrimination of the past" (p. 427). Moreover, a growing body of empirical evidence shows that incivility has negative consequences on individuals and organizations. Thus, incivility should be subject to the same regulations and policies as formal types of discrimination. In addition, incivility co-occurs with sexual and racial/ethnic harassment. Hence, multiple forms of interpersonal mistreatment need to be addressed simultaneously rather than in isolation, as is typically the case. As Lim and Cortina (2005) put it, "a concerted effort at eliminating all elements of a hostile work environment might be more effective and efficient" (p. 494).

Gender harassment has been identified as an important link between general incivility and sexualized harassment (i.e., unwanted sexual attention and sexual coercion; Lim & Cortina, 2005). Thus, gender should be actively investigated when assessing generalized incivility in order to detect gendered incivility, gendered bullying, and the interface between gender with other systems of inequality, such as race/ethnicity and sexual orientation. In addition, same-sex sexual harassment is a common occurrence, suggesting a need to focus on gender stereotyping rather than on sexualized harassment, which is more symptomatic of heterosexual sexual conflict between men and women. In fact, legal scholars have suggested that the term sexual harassment should be re-conceptualized as gender-norm harassment to accommodate the plurality of forms that sexual harassment now takes (Epstein, 1998; Franke, 1997; Schultz, 1998). Additional research and legal scholarship describing the link between gender stereotyping and discrimination are needed in order to make clear to policy makers the need to make gender-norm harassment, both overt and covert, illegal.

REFERENCES

Andersson, L. M., & Pearson, C. M. (1999). Tit for tat? The spiraling effect of incivility in the workplace. *Academy of Management Review, 24*, 452–471.

Baron, R. A., Neuman, J. H., & Geddes, D. (1999). Social and personal determinants of workplace aggression: Evidence for the impact of perceived injustice and the Type A behavior pattern. *Aggressive Behavior, 25*, 281–296.

Bastian, L. D., Lancaster, A. R., & Reyst, H. E. (1996). *Department of Defense 1995 sexual harassment survey*. Arlington, VA: Defense Manpower Data Center.

Berdahl, J. L., Magley, V. J., & Waldo, C. R. (1996). The sexual harassment of men? Exploring the concept with theory and data. *Psychology of Women Quarterly, 20*, 527–547.

Berdahl, J. L., & Moore, C. (2006). Workplace harassment: Double jeopardy for minority women. *Journal of Applied Psychology, 91*, 426–436.

Bernstein, A. (1997). Treating sexual harassment with respect. *Harvard Law Review, 111*, 445–527.

Blumenthal, J. A. (1998). The reasonable woman standard: A meta-analytic review of gender differences in perceptions of sexual harassment. *Law and Human Behavior, 22*, 33–59.

Buchanan, N. T. (2005). The nexus of race and gender domination: The racialized sexual harassment of African American women. In P. Morgan & J. Gruber (Eds.), *In the company of men: Re-discovering the links between sexual harassment and male domination* (pp. 294–320). Boston: Northeastern University Press.

Buchanan, N. T., & Ormerod, A. J. (2002). Racialized sexual harassment in the lives of African American women. *Women & Therapy, 25*, 107–124.

Code of Federal Regulations, Vol. 29, §1604.11 (2000).

Cortina, L. M., Fitzgerald, L. F., & Drasgow, F. (2002). Contextualizing Latina experiences of sexual harassment: Preliminary tests of a structural model. *Basic and Applied Social Psychology, 24*, 295–311.

Cortina, L. M., & Magley, V. J. (2003). Raising voice, risking retaliation: Events following interpersonal mistreatment in the workplace. *Journal of Occupational Health Psychology, 8*, 247–265.

Cortina, L. M., Magley, V. J., Williams, J. H., & Langhout, R. D. (2001). Incivility in the workplace: Incidence and impact. *Journal of Occupational Health Psychology, 6*, 64–80.

Deitch, E., Barsky, A., Butz, R. M., Chan, S., Brief, A. P., & Bradley, J. C. (2003). Subtle yet significant: The existence and impact of everyday racial discrimination in the workplace. *Human Relations, 56*, 1299–1324.

DeSouza, E., & Solberg, J. (2003). Incidence and dimensions of sexual harassment across cultures. In M. Paludi & C. A. Paludi, Jr. (Eds.), *Academic and workplace sexual harassment: A handbook of cultural, social science, management, and legal perspectives* (pp. 3–30). Westport, CT: Praeger.

DeSouza, E., & Solberg, J. (2004). Women's and men's reactions to man-to-man sexual harassment: Does the sexual orientation of the victim matter? *Sex Roles, 50,* 623–639.

DeSouza, E. R., Solberg, J., & Cerqueira, E. (2007). A cross-cultural perspective on judgments of woman-to-woman sexual harassment: Does sexual orientation matter? *Sex Roles, 56,* 457–471.

Dipboye, R. L., & Coletta, A. (2005). The dilemmas of workplace discrimination. In R. L. Dipboye & A. Coletta (Eds.), *Discrimination at work: The psychological and organizational bases* (pp. 425–462). Mahwah, NJ: Erlbaum.

DuBois, C.L.Z., Knapp, D. E., Faley, R. H., & Kustis, G. A. (1998). An empirical examination of same- and other-gender sexual harassment in the workplace. *Sex Roles, 9,* 731–749.

Employment Equal Opportunity Commission (2007a, May 17). *Sexual harassment.* Retrieved on November 2, 2007, from http://www.eeoc.gov/types/sexual_harassment.html.

Employment Equal Opportunity Commission (2007b, January 31). *Sexual harassment charges: FY 1997–FY 2006.* Washington, DC. Retrieved on November 2, 2007, from http://www.eeoc.gov/stats/harass.html.

Epstein, L. B. (1998). What is a gender norm and why should we care? Implementing a new theory in sexual harassment law. *Stanford Law Review, 51,* 161.

Ferris, G. R., Zinko, R., Brouer, R. L., Buckley, M. R., & Harvey, M. G. (2007). Strategic bullying as a supplementary, balanced perspective on destructive leadership. *The Leadership Quarterly, 18,* 195–206.

Fitzgerald, L. F., Shullman, S., Bailey, N., Richards, M., Swecker, J., Gold, Y., Ormerod, M., & Weitzman, L. (1988). The incidence and dimensions of sexual harassment in academia and the workplace. *Journal of Vocational Behavior, 32,* 152–175.

Fitzgerald, L. F., Swan, S., & Magley, V. J. (1997). But was it really sexual harassment? Legal, behavioral, and psychological definitions of the workplace victimization of women. In W. O'Donohue (Ed.), *Sexual harassment: Theory, research, and treatment* (pp. 5–28). Boston: Allyn & Bacon.

Franke, K. M. (1997). What's wrong with sexual harassment? *Stanford Law Review, 49,* 691–772.

Glomb, T. M., Richman, W. L., Hulin, C. L., Drasgow, F., Schneider, K. T., & Fitzgerald, L. F. (1997). Ambient sexual harassment: An integrated model of antecedents and consequences. *Organizational Behavior & Human Decision Processes, 71,* 309–328.

Haslett, B. B., & Lipman, S. (1997). Micro-inequalities: Up close and personal. In N. V. Benokraitis (Ed.), *Subtle sexism: Current practice and prospects for change* (pp. 34–53). Thousand Oaks, CA: Sage.

Hearn, J., & Parkin, W. (2001). *Gender sexuality and violence in organizations.* London: Sage.

Hebl, M. R., Foster, J. B., Mannix, L. M., & Dovidio, J. F. (2002). Formal and interpersonal discrimination: A field study of bias toward homosexual applicants. *Personality and Social Psychology Bulletin, 28,* 815–825.

Hepworth, W., & Towler, A. (2004). The effects of individual differences and charismatic leadership on workplace aggression. *Journal of Occupational Health Psychology, 9,* 176–185.

Hoel, H., Faragher, B., & Cooper, C. L. (2004). Bullying is detrimental to health, but all bullying behaviors are not necessarily equally damaging. *British Journal of Guidance & Counselling, 32,* 367–387.

Jennifer, D., Cowie, H., & Ananiadou, K. (2003). Perceptions and experience of workplace bullying in five different working populations. *Aggressive Behavior, 29,* 489–496.

Krieger, N., Waterman, P. D., Hartman, C., Bates, L. M., Stoddard, A., Quinn, M. M., Sorensen, G., & Barbeau, E. M. (2006). Social hazards on the job: Workplace abuse, sexual harassment, and racial discrimination—A study of Black, Latino, and White low-income women and men workers in the United States. *International Journal of Health Services, 36,* 51–85.

Lapierre, L. M., Spector, P. E., & Leck, J. D. (2005). Sexual versus nonsexual workplace aggression and victims' overall job satisfaction: A meta-analysis. *Journal of Occupational Health Psychology, 10,* 155–169.

Lim, S., & Cortina, L. M. (2005). Interpersonal mistreatment in the workplace: The interface and impact of general incivility and sexual harassment. *Journal of Applied Psychology, 90,* 483–496.

Lipari, R. N., & Lancaster, A. R. (2003). *Armed forces 2002: Sexual harassment survey.* Arlington, VA: Defense Manpower Data Center.

Mansfield, P. K., Koch, P. B., Henderson, J., & Vicary, J. R. (1991). The job climate for women in traditionally male blue-collar occupations. *Sex Roles, 25,* 63–79.

Martindale, M. (1991). Sexual harassment in the military: 1988. *Sociological Practice Review, 2,* 200–216.

Miner-Rubino, K., & Cortina, L. M. (2004). Working in a context of hostility toward women: Implications for employee's well-being. *Journal of Occupational Health Psychology, 9,* 107–122.

Miner-Rubino, K., & Cortina, L. M. (2007). Beyond targets: Consequences of vicarious exposure to misogyny at work. *Journal of Applied Psychology, 92,* 1254–1269.

Murrell, A. J. (1996). Sexual harassment and women of color: Issues, challenges, and future directions. In M. S. Stockdale (Ed.), *Sexual harassment in the workplace: Perspectives, frontiers, and response strategies* (pp. 51–65). Thousand Oaks, CA: Sage.

Neuman, J. H., & Baron, R. A. (1998). Workplace violence and workplace aggression: Evidence concerning specific forms, potential causes, and preferred targets. *Journal of Management, 24,* 391–419.

Pearson, C. M., Andersson, L. M., & Porath, C. L. (2000). Assessing and attacking workplace incivility. *Organizational Dynamics, 29,* 123–137.

Pearson, C. M., Andersson, L. M., & Porath, C. L. (2005). Workplace incivility. In S. Fox & P. E. Spector (Eds.). *Counterproductive work behavior: Investigation of actors and targets* (pp. 177–200). Washington, DC: American Psychological Association.

Pearson, C. M., Anderson, L. M., & Wegner, J. W. (2001). When workers flout convention: A study of workplace incivility. *Human Relations, 54,* 1387–1419.

Pearson, C. M., & Porath, C. L. (2002). *Rude awakening: Detecting and curtailing workplace incivility.* London, Ontario, Canada: Richard Ivey School of Business, University of Western Ontario.

Pryor, J. B., & Fitzgerald, L. F. (2003). Sexual harassment research in the United States. In S. Einarsen, H. Hoel, D. Zapf, & C. L. Cooper (Eds.), *Bullying and emotional abuse in the workplace: International perspectives in research and practice* (pp. 79–100). London and New York: Taylor & Francis.

Raver, J. L., & Gelfand, M. (2005). Beyond the individual victim: Linking sexual harassment, team processes, and team performance. *Academy of Management Journal, 48,* 387–400.

Richman, J. A., Rospenda, K. M., Nawyn, S. J., Flaherty, J. A., Fendrich, M., Drum, M. L., & Johnson, T. P. (1999). Sexual harassment and generalized workplace abuse among university employees: Prevalence and mental health correlates. *American Journal of Public Health, 89,* 358–363.

Rotundo, M., Nguyen, D. H., & Sackett, P. R. (2001). A meta-analytic review of gender differences in perceptions of sexual harassment. *Journal of Applied Psychology, 86,* 914–922.

Rowe, M. (1990). Barriers to equality: The power of subtle discrimination to maintain unequal opportunity. *Employee Responsibility and Rights Journal, 3,* 153–163.

Schneider, K. T., Hitlan, R. T., & Radhakrishnan, P. (2000). An examination of the nature and correlates of ethnic harassment experiences in multiple contexts. *Journal of Applied Psychology, 85,* 3–12.

Schultz, V. (1998). Reconceptualizing sexual harassment. *The Yale Law Journal, 107,* 1683–1805.

Stockdale, M. S., Visio, M., & Batra, L. (1999). The sexual harassment of men: Evidence for a broader theory of sexual harassment and sexual discrimination. *Psychology, Public Policy, & Law, 5,* 630–664.

Sue, D. W., Capodilupo, C. M., Torino, G. C., Bucceri, J. M., Holder, A.M.B., Nadal, K. L., & Esquilin, M. (2007). Racial micro-aggressions in everyday life. *American Psychologist, 62,* 271–286.

Texeira, M. T. (2002). "Who protects and serves me?" A case study of sexual harassment of African American women in one U.S. law enforcement agency. *Gender & Society, 16,* 524–545.

U.S. Merit Systems Protection Board (1981). *Sexual harassment in the federal workplace: Is it a problem?* Washington, DC: U.S. Government Printing Office.

U.S. Merit Systems Protection Board (1988). *Sexual harassment in the federal government: An update.* Washington, DC: U.S. Government Printing Office.

U.S. Merit Systems Protection Board (1995). *Sexual harassment in the federal government: Trends, progress, continuing challenges.* Washington, DC: U.S. Government Printing Office.

Vickers, M. H. (2006). Writing what's relevant: Workplace incivility in public administration—A wolf in sheep's clothing. *Administrative Theory & Praxis, 28,* 69–88.

Waldo, C. R., Berdahl, J. L., & Fitzgerald, L. F. (1998). Are men sexually harassed? If so, by whom? *Law and Human Behavior, 22,* 59–79.

Ward, J., & Winstanley, D. (2003). The absent presence: Negative space within discourse and the construction of minority sexual identity in the workplace. *Human Relations, 56,* 1255–1280.

Welsh, S., Carr, J., MacQuarrie, B., & Huntley, A. (2006). 'I'm not thinking of it as sexual harassment': Understanding harassment across race and citizenship. *Gender & Society, 20,* 87–107.

Willness, C. R., Steel, P., & Lee, K. (2007). A meta-analysis of the antecedents and consequences of workplace sexual harassment. *Personnel Psychology, 60,* 127–162.

Yoder, J. D., & Aniakudo, P. (1995). The responses of African American women firefighters to gender harassment at work. *Sex Roles, 32,* 125–137.

Chapter 5

Sexual Harassment and Male Dominance: Toward an Ecological Approach

Phoebe Morgan
James Gruber

The last quarter century has witnessed aggressive efforts at gender integration and gender equity by women's groups, government agencies, and policy advocates. Because wages and occupational status have historically been disproportionately higher among men, economic and labor parity has played a key role in efforts to desegregate male-dominated domains.[1] As a result, today unprecedented numbers of women are now doing work previously done by men, and an increasing number of high-paying, high-status occupations previously dominated by men have achieved or are close to achieving gender equity.[2] Yet, in the United States, men's wages are 25% higher than women's, over 90% of Fortune 500's CEOs are White men (Business Wire, 2000), and the labor market remains highly segregated (Kelly, 1991).

Research has consistently linked the problems of male dominance with sexual harassment (for an overview, see Morgan 2001). Despite laws and policies prohibiting it, sexual harassment continues to be a problem across all domains and is endemic where men predominate (Gruber & Morgan, 2005). In male-dominated domains, disproportionately more women (and men) experience sexual harassment and they report more severe forms of it. In domains of *high* dominance (where 85% or more of occupants are male), sexual harassment is especially prevalent. For example, while less than half (42%) of female U.S. government employees have been sexually harassed (U.S. Merit Systems Protection Board [USMSPB], 1995), two-thirds or more of the women working in the military sector report experiencing it (Bastian, Lancaster, & Reyst, 1996). Similarly, women working in paramilitary occupations like policing and firefighting have significantly higher rates of harassment than their civilian counterparts (Commission on Women, 1992; Brown, Campbell, & Fife-Schaw, 1995). In fact, the rate of harassment among women police officers may be as high as 80% (Martin & Jurik, 2006).

In male-dominated domains, sexual harassment is not only common, but pernicious. In addition to high victimization rates, the types of harassment and the consequences of it are more severe. Sexual bribery and sexual assault, for example, are experienced by a significantly higher portion of military and paramilitary women (Bastian et al., 1996; Embser-Herbert, 2005; Texteira, 2002; Yoder & Aniakudo, 1997) than in the general population. Reports of especially demeaning and violent harassment across a wide range of male-dominated occupations—from coal miners (Yount, 1991) to oil riggers (Holcombe, 1992) and even stock brokers (Smith, 2002)—add more evidence about the unique problems women face in male-dominated domains.

Historians have found ample evidence that, at least since the 19th century, the problems of male dominance and workplace sexual harassment have been inextricably linked (Baker, 2005; Bularzik, 1978). Since the 1970s feminists have conceptualized sexual harassment as a political problem (Farley, 1978; MacKinnon, 1979), an occupational hazard (Crull, 1981), and even a public health risk (Charney & Russell, 1994). Regardless of the type of problem sexual harassment is conceived to be, from a feminist perspective male dominance is a key, if not *the* central, factor affecting it. Sociologist Lin Farley (1978) broke theoretical ground by linking unwanted sexual attention to the dominance of patriarchal ideology. Specifically, Farley argued that the normalization of unwanted sexual attention is the *outcome* of a patriarchal system in which men's wants and needs are privileged over those of women's. Legal scholar Catherine MacKinnon (1987) concurred, but extended the theory further by envisioning male dominance as the primary marker of patriarchy and sexual harassment as both an outcome of *and* a contributor to male domination. In other words sexual harassment is not simply a product of male dominance; it also *reproduces* it. Social research of the last quarter century has consistently validated this feminist view.

But more recently the focus of sexual harassment research has drifted away from the study of institutionalized male dominance to psychological and organizational factors. This shift to micro-level analyses (for an in-depth critique, see Mueller, DeCoster, & Estes, 2001) has, among other things, led to an exploration of the psychological factors associated with research participants' definitions of and responses to "sexual harassment."

This tilt toward the psychological study of sexual harassment has been fueled in large part by the Sexual Experiences Questionnaire (SEQ) developed in the late 1980s by Louise Fitzgerald and her colleagues, which has become the most widely used measure of sexual harassment experiences in the world. Only recently has the widespread use of the SEQ been challenged (see Gutek, Murphy, & Douma, 2004). In particular, Gutek and her colleagues state that, at best, the SEQ is a measure of *psychological* sexual harassment. That is, Fitzgerald and her colleagues, as well as other researchers during the first decade of sexual harassment research, "tried to find out what kinds of experiences people had that might be considered sexual harassment and then wrote questions to try to capture these experiences" (p. 467). In addition to the SEQ, Fitzgerald's measure of "organizational tolerance" (i.e., whether leadership has a lax attitude toward enforcing sexual harassment policies) is assessed by asking employees about the likely responses of their supervisors or managers to *hypothetical situations* that involve unwanted sexual attention.

Our primary critique of recent trends in sexual harassment literature is that the problem of male dominance as a theoretical force and a stimulus for research models is "missing in action." In particular, we believe that sexual harassment theory and research has lost much of its feminist edge during the last two decades because of the prominence of organizational psychology paradigms over alternative critical feminist perspectives that link work to cultural production and reproduction of racial, social class, and gender inequality. Through an in-depth review and re-analysis of the existing research, the following pages make several theoretical propositions that, when viewed together, present an ecological model of the relationship between male dominance and sexual harassment. By "ecological" we mean that male domination occurs as the result of situated performances of masculinity that are influenced by a host of "external" or extra-situational factors, such as sex ratios, the dominance of cultural norms in the work domain (e.g., "sex-role spillover"), physical and social boundaries that demarcate work domains, collective identities of participants, and individual attitudes.

Recent innovations in men's studies have allowed us to understand male dominance as a far more complicated phenomenon than sexual harassment research has conceived it to be (for a thorough overview and critique of the masculinity literature, see Connell, 2000). This body of work places masculinity construction at the center of its analyses and critically examines the normalization of manhood and the social functions of manliness. Masculinity research sheds considerable light on how gender segregation and the subordination of women is socially justified and perpetuated. However, the subject of sexual harassment has been tangential at best in this body of work (for an exception, see Messerschmitt, 1993).

For ease of discussion, we present our analysis in three parts. Part one critiques the ways in which male dominance has been conceptualized in numerical terms. Part two draws upon recent masculinity theory to conceptualize male dominance in normative terms (e.g., domains where work roles or identities center around stereotypic masculine behaviors or images such as risk-taking, aggressiveness, sex talk, etc.) and highlights the variety of ways these stereotypes affect sexual harassment. In the third part we discuss the implications this multidimensional view of male dominance has for future sexual harassment research and policies. The outcome is a set of proposals based upon our ecological model that may serve as a basis for future research.

NUMERICAL DOMINANCE

Survey research consistently confirms a positive correlation between numerical dominance and sexual harassment. In domains where the sex ratio is skewed (i.e., the proportion of men greatly exceeds that of women), sexual harassment is likely to be prevalent (Gruber, 1998; Gutek, 1985; Gutek & Morasch, 1982). In fact, comparative analyses show that male predominance and sexual harassment correlate across domains as well as within them. A complication arises, however, because numerical dominance does not always (or necessarily) predict the existence of a work domain male culture. Nevertheless, numerical dominance has often been used as a proxy for normative dominance.

Proportionality

Drawing upon social role theory, Gutek and Morasch (1982) were the first to theorize the connection between sex ratio skew and sexual harassment prevalence. They argued that in environments where the sex ratio is skewed, cultural gender roles "spill over" into the workplace. While this occurs regardless of which sex predominates, sexual harassment is especially problematic when men are a significant majority. In domains where sex role spillover occurs, the climate becomes sexually charged and the treatment of women as daughters, wives, girlfriends, and mothers rather than as coworkers and supervisors is normalized. In coal mining, for example, where less than 7% of the workers are female, women are often typecast as flirts, tomboys, or ladies and then treated as such by their male coworkers (Yount, 1991). Similarly, in corporate offices, executive secretaries are hired and promoted on the basis of their abilities to perform as surrogate wives (Pringle, 1989) and are often conspicuously objectified as status-bearing possessions (Messerschmidt, 1993). Bond and her colleagues (2004) argued that job satisfaction for both women and men varied substantially between female- and male-dominated occupations because of cultural gender differences. Specifically, they hypothesized that workers' higher satisfaction in female-dominated jobs was the product of workplace norms that encouraged supportive and nurturing relationships, which contrasted with male-dominated jobs where emotional distance was typical.

Degree of Sexualization and Amount of Contact

In addition to conflating gender roles with work roles, men tend to sexualize interaction with the opposite sex more than women do (Gutek, Cohen, & Konrad, 1990; Stockdale, 2005). The "contact theory" of Gutek and her colleagues argues that routine contact with members of the other sex increases sociosexual behavior and workplace sexualization, especially in male-majority workplaces because men tend to sexualize interactions, irrespective of specific occupational or situational norms. In highly sexualized environments, for example, girl watching is accepted as innocent fun, as is the highly visible display of scantily clad "calendar girls" on walls or computer screens (Quinn, 2000).

An analysis of a random survey of Canadian women found that the amount of contact with men within a domain was a more significant predictor of sexual harassment than the number of men who work there (Gruber, 1998). Expectedly, in domains where the rate of contact with men is high, the atmosphere is sexually charged and sex and work roles are conflated; unwanted sexual attention such as flirting, requests for dates, sexual jokes, and proposals for sex is common. In addition, quid pro quo harassment is likely to be tolerated. By "quid pro quo" we refer to an often unspoken expectation that sexual favors can be traded for work-related rewards. Women who flirt or accept requests for dates or sex are rewarded by being hired, promoted, or given favorable assignments; those who refuse sexual offers risk being demoted or fired (MacKinnon, 1979). Labeled "the casting couch" by theatrical performers, quid pro quo harassment has frequently occurred at auditions (Farley, 1978).

While the problems of skewed sex ratio and high contact implicate the need for more aggressive efforts at integration, sex role spillover and the sexualization of the attitudinal climate suggest the need for greater efforts at promoting professional behavior. Consensual relations policies and mandated sexual harassment workshops are examples of the latter (Wonders, 1997). However, the fact that the problem of sexual harassment persists in light of increased integration and professionalism suggests the relationship between male predominance and sexual harassment is multifaceted.

Degree of Women's Visibility

Kanter's (1977) ethnographic study of corporate gender relations suggests the correspondence between sex ratio and sexual harassment may actually be curvilinear. She found that in departments where the numbers of women were especially small—one or two—men granted them token status and treated them affectionately. The tokens were infantilized and treated as little sisters, workgroup pets, or department mascots. However, as the number of women increased, they lost token status and, with that, the affection of their patronizing male coworkers. As the visibility of women increased, gender relations grew hostile.

As Cockburn (1991) explains, visibility affects gender relations in two ways. First, greater numbers foster a heightened sense of solidarity among women; as a result, they may feel more empowered to assert their work roles over their sex roles and therefore resist male sexual advances. Those who follow this path are likely to experience retaliation. Spurned judges, for example, have punished female attorneys by berating them in court (Angel, 1991). Thus, the visibility theory suggests retaliation-based sexual harassment will rise as women's profile increases.

Second, growing visibility creates the impression that a critical mass of women is taking over the domain. Such a perception produces backlash. Sexual harassment, then, becomes both an expression of anger and a tool of intimidation. Rather than infantilizing or objectifying, sexualized behavior becomes demeaning and humiliating. It creates an environment inhospitable to women that signals "you are not wanted here." For example, despite the fact that the U.S. Armed Forces have some of the most progressive gender integration policies in America, which resulted in the doubling of the number of women recruits in a decade (Titunik, 2000), in 2001 *nearly 80%* of female veterans claimed they experienced sexual violence while serving their country (USA Today, 2001). In short, the critical mass theory suggests that when men perceive their dominance is at risk, the rate of hostile environment harassment will increase.

Within a sexually charged environment, backlash will manifest in forms of more severe physical aggression. They may haze rather than initiate female newcomers. For example, in the Arizona Department of Corrections, new female corrections officers were required to practice body and cavity searches more frequently than their male counterparts (Morgan, 1999). In coal mining, the stripping and greasing down of newcomers initiates them to the culture and solidifies bonds between those who share it (Yount, 2005). Yet, when a small number of women are stripped and greased by a large number of men, for them an initiation ritual becomes an alienating experience. Likewise, in military academies, a site of rapid integration, upperclassmen traditionally initiate freshmen through demands for submission. A Pentagon survey found that within their first year of service 12% to 17% of all female cadets had been sexually assaulted (Lipka, 2005).

While numerical dominance and the prevalence of sexual harassment are related, these examples show that the relationship is neither necessarily linear nor positive. It is not simply that the more men that populate a domain, the more women will be sexually harassed. Among U.S. autoworkers, for example, the women who experienced the most sexual harassment were not tokens, but working in groups where their numbers (approximately a third of the group) made them a "threatening minority" (Gruber & Bjorn, 1982). Recent findings from a Dutch survey show that women are at the highest risk of sexual harassment in domains that are *somewhat* dominated by men. While approximately half of the female respondents working in either non-dominated or highly male-dominated workplaces experienced unwanted sexual behavior, a whopping 81% of those in somewhat male-dominant domains experienced it (Timmerman, 1990). So, numerical dominance is related to sexual harassment, but the nature of that relationship is contingent upon context.

In conclusion, numbers do matter, but in at least two different ways. First, in highly male-dominated settings where the majority of men hold traditional gender values, sex spillover is likely, as is the sexualization of social interaction. In these situations, unwanted flirting, touching, "ogling," and requests for dates or sex will seem normative and the exchange of sexual favors for work-related reward will be common. But, with the successful integration of more women, the more visible they become. With their higher profile comes women's resistance to quid pro quo harassment and an escalation of men's hostility. Once the character of a domain shifts from highly dominated to somewhat dominated, there arises the possibility that a critical mass of women is emerging. Men unwilling to relinquish their majority status (and the perks that come with it) respond with demeaning and humiliating forms of sexual harassment as a means to express outrage and to make the environment as inhospitable as possible for women.

NORMATIVE DOMINANCE

Applications of sex ratio, spillover, sexualization, contact, and critical mass theories make the connection between male predominance and sexual harassment prevalence clear but not complete. There are at least two common situations that illustrate the limitations of these theories. First is the sexual harassment of women by men in domains where men do not predominate. Second is the sexual harassment of men by other men.

With regard to the first situation, survey results indicate that even when the sex ratio is fairly even the sexual harassment of women is common. Timmerman's (1990) study of Dutch employees, for example, found that while sexual harassment rates in non-male-predominant domains was lower than where men are the majority, nearly half (48%) of the women in them experienced sexual harassment. In a Canadian survey of working women, those in gender-balanced work domains experienced levels of harassment similar to their peers in male-dominant settings (Gruber, 1998). In fact, even in situations where a minority of women have greater job status and authority over their male subordinates, they are harassed (Rospenda, Richman, & Nawyn, 1998). About half of college faculty professors are sexually harassed by their students (DeSouza & Fansler, 2003), as are attorneys by their clients (Laband & Lentz, 1998), and nurses by their patients (Hanrahan, 1997). Likewise, female executives, managers, and supervisors are sexually harassed by their subordinates at least as often as women without supervisory status.

As for the second situation, surveys show that 14% to 19% of men are sexually harassed at work, and they experience significantly more same-sex harassment than women do (USMSPB, 1981, 1988, 1995). Men harass women primarily through sexual comments or requests for relationships or sex; but they harass other men physically, mostly by inappropriate touching or body language (Stockdale, Wood, & Batra, 1999). So, while these two situations highlight the limits of predominance theory, they do not necessarily call for a discarding of it. In fact, they suggest that male dominance is at least two-dimensional: There is a normative component as well as a numerical one. By normative we refer to those psychological and sociological processes that construct male dominance as natural and sexual attention as inevitable and therefore tolerable.

Traditionality

Attitudinal and perceptional studies of psychologists have made significant progress toward linking normative male dominance to sexual harassment prevalence. In general terms, traditionality (i.e., the degree to which one believes that gender differences are "natural") normalizes the sexual, social, and economic subordination of women. Pryor and colleagues, for example, have found a relationship between men's propensity to sexually harass women and their attitudes. In particular, high LSH (likelihood to sexually harass) men hold adversarial sexual beliefs, find it difficult to assume the perspectives of others, and endorse traditional sex-role stereotypes (Pryor & Stoller, 1994; Pryor, Giedd, & Williams, 1995). Also, these men score high on scales of anti-femininity, toughness, dominance, and authoritarianism. Fitzgerald and Shullman (1985) note a similar link between traditional attitudes about gender roles among women and their resistance in labeling unwanted sexual attention as "sexual harassment." In contrast, Brooks and Perot (1991) found feminist ideology to be a significant predictor of the likelihood of defining situations as sexually harassing. Specifically, the more respondents embrace gender equality, the more likely they were to define unwanted sexual attention as harassing.

Thus, regardless of the number of men populating a domain, the men and women who rate high on the traditionality scale will more likely view unwanted sexual attention as just the price women must pay to participate in the paid labor force while those with feminist orientations are more apt to find unwanted sexual attention hostile and offensive. Traditionality theory, then, can account for the sexual harassment of women in domains where men do not predominate. Where the majority of those who populate the domain hold traditional values, most likely there will be a gendered division of labor and a disparate disbursement of power. In a highly traditional domain, it is normal for a minority of elite men to hold a disproportionate amount of power over a majority of subordinate women.

Hospitals are a case in point. In this domain, a high degree of traditionality is evidenced by a gendered division of labor such that medicine is predominately practiced by men and patient care is performed primarily by women. Despite the fact that the work and training of nurse practitioners is in many ways comparable to physicians, their status and pay is significantly less than physicians (About Women and Marketing, 1998). Furthermore female nurses are more likely than female physicians to be sexually harassed by male patients. Thus, in hospital rooms where nurses have the greatest authority, unwanted sexual harassment from male patients is common, but complaints about it are not (Hanrahan, 1997). Even though they didn't like it, nurses told Hanrahan sexual harassment was for them an unavoidable occupational risk.

In sum, in work domains where the majority of women and men hold traditional beliefs about gender, the prevalence of interactions that meet the Equal Employment Opportunity Commission's definition of sexual harassment will be high, but reports of sexual harassment low (Stambaugh, 1997; Morgan, 1999). But, as the number of women with feminist ideology grow, so will the number of reports and complaints about sexual harassment. Also, a feminist ideology can help buffer the negative impact of harassment on women's mental health and well-being (Rederstorff, Buchanan, & Settles, 2007).

Gender Regime

Traditionality theory cannot account for the harassment of men by other men, especially when the perpetrator and his target are both heterosexual. Gender performance theory, more commonly referred to as "doing gender" theory, offers an explanation. Ethnomethodologists

West and Zimmerman (1987) conceptualized gender as an interactive accomplishment. Most simply, what it means to be feminine or masculine is produced through social interaction. What is defined as "normal" for a man or a woman is the outcome of negotiations that extend over a period of time. When gender performance does not meet expectations, the actor is stigmatized and subject to social control. Gender is produced at every level of interaction, from interpersonal to organizational (Martin & Jurik, 2006). Gender norms change with ideological shifts and vary across types of interactions and within domains. Gender hegemony—the privileging of the roles, values, and beliefs of one group over another—is institutionalized by the state, media, religion, at home and at work, and structured by race, class, sexuality, and ability (Messerschmidt, 1993). Connell (2000) refers to this system of gender management as the "gender regime."

As a learned performance, there are variations in the degree to which men accomplish the hegemonic ideal (Connell, 1995). In fact, only a few rigorously practice it, and this group of "hyper-masculine" men is accorded elite status. Thus, the gender regime produces a hierarchy of men in which only a few men dominate the remaining majority. Sometimes men of privilege use intimidation and violence to sustain dominance, and men of lesser status use the same to resist subordination and increase their status (Collinson, 1992; Kaufman, 1987; Hearn, 1985). Sexual harassment, then, is a common tactic used by subordinate men to challenge the power of elite males. Conversely, sexual harassment is also a weapon used by elite men to defend against insubordination.

Organized Sexual Harassment

In a patriarchal society, one of the most unambiguous ways to demonstrate masculinity is to assert sexual, economic, or social dominance over women (MacKinnon, 1987). Thus, there is no place for women in a power pyramid based upon masculinity (Cockburn, 1991) and attempts to insert women into it destabilize the regime (Hatty, 2000). The need to preserve the dominance of men over women bonds men of all statuses—the elite hyper-masculine as well as the men they dominate. In fact, it is at the very sites of successful integration of women where cults of masculinity flourish (Connell, 1995).

At these sites, sexual harassment is an organized male-bonding ritual. Quinn's (2000) ethnography of girl watching, for example, reveals that the primary motivation of group ogling is not inherently hostile but more for sport. As with team sports like football, the sexual objectification of women becomes a game in which knowledge of the rules and willingness to play it establish insider status. From the girl watcher's point of view, ogling is harmless fun. It is, then, domination of women that bonds together all those within the masculine hierarchy.

Those who are uninitiated to the masculine order are inducted through group performances of ritualized sexual aggression. In military academies, the sexualized hazing of cadets is a long-standing tradition. A prerequisite for induction into a college fraternity is the ability to rise above the humiliation of being demeaned as homosexuals or subordinated as women.

It is not just the integration of women that destabilizes the hierarchy of men. Men who stand against the gender regime also threaten the stability of the masculine hierarchy. Men who choose cooperation over competition, treat women as equals, or who refuse to use force are gender rebels who risk becoming targets of what Stockdale (2005) terms "rejection-based" sexual harassment. In much the same way as women who "invade" male turf become targets of hostility and derision, so too nonconforming men are subject to verbal and physical aggression and excluded from routine male-bonding experiences.

Given the fact that only a few men have what it takes to achieve elite status and the vast majority are either working to prove their masculinity or resisting pressure to do so, it makes sense that the majority of men targeted for sexual harassment are harassed by heterosexual men and that the most common types of harassment they experience are sexualized acts of hostility and intimidation. Ironically, then, while the masculine regime is stabilized by homosocial rituals, it is destabilized by homosexuality. As a result, highly normative domains strongly prohibit homosexuality. For example, in the U.S. Armed Forces, homosexual behavior is a crime subject to court martial. When gays and lesbians challenged that policy by publicly owning their sexual orientations, the Clinton Administration attempted to restore order with the institution of "Don't Ask Don't Tell" policies. Yet, sexual harassment has become a common method for the informal sanction of homosexual behavior. Interestingly, false "outing," or just the threat of it is a common retaliation against *heterosexual* women who resist or complain about unwanted sexual attention, as doing so triggers formal mechanisms of social control (Embser-Herbert, 2005).

TOWARD AN ECOLOGICAL MODEL OF MASCULINITY IN ORGANIZATIONS

To this point we have examined how two different facets of male dominance—numerical and normative—affect sexual harassment prevalence and severity. For ease of discussion, we have explored each one independently; but, as our examples illustrate, these two types of dominance operate simultaneously. We have established that there are degrees to both dimensions. The sex ratio, for example, can be slightly, somewhat, or heavily skewed toward men. Similarly, attitudes about gender and feminist ideology can slide along a scale from very traditional to not traditional at all. The masculine regime—the habits, practices, and rituals that sustain male dominance—can be formal or informal, and the rules can be rigid, plastic, or somewhere in between. In light of our review and critique, the following sets forth a series of proposals for future research and policy making. For ease of discussion, they are summarized in this chapter's appendix.

Proposal I

The fact that sex ratios occur within both social and psychological contexts needs greater consideration. In operationalizing this variable, there are three dimensions that researchers should include: the *objective* count of women and men (the number of employees, participants, or members listed in formal documents); the *perception* that work domain members have of the numbers (the degree to which those populating a domain sense men or women predominate); and *changes* in both the actual number of men and the perceptions of the numbers. With regard to the second aspect, research suggests that in situations of stress majority group members are apt to inflate their estimates of the number of minority-status members who have entered their domains. Also, as we discussed earlier, a notable *shift* in numbers of women, even when they already constitute a sizable minority, may create an outbreak of misogyny. Therefore, an evaluation of male dominance should include a *sex ratio history* of the domain under investigation.

Proposal 2

The extent to which leadership can control male dominance impacts the effectiveness of policies preventing sexual harassment. This is likely to be problematic when employees work in domains that are physically isolated from those where leadership resides. A fire station, a police station, and a military barracks are prime examples of this type of separation. For example, firefighters may perceive the city government, chief's office, or even the Equal Employment Opportunity Commission director as far removed from their daily work lives and therefore ignorant of their reality (Baignet, 2005). They may resent and therefore ignore policies that mandate attitudinal or behavioral change.

In isolated settings such as these, a physical structure encompasses a social setting and blurs the distinctions between *occupation* and *organization*. In some areas within an organization there are distinct *occupational niches* where employees with similar job titles are functionally and spatially segregated from the rest of the organization. These similarities promote group identification and solidarity that may be enhanced further by similarity in ascribed characteristics (e.g., gender, race, age). The physical separation heightens the symbolic separateness of the work group. For example, Corroto's (2005) field study shows that a masculinist enclave can exist within an otherwise gender-diverse setting (a university) where men in a traditionally male occupation (architecture) claim physical space (studios) as male territory and use these areas to enact normatively male ritual activities (e.g., displaying sexual graffiti). From our experiences as sexual harassment consultants, a map of the work domain that includes the flow or patterns of movement of women and men within it not only creates a more vivid portrayal of social contact between the sexes but also delineates the boundaries (physical and/or symbolic) that may heighten sexual harassment targets' sense of entrapment.

Proposal 3

When male dominance is normalized through organized rather than individual processes, the impact of masculine norms on work domains is increased substantially. The spillover effect may be heightened considerably when hiring or promotion criteria or membership requirements to professional associations or unions codify the conflation of gender and occupational roles. For example, military and paramilitary physical fitness requirements that emphasize upper body strength normalize masculinity as an occupational requirement. Similarly, uniform requirements like those of the Hooter's restaurant (i.e., tight, low-cut T-shirts and miniskirts) institutionalize a sexually charged restaurant climate and thereby normalize unwanted sexual attention as an acceptable occupational hazard.

A key feature of the role of extra-organizational norms among groups of people is an occupational culture. What has not received research attention is an analysis of the factors that heighten tensions between organizational and occupational loyalty and identity. For male-dominated occupations this may be a primary source of male resistance to organizational policies and directives against sexual harassment as men begin their careers. For a number of jobs there is an extended socialization process that controls entry into an occupation and guides behavior during employment. There may be a formal training process wherein a candidate spends an extended period of time as a student or trainee. The training or socialization may occur in a setting that is physically, psychologically, and gender separate. Police academies and military boot camps are notable examples. The spillover of this socialization into formal work domains is accentuated by unique global occupational *identities* that link workers to groups or associations outside the work site. Professional associations, fraternal organizations, and unions not only help to sustain occupational identities at work but they also create global allegiances that extend far beyond the work site. Group solidarity is further enhanced through informal rituals and practices that bond members of an occupation at a work site (e.g., coal miner greasing, girl watching, after-work get-togethers at strip bars) that often contradict or attempt to undermine formal processes of an organization. These rituals may serve, among other functions, to heighten group boundaries.

So, as we try to understand why women police officers or members of military units experience higher levels of sexual harassment than women in the general working population, we need to move beyond their small numbers and the masculinist character of these occupations to a fuller understanding of the socialization processes that reinforce homosociality and male bonding.

Proposal 4

Collective *occupational identities* and personality characteristics and attitudes coincide. In other words, the behavior and attitudes men have about gender and sexuality are shaped not only by their training, initiations, and interpersonal experiences at work, but also by the socialization experiences that determine the kinds of work they do and how they do it. There is a self-selection process whereby men with certain attitudinal or personality characteristics are apt to choose some types of work over others, the kinds of people they choose to work with, and their interpersonal relations with coworkers and supervisors.

A key socialization variable is sexual orientation, specifically *homophobia*—one of the most popular measures of a tendency to sexually harass, according to John Pryor's LSH scale, which correlates significantly with a number of negative personality characteristics. To advance the research on personal characteristics and work roles we need research on personality types, attitudes, and proclivities that is *group-based*, specifically *occupation-based*. Research on personality types or attitudes of men in occupations that are numerically male-dominant would clarify the elements of and extend the meaning of normative dominance. The problem of male dominance isn't simply the number of men; it's the attitudes and orientations that are shaped and reinforced by homophobic and misogynist occupational cultures. For example, Kurpius and Lucart (2000) found that undergraduate members of military groups (e.g., Reserve Officers' Training Corp) had higher scores on authoritarianism than their peers.

One approach to accomplishing this might be to derive a mean score for all persons (or a sample of persons) within an occupation using measures such as the LSH, authoritarianism, anti-femininity, traditional masculinity, or other scales of this sort. A more ambitious project would involve charting change or continuity in personality and attitudes of trainees, cadets, students, and the like as they move into the formal occupational world. Such longitudinal research would provide a basis for understanding the impact of organizational variables on either reinforcing or challenging gender stereotyping and discriminatory behavior socialized through occupational cultures.

Proposal 5

A "trickle down" theory about sexual harassment predominates in both research and policy. By "trickle down" we mean that within any hierarchy—social, economic, or organizational—it is assumed that beliefs and practices among the elites trickle downward, influencing the thoughts and actions of subordinates (Hulin, Fitzgerald, & Drasgow, 1996). Within employment and educational organizations, policy implementations that embrace this view emphasize the importance of formal prohibition statements made by leadership. Legally, liability rests not so much on the type of harassment reported but on an organization's administration to respond effectively. The rationale is straightforward: If the administration does not take harassment seriously, neither will its employees. The trickle down model predicts that organizations with male-dominated leadership and/or leadership that tolerates sexual harassment and discrimination are more likely to have sexual harassment problems within the ranks.

However, the trickle down theory cannot easily account for "contra-harassment," the harassment of superiors by those of lesser status (Rospenda et al., 1998). Yet, in reality harassment of teachers by their students and supervisors by their subordinates is common. As Connell (2000) notes, within the hierarchy of men harassment is used both to maintain power and to usurp it. Men at the top harass those at the bottom as a means to exercise their superiority and maintain their elite status. In their quest for upward mobility, men of lesser status may harass their competitors (i.e., men with equal status) as well as those above them. As Acker (1990) concurs, in the hierarchy of men, women are not even at the bottom—they are outside it completely. Their attempts to "break in" can precipitate a hostile comradeship among all men.

One of most neglected aspects of sexual harassment research—most specifically in survey research—is collective resistance by men against formal policies and programs aimed at reducing harassment. Certainly, resistance to "authority" is a well-worn feature of masculinity in American popular culture. From Marlon Brando and James Dean of the postwar era to Clint Eastwood (Dirty Harry) and Sylvester Stallone (Rambo) of the 1980s to the rappers of hip-hop today, the image of a "real man" is one who resists the "system" and the incompetence and weakness (i.e., stereotypic feminine characteristics) it perpetuates. Perhaps the most glaring problem with the trickle down model of leadership is the fact that policies and programs developed to reduce sexual harassment may in fact encourage it! This was demonstrated aptly by Miller's (1997) field study of male active-duty Army soldiers. Rather than risking formal punishment by directly attacking the military's gender equity policies and practices, the men chose subversive tactics, or "weapons of the weak" (e.g., foot dragging, rumor mongering) to convey their displeasure in ways that were hidden from official scrutiny. In these types of situations the impact of sexual harassment on its targets stems not only from the severity but the pervasiveness of the behavior as well. The pervasiveness results from both instances of overt, active resistance to official policy, as well as a continuous stream of hostile and demeaning behavior under the radar of official scrutiny. Quinn (2000) describes the "paradox of complaining" wherein targets of harassment are silenced by the "humorous" thrust of public jokes or innuendos ("chain yanking"), which, though guised as "not personal," are insulting and humiliating. This resistance may become emboldened when its targets are intimidated or silenced into inaction, as is the case when the harassment experiences occur in relatively isolated settings.

We propose, then, that women and men will interact differently depending on where they are located in the organizational structure, and how this location is perceived. Researchers have conceptualized work domains as interchangeable on the rungs of an organization, and consequently we have missed the dynamics of power and powerlessness—in particular, women's roles as scapegoats among men who perceive themselves as powerless.

Proposal 6

In addition to the previous factors we've discussed, one could predict the rates at which men sexually harassed their female and male colleagues not only by these previous factors (physical isolation, masculinist occupational identity, etc.) but also by attitudes toward work and work processes. Simply put, nasty, alienating work environments create nasty interpersonal relationships. Of particular interest to us is how the *reaction* to alienation by men is along the lines of reaffirming traditional masculinity, including aggression, substance abuse, and homophobia. Gender regimes normalize aggression as appropriate for men and unacceptable among women.

In one of the first cross-national comparisons of sexual harassment experiences among blue- and white-collar women, Kauppinen and Gruber (1993) found that American autoworkers had significantly higher levels of harassment than all other workers. Part of the reason for this was their significantly higher levels of work alienation or bureaucratization. Specifically, autoworkers had higher workloads and less autonomy than American professionals or European workers, and these were strongly related to poorer social relationships. The impact of work structure and processes on job-related, psychological, and health outcomes is a well-studied area within sociology and psychology (see Blauner, 1964; Miller, 1980; Kohn, Naoi, Schoenbach, Schooler, & Slomczynski, 1990). Jobs that are routine, regimented, inflexible, highly monitored, or offer little mobility or opportunity result not only in low job satisfaction and high turnover but also in poor physical and mental health and a negative work climate. Unfortunately, the role of work structure or processes on sexual harassment has received considerably less attention than organizational "climate." For example, Fitzgerald, Drasgow, Hulin, Gelfand, and Magley (1997) do not include work bureaucratization variables at all in their analyses of the antecedents of sexual harassment. This is unfortunate because research that uses bureaucratization variables show that they have unique, independent contributions in predicting sexual harassment.

Sexual harassment is frequently found in a nexus of variable relationships that include bureaucratization, organizational climate, and work-related and psychological outcomes. Mansfield, Koch, Henderson, and Vicary (1991) found that women workers who held jobs that were characterized by monotony, isolation, and fatigue experienced more sexual harassment than women in other jobs. Perhaps the clearest distinction between the impact of work structure and work climate variables was demonstrated recently by Mueller et al. (2001). They found that centralized decision making, a lack of formal policies that protect employee rights, and rigid organizational structures with little job mobility predicted sexual harassment above and beyond job–gender context or organizational climate variables. They also raised provocative questions about the oft-cited relationships among sexual harassment and various outcomes such as job dissatisfaction, burnout, or turnover (Laband & Lentz, 1998), psychological well-being (Schneider, Swan, & Fitzgerald, 1997) and drinking (Richman, Rospenda, Nawyn, & Flaherty, 1997). When work structure variables were controlled, they found no significant relationships between sexual harassment and job dissatisfaction, job stress, or intentions to quit because "sexual harassment and negative work outcomes are related because they are [all] products of similar organizational contexts" (p. 13).

One of the significant ways in which work structure affects job outcomes and experiences at work is by its impact on organizational climate. As Kauppinen and Patoluoto (2005) note, conflict among workers in the form of bullying, intimidation, or violence is frequently found in workplaces where the pace of work has increased, concerns about retrenchment are widespread, or workloads have increased. Gutek (1985) argues that inappropriate or unprofessional behavior—drinking, sabotage, petty bickering—and sexual harassment or sociosexual behavior are correlated. In work environments where tension and conflict exist, *erotic warfare* often erupts as sex and sexuality become vehicles for expressing rivalry and dissatisfaction (Haavio-Mannila, 1992). Two studies (Kauppinen & Gruber, 1993; DeCoster, Estes, &

Mueller, 1999) that used regression analyses found that low solidarity or poor congeniality among coworkers was a strong predictor of sexual harassment. Richman and her colleagues (Richman, Rospenda, Nawyn, & Flaherty, 1997) found that environments with high levels of generalized workplace abuse had significant problems with sexual harassment, and these (in particular, generalized workplace abuse) in turn were significant predictors of depression, anxiety, and hostility for both male and female employees of a university.

There are some important implications of the research on work structure and organizational climate to male dominance. An important reason why male-dominated jobs are dangerous environments for women is because many of these jobs are highly bureaucratic (e.g., regimented, routinized, hierarchical) such as factory work or military or paramilitary jobs. Women who enter these jobs are apt to be sexually harassed as a result of two tensions: a direct threat to male power and privilege, or an already existing poor work climate brought about by alienating work. While the first tension has received considerable attention, the second needs further development. Specifically, while bureaucratic structures and processes produce similar outcomes on job (dissatisfaction, turnover) and psychological outcomes, the *reactions* to alienation seem to differ insofar as men seem more inclined to express their discontent through hostility and stereotyping.

CONCLUSION

It is our contention that a fuller understanding of sexual harassment can be found by a deeper consideration of the various ways that masculinity impacts work domains. To be sure, "male dominance" is multifaceted. A central focus of this study is the complex interrelationships between gendered numbers and norms, or "double dominance." The impact of male dominance in this regard has been lost in the shuffle of "organizational climate" theory and research.

Our critique of the literature and our proposals for further study are fueled by an ecological approach to human interactions. We begin with two assumptions: Work domains provide rich settings for "doing gender"; and the content of these gender performances are highly situational and impacted by the work context and by a variety of factors outside the domain. If a work domain is the "stage" for gendered performances, then we need to understand its unique structural and physical aspects because it matters whether the stage is in the middle of the organization or at its bottom (Proposal 5) or whether or not it is separate or unified (Proposal 2). It has long been understood that numbers, in particular ratios of women and men, shape interactions in work domains. What we have tried to do is provide a normative context to the numbers by focusing on factors that facilitate (or inhabit) the influence of traditional masculinity on work roles.

APPENDIX: PROPOSALS

1	Actual numbers, perceived numbers, and changes in numbers are intricately linked and provide a comprehensive view of a work domain.
2	The impact and subjective interpretation of numbers is related to social and physical space.
3	Numerical dominance is strengthened by normative dominance when it is mediated through socialization processes.
4	Normative male dominance is enhanced when personal characteristics intersect with workplace variables.
5	Male dominance is about power and leadership as well as powerlessness and resistance.
6	Male dominance, bureaucratization, and alienation are interrelated.

NOTES

1. Male dominance varies across social institutions, employment sectors, organizations, and work groups; thus, for ease of presentation, the term "domain" will be used to reference all of these.

2. By "gender equity" we mean that the proportions of women employed in these settings are 40% to 60%. However, because pay inequities and differences in status persist, gender parity remains an elusive goal.

REFERENCES

Acker, J. (1990). Hierarchies, jobs, bodies: A theory of gendered organizations. *Gender & Society, 2*, 139–158.

Angel, M. (1991). Sexual harassment by judges. *University of Miami Law Review, 45*, 817–841.

Baignet, D. (2005). Fitting in: The conflation of firefighting, male domination, and harassment. In J. Gruber & P. Morgan (Eds.), *In the company of men: Male dominance and sexual harassment* (pp. 45–64). Boston: Northeastern University Press.

Baker, C. (2005). Blue collar feminism: The link between male dominance and sexual harassment. In J. Gruber & P. Morgan (Eds.), *In the company of men: Male dominance and sexual harassment* (pp. 243–270). Boston: Northeastern University Press.

Bastian, L., Lancaster, A., & Reyst, H. (1996). *The Department of Defense 1995 sexual harassment survey*. Arlington, VA: Defense Manpower Data Center.

Blauner, R. (1964). *Alienation & freedom*. Chicago: University of Chicago Press.

Bond, M., Punnett, L., Pyle, J., Cazeca, D., & Cooperman, M. (2004). Gendered work conditions, health and work outcomes. *Journal of Occupational Health Psychology, 9*, 28–45.

Brooks, L., & Perot, A. (1991). Reporting sexual harassment: A predictive model. *Psychology of Women Quarterly, 15,* 31–49.

Brown, J., Campbell, E., & Fife-Schaw, C. (1995). Adverse effects experienced by police officers following exposure to sex discrimination and sexual harassment. *Stress Medicine, 11,* 221–228.

Bularzik, M. (1978, June). Sexual harassment in the workplace: Historical notes. *Radical America,* 25–43.

Business Wire (2000). As century closes, women's wage gap is still an issue. Retrieved on November 12, 2007, from http://findarticles.com/p/articles/mi_m0EIN/is_1999_Oct_13/ai_56257035.

Charney, D., & Russell, R. (1994). An overview of sexual harassment. *American Journal of Psychiatry, 15,* 10–17.

Cockburn, C. (1991). *In the way of women: Men's resistance to sex equality in organizations.* London: MacMillan.

Collinson, D. (1992). Managing the shopfloor: Subjectivity, masculinity and workplace culture. New York: de Gruyter Press.

Commission on the Status of Women (1992). *Report on the City of Los Angeles 1992 sexual harassment survey.* Los Angeles, CA: The City of Los Angeles.

Connell, R. (1995). *Masculinities.* Berkeley: University of California Press.

Connell, R. (2000). *The men and the boys.* Berkeley: University of California Press.

Corrigan, T., Connell, R., & Lee, J. (1987). Hard and heavy: Toward a new sociology of masculinity. In M. Kaufman (Ed.), *Beyond patriarchy* (pp. 139–191). New York: Oxford University Press.

Corroto, C. (2005). The architecture of sexual harassment. In J. Gruber & P. Morgan (Eds.), *In the company of men: Male dominance and sexual harassment* (pp. 271–293). Boston: Northeastern University Press.

Crull, P. (1981). The stress effects of sexual harassment on the job. *American Journal of Orthopsychiatry, 52,* 539–544.

DeCoster, S., Estes, B., & Mueller, C. (1999). Routine activities and sexual harassment in the workplace. *Work & Occupations, 26,* 21–49.

DeSouza, E., & Fansler, G. (2003). Contrapower harassment: A survey of students and faculty members. *Sex Roles, 14,* 529.

Embser-Herbert, M. (2005). A missing link: Institutional homophobia and sexual harassment in the U.S. military. In J. Gruber & P. Morgan (Eds.), *In the company of men: Male dominance and sexual harassment* (pp. 215–242). Boston: Northeastern University Press.

Farley, L. (1978). *Sexual shakedown.* New York: McGraw-Hill.

Fitzgerald, L., Drasgow, F., Hulin, C., Gelfand, M., & Magley, V. (1997). Antecedents and consequences of sexual harassment in organizations: A test of an integrated model. *Journal of Applied Psychology, 82,* 578–589.

Fitzgerald, L., & Shullman, S. (1985). The development and validation of an objectively scored measure of sexual harassment. Paper presented at the American Psychological Association, Los Angeles.

Gender wage disparity by type of job held (1998, December). *About Women and Marketing, 11.*

Gruber, J. (1998). The impact of male work environments and policies on women's experiences of sexual harassment. *Gender & Society, 12,* 301–320.

Gruber, J. (2003). Sexual harassment in the public sector. In M. Paludi & C. Paludi (Eds.), *Academic and workplace sexual harassment: A handbook for cultural, social science, management and legal perspectives.* Westport CT: Praeger Press.

Gruber, J., & Bjorn, L. (1982). Blue collar blues: The sexual harassment of women autoworkers. *Work and Occupations, 9,* 271–298.

Gruber, J., & Morgan, P. (2005). *In the company of men: Male dominance and sexual harassment.* Boston: Northeastern University Press.

Gutek, B. (1985). *Sex and the workplace.* San Francisco: Jossey-Bass.

Gutek, B., Cohen, A., & Konrad, A. (1990). Predicting socio-sexual behavior at work. *Academy of Management Journal, 33,* 560–577.

Gutek, B., & Morasch, B. (1982). Sex ratio, sex spillover and the sexual harassment of women at work. *Journal of Social Issues, 38,* 55–74.

Gutek, B., Murphy, R., & Douma, B. (2004). A review and critique of the sexual experiences questionnaire (SEQ). *Law and Human Behavior, 28,* 457–482.

Haavio-Manilla, E. (1992). *Work, family, and well-being in five North and Eastern European capitals.* Helsinki: Suomalainentiedeakatemia.

Hanrahan, P. (1997). How do I know if I am being sexually harassed? *National Women's Studies Association Journal, 9,* 43–63.

Hatty, S. (2000). *Masculinities, violence & culture.* Thousand Oaks, CA: Sage.

Hearn, J. (1985). Men's sexuality at work. In A. Melcalf & M. Humphries (Eds.), *The sexuality of men* (pp. 110–128). London: Pluto Press.

Hearn, J. (1987). *The gender of oppression.* New York: St. Martin's Press.

Hearn, J., & Parkin, W. (1995). *Sex at work.* Hertfordshire: Prentice Hall.

Holcombe, B. (1992). *Search for justice.* Walpole, NH: Stillpoint.

Hulin, C., Fitzgerald, L., & Drasgow, F. (1996). Organizational influences on sexual harassment. In M. Stockdale (Ed.), *Women & work: Sexual harassment in the workplace.* Thousand Oaks, CA: Sage.

Kanter, R. (1977). *Men and women of the corporation.* New York: Basic Books.

Katzenstein, M.R.J. (1999). *Beyond zero tolerance.* Lanham: Rowman & Littlefield.

Kaufman, M. (Ed.). (1987). *Beyond patriarchy.* Toronto: Oxford University Press.

Kauppinen, K., & Gruber, J. (1993). The antecedents and outcomes of women-unfriendly behavior. *Psychology of Women Quarterly, 17,* 431–456.

Kauppinen, K., & Patoluoto, S. (2005). Sexual harassment and violence toward police women in Finland. In J. Gruber & P. Morgan (Eds.), *In the company of men: Male dominance & sexual harassment* (pp. 195–214). Boston: Northeastern University Press.

Kelly, R. M. (1991). *The gendered economy.* Thousand Oaks, CA: Sage.

Kimmel, M. (1995). *Manhood in America.* New York: Free Press.

Kohn, M., Naoi, A., Schoenbach, C., Schooler, C., & Slomczynski, K. (1990). Position in the class structure and psychological functioning in the United States, Japan, and Poland. *American Journal of Sociology, 95,* 964–1008.

Kurpius, S., & Lucart, A. (2000). Military and civilian undergraduates: Attitudes toward women, masculinity, and authoritarianism. *Sex Roles, 43,* 255–265.

Laband, D., & Lentz, B. (1998). The effects of sexual harassment on job satisfaction, earnings, and turnover among female lawyers. *Industrial and Labor Relations Review, 51,* 594–614.

Lipka, S. (2005). Defense Department releases data on sexual assaults at military academies. *Chronicle of Higher Education*. Available from http://chronicle.com/daily/2005/03/2005032102n.htm.

MacKinnon, C. (1979). *The sexual harassment of working women*. New Haven: Yale University Press.

MacKinnon, C. (1987). *Feminism unmodified*. New Haven: Yale University Press.

Mansfield, P., Koch, P., Henderson, J., & Vicary, J. (1991). The job climate for women in traditionally male blue-collar occupations. *Sex Roles, 25*, 63–79.

Martin, S., & Jurik, N. (2006). *Doing justice, doing gender*. Thousand Oaks, CA: Sage.

Messerschmidt, J. (1993). *Masculinities and crime*. Lansing: Rowman & Littlefield.

Miller, J. (1980). Individual and occupational determinants of job satisfaction. *Sociology of Work and Occupations, 7*, 337–366.

Miller, L. (1997). Not just weapons of the weak: Gender harassment as a form of protest for Army. *Social Psychology Quarterly, 60*, 32–51.

Morgan, P. (1999). Risking relationships: Understanding the litigation choices of sexually harassed women. *Law & Society Review, 33*, 67–92.

Morgan, P. (2001). Sexual harassment: Violence against women at work. In C. Renzetti, J. Edelson, and R. Bergen (Ed.), *Sourcebook on Violence Against Women* (pp. 209–222). Thousand Oaks, CA: Sage.

Mueller, C., DeCoster, S., & Estes, B. (2001). Sexual harassment in the workplace. *Work and Occupations, 28*(4), 411–446.

Pringle, R. (1989). *Secretaries talk: Sexuality power and work*. London: Verso Press.

Pryor, J., Giedd, J., & Williams, J. (1995). A social psychological model for predicting sexual harassment. *Journal of Social Issues, 51*, 69–84.

Pryor, J., & Stoller, L. (1994). Sexual cognition processes in men high in the likelihood to sexually harass. *Personality and Social Psychology Bulletin, 20*, 163–169.

Quinn, B. (2000). The paradox of complaining: Law, humor and harassment in the everyday work world. *Law & Social Inquiry, 25*, 1151–1185.

Rederstorff, J., Buchanan, N., & Settles, I. (2007). The moderating roles of race and gender role attitudes in the relationship between sexual harassment and psychological well-being. *Psychology of Women Quarterly, 31*, 50–61.

Richman, J., Rospenda, K., Nawyn, S., & Flaherty, J. (1997). Workplace harassment and the self-medication of distress. *Contemporary Drug Problems, 24*, 179–200.

Rospenda, K., Richman, J., & Nawyn, S. (1998). Doing power: The confluence of gender, race, and class in contrapower sexual harassment. *Gender & Society, 12*, 40–60.

Schneider, K., Swan, S., & Fitzgerald, L. (1997). Job-related and psychological effects of sexual harassment in the workplace. *Journal of Applied Psychology, 82*, 401–415.

Smith, R. (2002, December 17). Salomon is told to pay broker $2.5 million. *Wall Street Journal*, p. C–1.

Stambaugh, P. M. (1997). The power of law and the sexual harassment complaints of women. *National Women's Studies Association Journal, 9*, 23–42.

Stockdale, M. (2005). The sexual harassment of men: Articulating the approach-rejection theory of sexual harassment. In J. Gruber & P. Morgan (Eds.), *In the company of men: Male dominance and sexual harassment* (pp. 117–142). Boston: Northeastern University Press.

Stockdale, M., Wood, M., & Batra, L. (1999). The sexual harassment of men: Evidence for a broader theory of sex harassment and sex discrimination. *Psychology, Public Policy and Law, 5*, 630–664.

Texteira, M. (2002). Who protects and serves me? *Gender & Society, 16*, 524–545.

Timmerman, M. (1990). *Werkrelaties tussen vrouwen en mannen ongewenste intimiteiten in arbeidssituaties.* Amsterdam: Sua.

Titunik, R. (2000). The first wave: Gender integration and military culture. *Armed Forces & Society, 26*, 229–257.

U.S. Merit Systems Protection Board (1981). *Sexual harassment in the federal government.* Washington, DC: U.S. Government Printing Office.

U.S. Merit Systems Protection Board (1988). *Sexual harassment in the federal government: An update.* Washington, DC: U.S. Government Printing Office.

U.S. Merit Systems Protection Board (1995). *Sexual harassment in the federal workplace: Trends, progress & continuing challenges.* Washington, DC: U.S. Government Printing Office.

Violence against women in the military (2001, August 18). *USA Today,* p. 14.

West, C., & Zimmerman, D. (1987). Doing gender. *Gender & Society, 1*, 125–151.

Wonders, N. (1997). Politics of the policy process. In B. Sandler and R. Shoop (Eds.), *Sexual harassment on campus.* Boston: Allyn & Bacon.

Yoder, J., & Aniakudo, P. (1997). Outsider within the firehouse. *Gender & Society, 11*, 324–341.

Yount, K. (1991). Ladies, flirts and tomboys. *Journal of Contemporary Ethnography, 19*, 396–422.

Yount, K. (2005). Sexualization of work roles among men miners: Structural and gender-based origins of "harazzment." In J. Gruber & P. Morgan (Eds.), *In the company of men: Male dominance and sexual harassment* (pp. 65–91). Boston: Northeastern University Press.

Chapter 6

Challenges for Women of Color

Darlene C. DeFour

When people say that they want to focus only on gender, I wonder which aspect of myself I should leave at home when I go in to work. Should I leave home race today? Or should I leave home my gender?

(Told to the author)

Demographers predict that by 2050 half or nearly half of the population will be of color (Armas, 2007). In some states people of color are already the majority or near majority of the population. This boost in diversity is the result of a few factors, including: the predicted small decline in the non-Hispanic white population, continued large increases in the Hispanic and Asian populations, and the continued growth of the Black population. Add to these factors the increases in populations of immigrant of color and one can predict the characteristics of the labor force in the future. The enlargement of a multicultural population will mean a workforce that is more culturally diversified.

The workplace has continued to become more diverse in terms of gender over the years. There have been steady increases in women in the United States who are employed outside of the home. Over 60% of women who are 16 and older are members of the workforce (Bureau of Statistics, 2004).

Race and ethnicity are not current predictors of whether or not women are working outside of the home. According to the Bureau of Statistics (2004), 62% of Black women, 59% of Asian women, 59% of European-American women, and 58% of Latina women are in the workforce. While race/ethnicity may not strongly predict whether or not a woman is employed outside of the home, it can shape what she encounters while there. Race/ethnicity can influence the type of employment (Essed, 1991), stereotypes held about her abilities (St. Jean & Feagin, 1998), and her salary (Bureau of Statistics, 2004). Collins (2000) contends that the experiences of women cannot be investigated in terms of gender only. Collins's point is well taken in terms of salaries. Although women typically make less money than men, the amount varies across ethnicities. Thus a complete analysis of working women's experiences must consider identities in addition to gender. Looking at gender only when considering salaries would not take into account the milieu in which women operate. Feminists of color assert that all experiences should be analyzed using a framework that considers interlocking systems of oppression. This would include considering gender, race, class, ethnicity, and sexual orientation. Although the exploration of how the intersection between gender and all identities is important to consider, the focus of this chapter will be on the gender–race/ethnicity intersection. Collins's analysis suggests that it is important to look at the unique experiences of women of color.

Although great strides have been made, women continue to experience barriers to their success based on their sex. These obstacles are exhibited in terms of prejudice (negative attitudes about women's abilities); discrimination (treating women differently because of their sex); and stereotyping (beliefs about women's talents and abilities). The experiences of men and women of color with work and the workplace can be affected by race and ethnicity (St. Jean & Feagin, 1998). The obstacles based on sex can take unique forms for women of color (e.g., racialized sexual harassment) (Buchanan, 2005). It is important that we examine how the confluence of race and gender can influence the work lives of women of color.

In this chapter we will first look at definitions of sexism and racism and new definitions that incorporate simultaneously experienced gender and race discrimination. We will then look at specific ways women of color experience workplace discrimination. Finally, we will discuss frameworks for combating gender racism in the workplace.

CONCEPTUALIZING DISCRIMINATION: GENDER AND RACE

Gender discrimination and race discrimination have been conceptualized in a variety of ways (e.g., Glick & Fiske, 1996, 2001; Dovidio, 2001; Jones, 1997). These varying conceptualizations are relevant here in that they reflect the ways that unfair treatment may manifest in the workplace. Trends in conceptualizations of gender and race discrimination have followed similar paths. Initial research focused on blatant forms of the behaviors and took the perspective of the perpetrator. Current research examines hidden forms of discrimination and includes perspectives of the target (e.g., Essed, 1991; Swim & Stangor, 1998). How have gender and race discrimination been conceptualized?

SEX DISCRIMINATION

Glick and Fiske (1996, 2001) have delineated the contours of sexism in their work on ambivalent sexism. According to their work, attitudes toward women are not necessarily hostile; however, these attitudes still serve to undermine women and maintain subservient roles. They describe two forms of sexism: hostile sexism and benevolent sexism. Hostile sexism is based on a dislike of or an antagonism toward women. Women are viewed as trying to control men. Women may be seen as using their sex and/or sexuality to get ahead. This is the form of sexism that most people would define as sexism. Conversely, with benevolent sexism there is no overt hatred of women. In fact, women may be revered. They are perceived as being in need of help and protection. Women are seen as having a particular "place" in society. Benevolent sexism is defined as a set of interrelated attitudes toward women that are sexist in terms of viewing women stereotypically and in restricted roles but are subjectively positive in feeling and tone (for the perceiver) and tend to elicit behaviors typically categorized as prosocial (i.e., helping) or intimacy-seeking (i.e., self-disclosure) (Glick and Fiske, 1996, p. 491).

The work of Glick and Fiske (1996, 2001) is important in that it makes clear critical features of sexism. First, their work has shown the multidimensional nature of sexist thought. Second, sexism may not appear as blatant hostility, in some cases it is behavior that may appear to be supportive of women. Third, sexist beliefs are not harmless in that they are associated with unequal treatment.

Benokaraitis (1997) also conceptualizes sexism as a multidimensional construct. Sex discrimination is defined as "unequal and harmful treatment of people because of their sex (i.e., biological differences between males and females, which include hormones, chromosomes, and anatomical characteristics)" (p. 7). She further posits that sex discrimination comes in three general manifestations: blatant sex discrimination, subtle sex discrimination, and covert sex discrimination. Blatant sex discrimination is defined as "unequal and harmful treatment of women that is intentional, quite visible, and can be easily documented" (p. 7). Some examples of blatant sexism cited are sexual harassment, sexist language and jokes, gendered physical violence (including rape and wife abuse), and unfair treatment in societal institutions (e.g., the family, employment, education, politics) (Benokaraitis). Subtle sex discrimination is defined as "unequal and harmful treatment of women that is typically less visible and obvious than blatant sex discrimination." It is behavior that is frequently not seen as sexism or perceived at all. This behavior is frequently not seen because it has become part of the societal norm. It has been normalized; thus it is not viewed as damaging. When women complain about this form of sexism they are frequently accused of being too sensitive. Benokaraitis outlines nine forms of subtle discrimination. They include condescending chivalry, supportive discouragement, friendly harassment, subjective objectification, radiant devaluation, liberated sexism, benevolent exploitation, considerate domination, and collegial exclusion. Covert sex discrimination was defined as "the unequal and harmful treatment of women that is hidden, purposeful, and often, maliciously motivated" (p. 12). An essential feature of this form of sexism is that it is intentional. Males deliberately strive to guarantee that women do not succeed. Two common forms of covert discrimination are manipulation and sabotage. This form of sexism frequently occurs in educational and employment settings.

Benokaraitis's (1997) subtle sex discrimination construct shares much with Glick and Fiske's (1996, 2001) benevolent sexism construct. They both point to an ideology that makes particular discriminatory behaviors toward women part of the fabric of life.

RACE DISCRIMINATION

There is a long history of research on racism and prejudice (e.g., Allport, 1958; Brewer, 1979; McConahay, 1986; Jones, 1997; Dovidio, 2001; Swim & Stangor, 1998). Current research findings point to the multidimensional nature of racial discrimination. As the societal context has changed, the nature of racial prejudice and discrimination has changed with it. As with sexism, the forms that race discrimination takes can be overt and hostile or subtle and seemingly not related to the social category (in this case, race). These concepts of racism were initially focused on attitudes and behaviors toward Black Americans but have now been broadened to include other groups of color.

Early research on race discrimination concentrated on what is now called "old-fashioned racism." Old-fashioned racism is a form of racism where people support derogatory statements about the abilities or intelligence of Blacks and other people of color or support obviously racist social policies (e.g., racially segregated schools). Symbolic racism/modern racism is a less overt form of race discrimination. Racism is not expressed as overt hostility toward Blacks and other groups of color. In this form of racism individuals are not "anti-Black." They do not say that Black people should be denied opportunities because they are Black and innately inferior. Instead Black people and other underrepresented groups are seen as not adhering to important social American values such as hard work, being promoted on the basis of merit, and so on. They (Black people) want special treatment. This form of discrimination and prejudice is expressed in terms of endorsing statements like "Blacks are pushing too hard" and "Over the years blacks have gotten more than they deserve" (McConahay, 1986). It is associated with being against public policies like busing for school integration.

Analyses of discrimination have continued to evolve to explain seeming inconsistencies between attitudes and behavior. Dovidio (2001) and Dovidio and Gaertner (2000) posit aversive racism as a form of racism that they view as most typical of well-educated liberal Whites in the United States. (It is important to note that these are people who women of color are likely to encounter in the workforce as colleagues and employers.) They characterize aversive racism as a phenomenon that explains how many Whites who consciously, explicitly, and sincerely support egalitarian principles and perceive themselves to be nonprejudiced also harbor negative feelings and beliefs about Blacks and other historically disadvantaged groups. These unconscious negative feelings and beliefs develop as a consequence of normal, almost unavoidable and frequently functional, cognitive, motivational, and social cultural processes (Dovidio & Gaertner, p. 618).

The processes that are a part of this conceptualization of discrimination are general social psychological processes. The processes include cognitive (the seemingly natural process of placing people in categories that also activates racial bias and stereotypes), motivational (the need for individual and group power, status and control), and sociocultural (viewing these behaviors and thoughts as normal and natural and as a result adopting behaviors that perpetuate cultural stereotypes and social structures that maintain the status quo). Context affects whether or not discriminatory behaviors will be expressed. Discriminatory behavior will only be expressed in situations where "bias is not obvious or can be rationalized on the basis of some factor other than race" (Dovidio & Gaertner, 2000, p. 315).

GENDERED RACISM: THE INTERSECTION OF RACISM AND SEXISM

Although the literature on race and gender discrimination has become more complex, there is still a major gap in the literature. Conceptualizations of racism and sexism treat them as separate forms of bias. What then of people who exist in a space that crosses two devalued social categories? What then of people who are or can be discriminated against on the basis of both their sex and their race? Theorists have attempted to fill this omission in the literature with the concept of "gendered racism" (Essed, 1991; St. Jean & Feagin, 1998). The concept is based on the idea that for women of color the experiences of racism and sexism are interconnected. It is not possible to pull one apart from another. "These two concepts narrowly intertwine and combine under certain conditions into one, hybrid phenomenon" (Essed, p. 31). Gender roles of women of color are perceived through a lens of racial oppression. Viewing women of color in this way lends itself to particular negative images about their nature, talents, beliefs, and capabilities.

WORKPLACE EXPERIENCES OF WOMEN OF COLOR

Matlin (2008) describes two forms of discrimination that specifically relate to the workplace. They are access and treatment discrimination. Access discrimination refers to bias that is involved in the process of hiring. Treatment discrimination involves what happens after the person has been hired.

Women of color are frequently invisible in workforce statistics. Statistics are often reported in terms of gender or ethnicity but not both. Data are broken down in terms of "women" and "minorities." Some researchers have suggested that in some white-collar jobs we should be less concerned about access in terms of recruitment at entry-level positions (e.g., corporate management) because women of color are represented there. The greater concern is higher level advancement (e.g., Giscombe & Mattis, 2002). This is probably not the case in all forms of work. We do know that women of color are concentrated in certain fields and in low-paying jobs. Lack of access to higher paying jobs can be attributed to a number of factors including restricted access to educational opportunities and stereotyped ideas about skills and abilities. In some instances qualified women of color are not hired because the person does not fit the employer's preconceived notion of a successful applicant (St. Jean & Feagin, 1998).

EMPLOYMENT AND SALARIES

Clearly gender plays a role in women's work experiences. Women are likely to make less than men who work in a similar position. A recent report by the AAUW (2007) indicates that by the first year out of college women working full-time make less money than men. The discrepancy in salary increases over time. After the first year women earn 80% of what men make; after 10 years they earn 69% of what men receive. This difference is attributed to sex discrimination in that one-fourth of the discrepancy remains unaccounted for after factors that influence salary level are held constant. Workplace sex discrimination comes in multiple forms, including hiring rates, promotion, salaries, sexual harassment, occupational segregation, being mommy-tracked, and undervaluing women workers (WAGE, retrieved October 22, 2007). In addition, over the life of a career the unexplained portion of the salary gap increases. Thus we know that gender influences how much a person makes. However, both gender and race/ethnicity combined have an impact on how much money a women earns. Race and gender interact to influence salaries. The wage gap is not the same for all women. In 2004 median incomes by race and group were as follows: White men $45,542; White women $32,486; Black men $31,305; Black women $27,730; Hispanic men $26,679; Hispanic women $23,444; Asian men $45,870; and Asian women $35,975. The median income for Asian women was more than that for all women and more than the income of Black and Hispanic men. Thus all women are not equally affected by the wage gap.

MENTORING

Having a mentor is an important part of career development. Women of color frequently report not having mentors and being excluded from formal and informal networks at work. This appears to be the case in different fields. ABA Commission on Women (2006) conducted a study in an attempt to understand the high attrition rate of women of color lawyers in private law firms. Women of color lawyers in private firms report having mentors; however, although they had mentors, having a mentor did not appear to work for them as it did for White men. Traditionally, having a mentor increases access to important assignments, opportunities for advancement, and incorporation into the life of the organization. Even with mentors the women of color were still excluded from the internal networks within the firm. Having a mentor also did not increase the likelihood that they would have more contact with clients or get work assignments that would allow them to earn more billable hours. Numbers of billable hours is important because they determine who becomes a partner in a law firm. Women of color associates reported that the types of assignments that they had appeared to be tied their race and gender. They reported that contact with clients occurred only when their race or gender was beneficial to the firm. During these meetings their presence was more like "window dressing" to put the client at ease, and they did not play a substantive role.

In a study of resilience and resistance strategies of women of color faculty, Thomas and Hollenshead (2001) found that women of color at their academic institution were less likely to have mentors than were White women, White men, and men of color. Women of color's mentors were more frequently individuals who were not located in their campus units or departments or their academic institutions. They were more likely to use nontraditional forms of mentoring structures. Instead of having one individual who was older and more experienced, women of color used groups of peers. Women of color also used the ethnic minority sections of their professional organizations to find individuals who could assist them with a specific issue.

Although not focusing on the experiences of women of color, Kaminiski (2004) describes how mentoring and social networks can work to promote career development in academia. The mentor of a junior male faculty member who came to her campus the same year that she did received protection from his mentor. His mentor interceded to prevent him from having to work on campus and departmental committees. If the faculty member was asked, his mentor told the department head that the person needed time to work on his research so he should be excused. In contrast, Kaminiski was assigned to work on the executive committee, which is the departmental committee that required the most work. In addition to this, the junior faculty's mentor taught one of his courses for him. These things gave him more time to do his work and focus on receiving tenure. In academia receiving tenure and getting promoted are essential parts of career development.

Kaminiski (2004) also describes another exclusionary practice. Male faculty members went to lunch together; women were never invited to attend. This is another example of exclusion from internal networks. When asked about this faculty would say that they are friends or that they were discussing things that women would not be interested in. This is an example of rationalizing the practice by using reasons other than race and gender. It should be noted that these networks and informal gatherings serve multiple functions. First, they make a person feel like they are part of the fabric of the work group. Women of color in academia and other predominately White workplaces frequently describe feelings of alienation and isolation (Myers, 2002; St. Jean & Feagin, 1998). These informal gatherings set up relationships that can lead to working on projects. In addition, during informal meetings information about work is passed on (e.g., unwritten rules).

All of these point to subtle forms of sexism, benevolent sexism, and gendered racism. These examples of practices that appear not to be linked to race or gender nevertheless affect women's career trajectories.

OTHER FORMS OF GENDERED RACISM

Results of research suggest that women of color frequently feel that their work is judged through a lens of gendered racism. Themes that have arisen in numerous studies include:

1. Feeling that their work is viewed as unimportant. In academia it is especially not valued if the person is studying race and gender. This leads them to being asked to perform more service functions (Myers, 2004; Thomas & Hollenshead, 2001).

2. Feeling a lack of respect from colleagues for their work and research agendas.

3. Feeling of being used by their organizations or in academia their departments. They are asked to participate if the issue pertains to race or gender but not for other issues.

4. Feeling that they are judged by different standards and having to prove oneself over and over again (Myers, 2004; St. Jean & Feagin, 1998).

5. Feeling that they are under constant observation.

6. Not being made aware of the unwritten rules in their organization (Thomas & Hollenshead, 2001).

Women of color also reported that competent behavior such as using Standard English or writing well was viewed with surprise as an anomaly and meriting special praise (St. Jean & Feagin, 1998). Speaking Standard English was viewed as going against unconscious views of women of color's abilities. In addition, women still faced occupational ceilings. Women of color are only allowed to rise to a certain level. Employers continue to have stereotypes of Black women and other women of color, which include believing they are not particularly competent. Women of color are viewed as affirmative-action hires. A person who is hired via affirmative action is seen as not being competent (St. Jean & Feagin). The person is seen as being a part of the organization only because of the policy. They are viewed as covering two affirmative action categories—gender and race. In addition, women discuss being referred to in ways that reflect stereotypes about women of color (e.g., subtly suggesting that their form of dress makes them look like a prostitute) (Buchanan, 2005). Employers and others feel comfortable making comments about natural hairstyles. An example of this is a recent comment made during a presentation by an editor from *Glamour* magazine to members of a law firm where she indicated that wearing natural hairstyles was inappropriate for the practice of law.

WHAT CAN BE DONE ABOUT GENDERED RACISM IN THE WORKPLACE?

In combating racism and sexism in the workplace, multiple strategies must be used that deal with the multidimensional nature of the problem. The key is that workplaces must pay active attention to this issue. Creating workplace conditions that will allow women of color to flourish will not happen by chance. Giscombe & Mattis (2002) maintain that attempting to achieve diversity based on the business model (i.e., Do it because diversity is good business—it will lead to increases in profits.) is not really effective. Using this model does not promote social change. They believe that diversity programs should have a social justice agenda underlying its programs. Triandis (2006) suggests that, to combat these issues, organizations must develop a cultural intelligence. Cultural intelligence means "the capability of being effective across cultural settings" (Ng & Earley, 2006). In this context it would mean taking into consideration gender and race when thinking about how behaviors will be perceived. Triandis believes that there are a few practices that lend themselves to being culturally intelligent. These include not forming judgments until information about the person is gathered, and paying attention to the situation. As pointed out earlier in the chapter, unfair treatment of women of color is often the result of making judgments based on stereotypes.

Kaminiski (2004, p. 106–107) outlines strategies that can be used at, in, or by departments in academic settings. These include:

1. Transparency in decision making—making both the process and outcome public to everyone.
2. Fairness in performance evaluation—making sure that everyone has the same information about what evaluations will be based on.
3. Tracking resources distributions—providing the same level of support for all, men and women; this case it should be true across racial lines as well.
4. Inclusivity—finding a way for members of the department to perceive themselves as belonging to a common group.
5. Labor unions—using them to promote diversity and to fight back if equity is violated.

Research on the experiences of women of color in the workforce has evolved; however, there is still a need to continue to uncover how other aspects of their identities simultaneously impact their work experience. How do race, gender, class, sex, and sexual orientation intersect and interact? By looking at these intersections we will get more insight into the work lives of all women.

REFERENCES

AAUW (2007). Behind the Pay Gap.

ABA Commission on Women in the Profession (2006). Visible invisibility: Women of color in law firms. Retrieved on October 1, 2007.

Allport, G. W. (1954). *The nature of prejudice*. Reading, MA: Addison-Wesley.

Armas, G. C. (2007). Census bureau predicts diverse U.S. future. In P. S. Rothenberg (Ed.), *Race, class and gender in the United States* (pp. 203–205). New York: Worth.

Benokaraitis, N. V. (1997). Sex discrimination in the 21st century. In N. V. Benokaraitis (Ed.), *Subtle sexism* (pp. 5–33). Thousand Oaks, CA: Sage.

Brewer, M. B. (1979). Ingroup bias in the minimal intergroup situation: A cognitive motivational analysis. *Psychological Bulletin, 86,* 307–324.

Buchanan, N. T. (2005). The nexus of race and gender domination racialized sexual harassment of African American women. In J. E. Gruber and P. Morgen (Ed.), *In the company of men: Male dominance and sexual harassment* (pp. 294–320). Boston, MA: Northeastern University.

Collins, P. H. (2000). Gender, black feminism and black political economy. *Annals of the American Academy of Political and Social Science, 568,* 41–43.

Dovidio, J. F. (2001). On the nature of contemporary prejudice: The third wave. *Journal of Social Issues, 57,* 829–849.

Dovidio, J. F., & Gaertner, S. L. (2000). Aversive racism and selection decisions: 1989 and 1999. *Psychological Science, 11,* 315–319.

Essed, P. (1991). *Understanding everyday racism.* Newbury Park, CA: Sage.

Giscombe, K., & Mattis, M. C. (2002). Leveling the playing field for women of color in corporate management: Is the business case enough? *Journal of Business Ethics, 37,* 103–119.

Glick, P., & Fiske, S. T. (1996). The Ambivalent Sexism Inventory: Differentiating hostile and benevolent sexism. *Journal of Personality and Social Psychology, 70,* 491–512.

Glick, P., & Fiske, S. T. (2001). An ambivalent alliance. Hostile and benevolent sexism as complementary justifications for gender inequality. *American Psychologist, 56,* 109–119.

Higginbotham, E. (2004). Invited reaction: Black and white women managers: Access to opportunity. *Human Resource Development Quarterly, 15,* 147–152.

Hite, L. M. (2004). Black and white women managers: Access to opportunity. *Human Resource Development Quarterly, 15,* 131–146.

Jones, J. M. (1997). *Prejudice and racism* (2nd ed.). New York: McGraw-Hill.

Kaminiski, M. (2004). Running into the wind: The experience of discrimination in an academic workplace. In J. L. Chin (Ed.), *The psychology of prejudice and discrimination—Bias based on gender and sexual orientation, Volume 3* (pp. 93–111). Westport, CT: Praeger.

Matlin, M. W. (2008). *The psychology of women* (6th Ed.). Belmont, CA: Thomson Wadsworth.

McConahay, J. B. (1986). Modern racism, ambivalence, and the modern racism scale. In J. F. Dovidio & S. L. Gaerner (Eds.). *Prejudice, discrimination and racism* (pp. 91–125). Orlando, FL: Academic.

Myers, L. W. (2002). *A broken silence: Voices of African American women in the academy.* Westport, CT: Greenwood.

Myers, L. W. (2004). Black women coping with stress in academia. In J. L. Chin (Ed.), *The psychology of prejudice and discrimination. Bias based on gender and sexual orientation, Volume 3* (pp. 134–149). Westport, CT: Praeger.

Ng, K., & Earley, P. (2006). Culture and intelligence. *Group and Organization Management, 31,* 4–19.

St. Jean, & Feagin, J. R. (1998). *Double burden: Black women and everyday racism.* Armonk, NY: M. E. Sharpe.

Swim, J. K., & Stangor, C. (Eds.). (1998). *Prejudice: The target's perspective.* San Diego, CA: Academic.

Thomas, G. D., & Hollenshead, C. (2001). Resisting from the margins: The coping strategies of Black women and other women of color faculty members at a research university. *Journal of Negro Education, 70,* 166–176.

Triandis, H. C. (2006). Cultural intelligence in organizations. *Group and organizational management, 31*(1), 20–26.

WAGE. Retrieved October 22, 2007, from http://www.wageproject.org.

U.S. Department of Labor, Bureau of Labor Statistics. (2004). *Quarterly Census of Employment and Wages.* Washington, DC: Author.

Chapter 7

On Being a Woman Chiropractor: In My Own Voice

Patricia Campbell

"God, you're beautiful."

"I want you so bad."

"What a honey-mummy you are."

These are all comments I have received from male patients of all ages, from 20 to 70+, from first meeting to having treated them for many years. I was stunned—*I'm your doctor not your girlfriend*—then I was angry—*How dare you treat me that way*. Mostly, I blamed myself. I looked at what I wore, how I treated people, how I looked—it had to be me. I changed how I dressed, what I looked like. I cut my hair short, wore jackets and layers to hide myself, restricted my time with patients, especially men, and stayed with office hours not seeing patients after hours as emergencies. I did not go out in public alone, I tried to have my children, husband, or friend with me, I put in a swimming pool instead of going to the beach—two blocks away. I hid the vehicle so people would not know I was at home, even though I live in a small town where everyone knows everyone else—the people you work with are the parents at your child's school and their children are friends with your children and you see the same people at the arena, fitness club, and grocery store. I still believed it was something I was doing, it was my fault.

Then at a seminar 4 years into practice, I went to lunch with seven other women, and as the stories began to pour from them I realized I was not alone and patients behaving badly was a very large, silent problem. The solutions were as varied as the women at the table. One confronted a patient head-on and even banned him from the office.

Others like myself took personal responsibility and changed ourselves; others ignored it and thought we were over-reacting.

All the changes I made did little to improve the situation. The comments continued and even increased as people commented on the new look and gave their own opinion—"Grow your hair; I so like long blond hair."

Chiropractic college was an idyllic setting, intimate with only 800 staff and students, sheltered from the real world with support and guidance at every step, an atmosphere of respect, equality, and gender neutrality. Discussions about sexual harassment and abuse focused on the actions of male doctors who misused their authority. The doctor was responsible for the doctor–patient relationship. No mention was made about patients misbehaving or having anything other than the utmost respect for doctors.

With this sheltered and naïve attitude, I opened my own office at 26 years of age. A bubbly and vivacious young woman with a ready smile and warm approach, I welcomed everyone into the office and into care. As time went on, I began to wonder about comments certain patients made, their over-interest in my personal life, attention to me which was not in line with their care. I put it off to small-town life, a "high" profile of a doctor in the community, concern from the patients. I am a doctor, I was to be respected and appreciated, revered for my concern and knowledge—not hit on like I was at the bar.

Like any good doctor when faced with a problem, I began to research sexual harassment in the medical community. The lack of research was shocking and what I did find was strangely comforting. My excuses and self-blame were normal responses, and it was very common for females to be treated as women first and professionals second.

Because chiropractic and medicine are male-dominated fields, my mentors and older male colleagues had no experience with harassment and really didn't think it existed. The regulatory college and the rules and guidelines that govern the profession reflected a similar standpoint. The doctor is responsible for the patient–doctor relationship, and the doctor is held accountable for it.

One story shared with me and shared now with permission highlights how complicated and stressful harassment can be and how difficult dealing with it is.

It was a routine request, "May I see you after work for an adjustment?" Sure, this was a patient she had treated for 6 years and also treated his family and several friends—a great patient and an excellent ambassador for the office.

After the adjustment, they walked out of the treating room into the reception area. He stood in front of the exit door and she sat on the second step of the stairs a few feet away. Suddenly, he began to move toward her, she extended her hands to stop him. He grabbed her hands. In an instant, her world was upside down, laid out on the stairs with him straddling her hips, hands pinned above her head. She had to listen while he told her how much he wanted her and how long he had wanted her. Calmly, she tried to explain to him how such an affair was against her moral, professional, and social standards, as well as the trouble she would get into. He would hear none of it as he replied, "Trust me, I won't tell."

This situation was complicated by several factors:

1. She lived in a small town and these were her patients, friends, and colleagues—socially and professionally;
2. His mother taught at her children's school;
3. He was 20 years old and she was in her thirties;
4. The regulatory college has a zero tolerance policy against sexual abuse and does not care about the situation, only the letter of the law;
5. She is the doctor, with the power and authority, how could she let this happen;
6. Her reputation could be ruined and livelihood destroyed.

He left that night, understanding her point of view; yet, terrified, embarrassed, and scared, she said nothing for years. As a result of stress and panic attacks brought on by this encounter, she has left practice.

From my research, I have found sexual harassment of female doctors is the norm not the exception. Harassment will continue and even escalate if ignored. Certain men will treat a professional as a woman first and a doctor second. The regulatory bodies and professional associations believe this to be the doctor's responsibility and fault. Social standards and perceptions of health care professionals are changing and the respect and awe once experienced for doctors has diminished to the point of a hired consultant.

With more women entering the male-dominated health care fields, rules, regulations, and attitudes must change and support systems be developed and instituted to deal with this silent epidemic.

Chapter 8

Relationships with Men

Donna Castañeda
Breena E. Coates

Two-thirds of women in the United States over age 20 are in the paid workforce—when women in the armed forces are included, the proportion of women who work reaches 70% (U.S. Census Bureau, 2003). Thus, a large number of women spend a significant amount of their waking hours at work (Sayer, 2005) and, not surprisingly, the workplace is where many women encounter persons with whom they develop important relationships. Researchers increasingly understand that relationships are at the center of organizational life and it is through them that much of the work gets done (Blatt & Camden, 2007; Ragins & Dutton, 2007; Wilson & Ferch, 2005). Positive relationships with co-workers, subordinates, and superiors are critical to a woman's job satisfaction, motivation, and career advancement, and just as importantly, contribute favorably to the core competencies and end products of a particular organization. Even conceptions of effective leadership are changing to reflect the importance of relational interactions and the skills that are most useful in these, such as empathy, authenticity, and humility (Badarraco, 2002; Collins, 2001; see Fletcher, 2007 for a discussion).

Relationships that women develop with other women are important and may provide them with social support (Andrew & Montegue, 1998; Aronson, 1998; Lu & Argyle, 1992; Mays, 1985; Nyamathi, Bennett, Leake, & Chen, 1995; Severance, 2005), opportunities for companionship and enjoyable social interaction (Fehr, 1996; Severance, 2005), intimacy (Fehr, 2004; Parks & Floyd, 1996a; Sapadin, 1988), instrumental assistance (Nyamathi et al., 1995; Patterson & Bettini, 1993; Walker,

1995), and they contribute to their social and personal identities (Johnson & Aries, 1983). This chapter, however, focuses on women's relationships with men in the workplace and examines the nature of these relationships, why they may be important, and the consequences, both positive and negative, they may have for women. Although many categories of workplace relationships with men could be addressed, this chapter will focus on two of these—women's workplace friendships and romantic relationships with men.

Women's relationships with men at work are varied and they often develop out of the particular roles that women take in the workplace—men may be colleagues, coworkers, supervisors, staff that women supervise, managers, mentors, teammates, leaders, or team members that women lead. Just as in relationships outside the workplace, women's relationships with men at work can include instrumental or expressive qualities, or a combination of these elements, and their relationships with men can range from being close and intimate to superficial in quality (Lobel, Quinn, Warfield, & St. Clair, 1994). Women may also view and possibly label some of these relationships as friendships or romantic relationships. Nevertheless, the workplace is unique in that it is an arena where connection with others occurs along with demands for individual achievement and productivity (Quick, Gavin, Cooper, & Quick, 2004; Wilson & Ferch, 2005). Despite being a location where people sometimes meet others with whom they develop close and long-lasting relationships (Kalmijn & Flap, 2001), work requirements may necessitate, even motivate, intense competition and acrimony. This duality can create conflicts, contradictions, and stress for women. Despite more women being integrated into higher levels of organizational structures today, the implicit and sometimes explicit gender, class, sexual orientation, and ethnic/racial hierarchies and power relations that permeate and organize the workplace (Acker, 1990; Hurtado, 1996; Stobbe, 2006) may make women particularly vulnerable to negative consequences of relationships with men in the workplace, such as discrimination and sexual harassment. This reality of the workplace is always present and plays an important role in how women experience relationships with men.

FRIENDSHIPS WITH MEN IN THE WORKPLACE

Definitions of friendship abound, but they share common features such as notions of intimacy, trust, loyalty, liking, and shared interests (see Fehr, 1996: Berman, West, & Richter, 2002; Sapadin, 1988). Implicitly, or sometimes explicitly, definitions of friendship include the notion that they are entered into and maintained voluntarily and that, unlike other significant relationships, friendships in Western cultures are not formalized through familial or societal structures or obligations

(Fehr, 1996; Stein, 1993). In fact, the imposition of rigid role structures may be viewed as antithetical to formation of true friendship bonds (Bell & Coleman, 1999).

On the other hand, women's friendships with men in the workplace differ from those that occur outside of work, in that those within the workplace are, to a large extent, non-voluntary (Duck, 2007). In reality, choices of friends outside the workplace are not totally voluntarily made either. We are most likely to become friends with those who are of the same gender, similar in age, social class, sexual orientation, race/ethnicity, and who live in the same geographic area (Castañeda & Burns-Glover, in press; Cook, Bruin, & Crull, 2000; O'Boyle & Thomas, 1996; Rose, 1995; Serafica, Weng, & Kim, 2000; Way & Chen, 2000). To some extent, women choose their friends at work, certainly, but they may not realize the extent to which these choices are curtailed, bounded, or influenced by the specific work context. This may seem unimportant, but in a friendship outside work for example, the affective and relationship processes such as caring, trust, fairness, intimacy, and so on are developed and negotiated with the implicit understanding that if the relationship proves unrewarding, it may be exited. In the workplace, however, women must often continue to interact, work, and complete tasks with men even after a friendship has waned or even failed. The implications this may have for women's work life, both for its day-to-day quality and its influence on their success or advancement in the workplace, may be quite serious in comparison to friendships outside the workplace.

The social and relational nature of work plays a primary role in organizational life (Ragins & Dutton, 2007) and, although organizations are not bound to do so, more and more of them recognize the need to provide employees with not only a job and salary but also a pleasant and positive work environment. Organizations may therefore use strategies that promote workplace friendships, such as development of an atmosphere of openness, encouraging employees to act in a friendly manner with each other, training of supervisors and staff in how to develop positive relations at work, providing opportunities for workers to socialize with one another, and so on (Berman, West, & Richter, 2002). Nevertheless, the desire to create a positive and socially enjoyable workplace is not the only motivation for organizational managers. Organizations also understand that workplace friendships, or at least the opportunity for them in the organization, are linked to important work-related outcomes, such as job satisfaction, decreased employee turnover intentions, greater work involvement, greater readiness for organizational change, and greater commitment to the organization (Madsen, Miller, & John, 2005; Morrison, 2004; Nielsen, Jex, & Adams, 2000; Riordan & Griffeth, 1995). Workplace friends usually spend time together that goes beyond the needs of their job specifications, and they are able to communicate about and interact around both personal and work-related topics (Sias & Cahill, 1998). In fact, communication about work-related topics with workplace friends tends to be more in-depth, efficient, and useful than with nonwork friends (Ray, 1987). The ability to be sociable and get along with co-workers may be essential to movement from lower- to higher-level positions in the organization and in determining the "fit" of an individual for a job promotion (citation). Friendships at work help provide a pleasant work experience, help workers "get through the day," and may even spill over into and contribute to socializing activity outside work (Pettinger, 2005). Through creation of positive relationships and reduction of conflict, the effects of a workplace that facilitates friend-ships may extend and promote an organization's effectiveness even into the future (Massey, 2005).

For women, workplace friendships with men may be especially im-portant. Men continue to be most likely to hold positions of power in organizations, and the informal relationships women have with men can affect their advancement in the organization, their ability to effec-tively navigate the social and political work hierarchy, and their access to support and patronage. For example, mentor/protégée relationships can be formal in nature, where a mentor and protégée are assigned to each other by the organization, or they can be informal, where they grow out of mutual identification of needs, interpersonal comfort with and attraction to each other, and perceptions of competence in each other (Ragins & Cotton, 1999). In other words, informal mentor rela-tionships have many of the qualities of friendship and, compared to formal mentoring relationships, different consequences for work out-comes. First, informal mentors are related to greater pay compensation for both women and men than formal or no mentors. Furthermore, women report greater coaching, counseling, role modeling, social, and friendship functions with informal mentors than with formal mentors, whereas men find formal and informal mentors equally helpful in these areas. Finally, women with a history of informal and formal rela-tionships with *male* mentors, compared to such relationships with *female* mentors, tend to receive greater pay compensation (Ragins & Cotton, 1999).

Despite the usefulness to women of informal mentors, they tend to rely more heavily than men on formal relationships and organizational structures to promote their careers (De Vries, Webb, & Eveline, 2006; Pazy, 1987). These formal programs have been useful for women, and they have helped recreate, to some extent, the informal relationships or networks from which women may be excluded. However, a range of formal and informal workplace relationships with men are needed by women, including those that they consider to be friendships (Gibson, 2005). Not all women have access to a one-on-one developmental relationship with a powerful mentor, and, in fact, such a model may not be needed for women to be successful in their work lives. Informal networks and friendships with peers may be quite helpful to women and provide them with helpful role models, social support, instrumental advice, and career-development information. Furthermore, when women are in a mixed-gender employment situation, their informal relationships with men are related to their greater influence and centrality in the organization. Nonetheless, women often have difficulty developing the informal relationships with men that are beneficial to their careers, and their informal relationships at work tend to be more restricted and with less powerful employees (Brass, 1985; Cannings & Montmarquette, 1991). Of course, many other factors play a role in this finding, such as job level, gender composition of the workplace, access to high-level employees, and aspects of the job such as location, hours, full- or part-time status, and so on, but clearly friendships with men are important for women to develop in the workplace.

The development of friendships by women is influenced by many variables that can range from the individual and interpersonal to contextual variables at larger levels of analyses, such as the social network, community, and national cultural level (Adams & Allan, 1998), but the workplace in particular contains the situational elements that facilitate friendship, such as proximity (Festinger, Schacter, & Back, 1950), shared tasks and activities, and repeated exposure (Saegert, Swapp, & Zajonc, 1973) that lead to familiarity and liking. However, workplace friendships are especially influenced by the specific aspects of the work context (Sias & Cahill, 1998). For example, workers are more likely to develop intimate relationships when a supervisor's behavior is perceived to be unfair, unsupportive, or she/he appears unwilling to recognize employee accomplishments or contributions (Odden & Sias, 1997; Sias & Jablin, 1995). Friendships may also move from superficial to deeper levels as a result of workplace factors. In one study of friendship development in the workplace, for instance, progression from acquaintance to friend was most frequently related to physical proximity. On the other hand, progression from friend to close friend and from close friend to almost best friend was most frequently related to work problems, such as a difficult supervisor or coworker, or problematic organizational changes, as well as personal life events or problems (Sias & Cahill, 1998). In these cases, workplace friends can provide support, advice, and guidance that strengthen bonds between individuals. This study highlights workplace factors as an influence on friendship development, but it also demonstrates how the line between work and personal lives is much less distinct than is generally thought.

In general, women tend to have a greater desire for social ties in the workplace than do men (Konrad, Richie, Lieb, & Corrigall, 2000), but women are more likely to become friends with female than male coworkers (Elesser & Peplau, 2006; Markiewicz, Devine, & Kausilas, 2000). Men are also more likely to become friends with male rather than female coworkers, and this same-gender preference is indicative of the greater shared interests and comfort women and men may have with same-gender friends (Ibarra, 1992). Just as in relationships outside the workplace, women tend to show greater orientation to interpersonal relationships within the workplace than men. For example, women are more likely to engage in electronic and face-to-face relationship-oriented communication with other employees than are men, and they are more likely than men to report communication about nonwork topics with coworker friends (Harper, 2005; Lobel et al., 1994). These patterns imply that traditional constructions of gender surrounding friendships outside the workplace (i.e., that women are more relational than men and are more satisfied with same-gender friendships than cross-gender friendships), continue to operate in the workplace. However, other research suggests a more complex picture of friendship in organizations. For instance, in contrast to friendships outside the workplace where friendships with women are routinely rated as more satisfying by both women and men (Adams, Blieszner, & De Vries, 2000; Cheng, Chan, & Tong, 2006; Hays, 1985; Parks and Floyd, 1996), one study found that across varying job categories (lawyers, information technology workers, and managers in mid- to large-size organizations), friendships with women were not consistently rated as more satisfying than those with men (Markiewicz et al., 2000). This study also found that higher evaluation of the quality of a relationship with a male friend was related to greater salary, whereas greater efforts to spend time interacting with female friends was related to lower salary. Furthermore, tensions and strains in relationships with male friends at work resulted in lower job satisfaction for women.

Taken together, these results suggest that friendships with men are more highly linked to career success than those with women. As mentioned previously, in many job settings men tend to occupy the high power positions, thus, they may be more able to contribute to women's career success. Conversely, because they hold more positions of power in organizations, conflicts with male friends may be particularly distressing for women.

Women may have a greater desire than men for social ties in the workplace, but this should not obscure the fact that women's motivations for workplace friendships may also be related to their desire to facilitate their work and advance their careers (Markiewicz et al., 2000; Randal & Ranft, 2007). Contrary to common assumptions, women can be just as ambitious and concerned about achievement as men (Paludi, 1990), and the networking activities and informal relationship building that women engage in at work may be part of their effort at career development. In fact, when women's motivations for coworker relationships are primarily based upon their desire to facilitate or advance their work, rather than primarily related to development of social ties, they engage in greater information exchange outside their organizations, which provides them greater opportunities to find other jobs (Randal & Ranft, 2007).

The gender composition of an organization and a woman's position in the organizational hierarchy can also influence women's development of friendships with men. Both women and men at lower levels in the organizational hierarchy are more likely to develop workplace friend-ships than those at higher organizational levels (Mao, 2006). This pattern may differ depending on organizational culture—for example, some organizations emphasize collegiality or egalitarian structures, others emphasize these to a lesser extent. It may also vary on the basis of the advancement and promotion rules within an organization. Where these rules are explicit and clear, friendships may benefit, as opposed to work situations where they are vague or arbitrary. In such organizations, friendship development may suffer because of competition between workers and perceived unfairness in the evaluation process.

Being in the minority in the workplace or in a specific work team is associated with greater visibility, but also with greater stereotyping and social isolation (Kanter, 1977). Thus, women in largely male work situations have even greater difficulty in establishing the friendships with men that are crucial to career advancement. Greater status may not alleviate these difficulties—women in the minority who have a higher status than their male team members tend to be especially iso-lated (Goldner & Strong, 1987). Not only are these women excluded from male friendship networks in the workplace, but they themselves may be reluctant to develop friendships with other women in the workplace because of differences in status and power.

Despite this, the workplace may be a context where differences, par-ticularly in demographic characteristics such as age, ethnicity, social class background, and even gender, may be more easily transcended than in nonwork contexts. Commonality in work requirements and environment may facilitate friendships, and this may be increasingly true as organizations become more diverse. A factor that may be criti-cal in this process is the passage of time. The longer people are to-gether, the less important become visible differences, whereas less visible differences, such as attitudes, values, and personalities, increase in their importance over time (Cable & Judge, 1996; Elfinbein & O'Reilly, 2007; Harrison et al., 2002; Ostroff & Rothausen, 1997).

BARRIERS TO WORKPLACE FRIENDSHIPS WITH MEN

As stated earlier, friendships with men in the workplace can have positive effects on women's work lives, but a number of barriers exist that make development of such relationships difficult. For instance, in interviews with professional-level women and men, Elesser and Peplau (2006) found that, with regard to cross-gender friendships, these workers were concerned that coworkers might perceive a cross-gender friendship as sexual or romantic in nature and organizations may have explicit policies against such relationships. Men were also concerned that their friendly behavior would be misinterpreted by female coworkers as sexual harassment. For their part, women were concerned that male coworkers felt uncomfortable in their presence and therefore men avoided interacting with them. Elesser and Peplau found that men did change their behavior when interacting with women—men joked less with women than with men and were less likely to engage in behaviors that could be interpreted as sexual harassment, such as meeting in an office alone with a woman.

Elesser and Peplau (2006) have referred to these barriers to cross-gender friendships as the "glass partition." Many work arenas are male-dominated, and women in these situations are at a greater disadvantage than their male counterparts in developing the friendships that facilitate and advance their careers. In particular, women may be less able than their male coworkers to develop friendships with male superiors in the workplace. Cross-sex superior–subordinate friendships are especially fraught with perceived sexual harassment content (Powell, 2001); thus, they may be avoided by male superiors. Even when women do establish friendly relationships with supportive male superiors, these men may overstep their bounds to subordinate women workers, thus leading to sexual harassment claims (*Bryson v. Chicago State University* 96 F3d 912, 1996). Nonetheless, relationships with superiors can be key to women's vocational development. Superiors are crucial role models and they may even take on mentor roles with subordinates, but with fewer opportunities to interact and develop relationships with male superiors, women have less access to the mentor process (Dreher & Cox, 1996; Paludi, 1990; Ragins & Cotton, 1999).

Other factors unrelated to sexual harassment concerns can influence women's friendship development with men in the workplace. The tokenism theory, posited by Kanter (1977a), argues that many organizations fill a perceived gap in gender equality with "token" women, particularly in the upper echelons of the enterprise. However, being in the minority in a workplace or in a specific work team is associated with greater visibility and resultant stereotyping and isolation (Kanter, 1977a, 1977b). Thus, women in largely male work situations have even greater difficulty establishing the friendships with men that are crucial to career advancement. They are excluded from informal networks where important information is exchanged along with friendship and camaraderie. These traditional male alliances, sometimes called the "old boy-ocracy," continue to present barriers to career effectiveness for senior-level professional women (Swiss, 1996). Even when women are allowed into the relationship, they have reported the feeling of "not fitting in" and experienced a constant uneasy need to change their behavior to match the behavior of male colleagues (Cox, 1994; Kanter, 1977). Greater status may not alleviate these difficulties—women in the minority who have a higher status than their male team members tend to be especially isolated. Such isolation of executive women spills over into relationships with female subordinates—women themselves may be reluctant to develop friendships with other women in the workplace because of differences in status and power (Goldner & Strong, 1987).

Other factors influence women's friendships with men. First, while women may desire friendships with men in the workplace, they may simply not have enough time to devote to friendship development. While both women and men work, women with children are responsible for a greater share of the work surrounding family matters, such as taking children to medical appointments, grocery shopping, school visits, etc., and these may cut into their lunch and break times during the work day. Also, while men have increased the amount of time they devote to family matters (although it is still less than that of women), a gap in the amount of free time for leisure activities has emerged with women's free time decreasing compared with that of men (Sayer, 2005). Thus, women's friendships at work, as well as out of work, must compete for time with other demands, particularly those related to family matters.

Another factor that can influence women's friendships with men is sexism. Women report encounters with sexism at a rate of one or two sexist incidents weekly (Swim, Hyers, Cohen, & Ferguson, 2003) and these occur across women's daily activity domains, including work. These encounters are common, even mundane, but they still negatively impact women's psychological mood and self-esteem. In workplace friendships with men, women may increase the possibility of these experiences, relative to their friendships with women, and this may be another element that influences women's experience of and desire for friendships with men. Women in nontraditional occupations such as construction, mining, law enforcement, etc., may be especially subject to sexist incidents, and development of friendships with men in these occupations may be particularly difficult (Harrington & Lonsway, 2007; Ilies, Hauserman, Schwochau, & Stibal, 2003; Lafontaine & Tredeau, 1986).

For lesbians, bisexual women, women of color, and other women from diverse backgrounds, friendships with men in the workplace take on other dimensions. Biases against them may stem not only from their gender, but also from their ethnicity, race, or sexual orientation (Hurtado, 1996; Martin, 1994). Like sexism, the experience of everyday racism is a frequent and common occurrence for women of color (Martin,

1994; Swim, Hyers, Cohen, Fitzgerald, & Bylsma, 2003), and this can influence how women approach friendships with men in the workplace. They themselves may curtail or carefully monitor their behaviors in relationships with men (and European-American women) to avoid stereotypes, to "fit in," or to succeed at work. For example, a study of Latina managers found that regardless of their generation level, awareness of prejudice and discrimination influenced how open they were with non-Latina/o coworkers and the extent that they revealed aspects of their family lives to them (Hite, 2007). Lesbian women's friendships with men are influenced by the heteronormativity of organizational practices; that is, the notion that heterosexuality is ubiquitous, normal, and unquestioned in the workplace (Bruni, 2006; McDermott, 2006). Although it may vary depending on the particular organization, its policies, and the history and personality of individual women, performance of lesbian, bisexual, or transgender identities in the workplace always entails a calculation/risk assessment process that can be psychologically costly for women (McDermott, 2006). Part of this calculation/risk assessment process may include greater wariness of friendships with men in the workplace on the part of women, particularly in employment settings where hostility toward differing sexual identities is present. Openly lesbian or bisexual women have reason to be fearful as, with openness about their sexual orientation, they may become targets of intimidation, harassment, or discrimination (Ragins, Cornwell, & Miller, 2003; Ragins, Singh, & Cornwell, 2007; Taylor & Raeburn, 1995). Lesbian and other sexual minority women may rightly understand that knowledge of their sexual orientation can influence actual job outcomes, such as promotions (Ragins & Cornwell, 2001). On the other hand, even if they are willing to develop friendships with heterosexual men in the workplace, social segregation or even ostracism of lesbian women in organizations, particularly when they take an openly activist stance, may affect their ability to initiate, develop, and maintain these friendships (Taylor & Raeburn). This social exclusion may not even be particularly apparent to those affected by it—one woman employed in an academic setting explained that "I suffered horrible ridicule and discrimination in the department but usually didn't know about it until after it occurred. You see, I was so far outside the networks that no one even told me about all of the events I was missing" (Taylor & Raeburn, p. 265).

A more subtle concern for women surrounding friendships with men in the workplace, and one they themselves may not be aware of, is that relationality, and the responsibility for developing connections with others, is not a gender-neutral process in organizations nor the larger society (Abrams, 1998; Cancian, 1987; Miller, 1976). While organizations are beginning to appreciate the importance of positive relationships, women are more likely than men to be expected, even assigned,

to create the conditions for these relationships (Fletcher, 2007). However, because relationality is consistent with femininity, and femininity
is associated with powerlessness and dependence, the skills needed to
facilitate and enhance positive relationships in the workplace may be
ones that are not taken seriously, rewarded, or recognized (Fletcher,
2007). Competence at work is many times associated with displays of
masculine behavior for both women and men and displays of relational
skills and behavior by women, while they may be viewed as "nice,"
may not contribute to perceptions of job competence or expertise
(Fletcher, 1999; 2007). Enacting relationality in the workplace is certainly positive and may be helpful for women, but unlike for men, it
contains a greater potential for detracting from their evaluation as competent and valued workers. Greater attention and research must be
done to more fully explicate these gender dynamics and processes and
implications for them for women in the workplace.

ROMANTIC RELATIONSHIPS WITH MEN IN THE WORKPLACE

In addition to friendships, women may also develop romantic relationships with men at work. These relationships are typically referred
to in the literature as "workplace romances" and indicate a relationship between two individuals in the same organization that includes
mutual sexual attraction that is consensually and autonomously acted
upon by both participants in some form of intimate behavior, such as
dating and or sexual activity (Mainiero, 1993; Pierce, Byrne, & Aguinis,
1996). The setting for workplace romances is often perceived to be an
office. In fact, the term "office romance" is sometimes colloquially used
to refer to these relationships, and workplace romance research has
focused primarily on those that take place in white-collar settings.
However, the organizational setting of these relationships can vary and
can include factories, hospitals, retail businesses, construction sites, res-
taurants, and shop floors. The individuals' connection to the workplace
can be varied as well and can include coworkers, vendors, team members, clients, and contractors. They may work side by side, in different
offices, different divisions, or even in different geographic locations,
such as different neighborhoods, cities, states, or countries.

For the most part, the prevailing image of workplace romantic partners is that they are heterosexual and European-American, although,
clearly, this does not have to be the case. Nevertheless, researchers are
only recently beginning to recognize the importance of studying same-
sex workplace romances and the role of culture, social class, and ethnicity in them. Indeed, same-sex workplace romances may be subject
to greater implications for participants because they tend to receive
more negative responses from society in general (see Riach & Wilson,
2007). Furthermore, at least in some workplaces, those from already

marginalized groups (the working class, certain ethnic or cultural groups) who engage in workplace romance behavior may be more likely to be targeted for enforcement of existing workplace sexual harassment policies than those from socially dominant groups (Williams et al., 1999).

The existing literature on workplace romance tends to emphasize the legal, emotional, and work performance pitfalls of these relationships (Powell & Foley, 1998; Williams et al., 1999). In fact, much of the advice to organizations focuses on how to manage or restrict such relationships, and they are exhorted to develop written company policies surrounding them. Part of the difficulty for employers, however, is that while a plethora of advice on how to manage workplace romance is available, little of it stems from empirical research. For example, of key interest to employers are the potential effects of workplace romances on job performance, but that message is mixed. Some studies show that involvement in a workplace romance does not result in decrements in work performance, and in some cases it is related to improvement in various aspects of work performance (Dillard, 1987; Pierce, 1998). In fact, involvement in a romantic relationship, whether in or out of the workplace, has been positively linked to one's own work motivation, job involvement, and satisfaction with type of work (Pierce, 1998). In at least one study, motives for engaging in a workplace romance affected work performance. In this case, women, and to a lesser extent men, who engaged in workplace romance out of love motives were more likely to increase their work performance and job involvement than those who engaged in a workplace romance out of job-related or ego motives (Dillard, 1987).

The definitive study of the prevalence of workplace romance has yet to be done, but available research suggests the workplace is an arena in which intimate romantic and sexual relationships are frequently formed. According to an American Management Association survey conducted among its members and customers, 26% of men and 36% of women report having dated a workplace colleague. The proportion was higher among workers under 49 years of age (37%) compared with workers 50 years of age and above (22%). More men had dated a subordinate (20%) compared with 2% for women, while more women had dated a superior (18%) compared with 5% for men. In another survey of 610 employees representing a variety of industries across the United States, 58% reported engaging in an office romance, up from 46% in the same survey two years prior (Vault, 2005, September). The results in this survey were not broken down by gender, but 14% reported dating a superior and 19% reported dating a subordinate.

Not only is the prevalence high for those who report engaging in a workplace romance, but many workers report having been exposed to a workplace romance on the part of their coworkers. In one of the first studies of the extent of workplace romance, Quinn (1977) found that 62% of respondents said they knew of at least one of these relationships. Later, Anderson and Hunsaker (1985) found that 86% of respondents had been exposed to one or more workplace romantic relationships. Most recently, the Vault survey found that 43% of respondents knew of a currently occurring romantic relationship in their organization.

Of special note is that, while organized settings such as family and neighborhood networks continue to influence choice of marriage partner, social network research has found that, since 1945, the workplace (along with schools) has increased in its importance as a site from which marriage partners are selected (Kalmijn & Flap, 2001). For example, 22% of respondents in one survey reported meeting their spouse or long-term significant other in the workplace (Vault, 2005); in another survey, 45% of women and 43% of men who engaged in a workplace romance reported that the relationship had ended in marriage (American Management Association, 2003).

Internet relationships notwithstanding, who we end up with in a close relationship is limited to those we are actually able to meet and interact with, and the workplace provides a pool of persons to choose from and an organized setting for social interaction.

Not only are romantic relationships common at work, but the workplace is also a location in which a fair amount of sexual activity occurs (for a discussion, see Castañeda, 2006). Sexual behavior includes kissing, hugging, fondling, sexual intercourse, and other physical, sexually stimulating behavior, but it may be more broadly conceived to include flirtation behavior, requests for dates, sexual comments or jokes, and sexual language. This behavior may be considered by participants as consensual and nonharrassing or as offensive, coercive, and sexually harassing (Gutek, Cohen, & Konrad, 1990). In an investigation of the predictors of this broad spectrum or sexual behavior in the workplace, Gutek and her colleagues found that a greater amount of contact with the other gender in the workplace predicted, first, a more sexualized work environment, and this in turn was predictive of greater sexual behavior in the workplace. Overall, women reported greater sexually harassing behavior than men, but women and men were equally likely to report nonharrassing sexual behavior in the workplace, and this behavior was much more commonly experienced than sexual harassment (Gutek et al., 1990). However, while the two types of sexual behavior exist in the workplace, sexual harassment behavior also increased. This result points to the role of social and cultural power differentials between women and men—because we live in a world where women are secondary to men and where heterosexuality is the expected norm and guides gender relations in organizations, for women sexuality at work always holds the potential for an acting out of these power relations (Mills, 1989; Riach & Wilson, 2007).

The only study by Gutek and her colleagues highlights that the phenomenon of sexuality at work is not always coercive and contains multiple facets and interpretations by workers. For instance, the contradictory nature of sexuality in the workplace (i.e., that it can be an act of resistance to managerial control and regulation, as well as an expression of hierarchies of oppressive power) is obscured by the more pronounced focus on its potential coercive effects on workers, particularly women. More nuanced thinking on organizational sexuality refers, instead, to "... a multileveled understanding of power and resistance in which struggles around sexuality have manifold consequences" (Fleming, 2007, pg. 240). Sexuality, gender, power, resistance, control—all of these processes in the workplace intersect in complex ways that are not always easily mapped out in an unambiguous manner and how they are expressed, evaluated, interpreted, and experienced by women very much depends on the political context of a particular work setting (Fleming). This more subtle point is often overlooked, but once brought to the forefront it suggests a much wider spectrum of women's experiences with sexuality and romantic relationships with men in the workplace that may be missing from organizational theory and research.

That said, however, one of the predominant organizational concerns surrounding workplace romance is the potential for sexual harassment claims that may result when the relationship fails. Some data indicate a link between the two. In a survey conducted by the Society for Human Resource Management, a quarter of the respondents indicated that sexual harassment claims in their organizations were caused by workplace romances. Of particular concern are dissolved hierarchical relationships, especially direct reporting ones, because they are thought to contain greater potential for sexual harassment claims for a number of reasons. First, even though negative feelings may exist on the part of one partner or both partners, they must continue to work with one another after the relationship is over. In addition, the lower-level partner in such relationships may have had job-related motives for entering the relationship that have now been thwarted, and this could lead to resentment. Finally, a power differential between the two exists that could lead to sexual coercion or discriminatory managerial decision making (Pierce & Aguinis, 1997).

Sexual harassment is a serious legal and ethical event and should be dealt with accordingly; however, with respect to a dissolved workplace romance, judgments of responsibility for the sexual harassment and decisions about subsequent managerial intervention do not stem solely from the objective behaviors of the former relationship partners. The characteristics of observers and aspects of the former workplace romance play a role in perceptions of responsibility and intervention decisions. For example, Pierce, Broberg, McClure, and Aguinis (2004) found that assessment of the immorality of the sexually harassing behavior mediated decisions about whether the accused or complainant had greater responsibility for the behavior. Assessment of responsibility, in turn, influenced disciplinary action decisions that ranged from no response to punitive responses. However, assessment of the immorality of the behavior was influenced by factors unrelated to the specific harassing behavior. If the prior workplace romance had been hierarchical, the company had a workplace romance policy in place, and the sexually harassing behavior was quid pro quo rather than hostile environment harassment, assessment of the immorality of the sexually harassing behavior occurred.

Motives for engaging in a workplace romance, as well as gender of the relationship partner, play a key role in perceptions of judgments of responsibility for sexual harassment behavior. In one study where a woman was the sexual harassment complainant and a man was the accused, perceptions of job motives of the accuser and complainant affected judgments of responsibility for the sexual harassing behavior. In this case, the accused was considered most responsible when he had an ego motive and the complainant had a love motive, and least responsible when he had a love motive and the complainant had a job-related motive for participation in the relationship. Conversely, the complainant was judged as most responsible for the harassment when she had a job-related or ego motive compared to a love motive and the accused had a love, not ego, motive for participation in the relationship. This study also found that observers considered disciplining the accused as an appropriate action when the romance had been a hierarchical one, but if the complainant in a hierarchical workplace romance was perceived to have a job-related motive, male but not female observers did not consider company-funded counseling as an appropriate intervention (Pierce, Aguinis, & Adams, 2000).

This research provides insight into the complex cognitive processes that contribute to coworker responses to sexual harassment claims by those who have participated in a workplace romance. They demonstrate, once again, the importance of *perceived* motives for the romance on the part of observers and that, even if erroneous, these perceived motives cannot be taken lightly. However, a more fundamental and crucial issue surrounding workplace romances and sexual harassment remains unexamined. While women are acknowledged to more likely be the victim of sexual harassment, the reasons for this are not questioned. Therefore, the deeper causes for sexual harassment behavior are not addressed. The rationale for organizational attempts to prevent it is usually based upon its threats to the organization (e.g., low staff morale, high turnover, and lowered productivity), and less upon its harmful impact on women (Bennett-Alexander & Hartman, 2004; see Robinson v. Jackson Shipyards, Inc., 760 F. Supp. 1486 (M.D. Fla Jacksonville Div., 1991); Samuels, 2003). The view implicit in advice to organizations is that sexual harassment is the result of individual, aberrant behavior and is containable and readily resolved by following a checklist of managerial actions. What this traditional approach to sexual harassment obscures is the highly gendered power relations in organizations that structure and perpetuate women's inequality in the workplace (Acker, 1990; Hurtado, 1996). One expression of this workplace inequality is sexual harassment.

This may be one reason women tend to have more negative attitudes toward workplace romantic relationships than men (Pierce, et al., 1996), especially hierarchical romances (Jones, 1999). They may correctly understand that women in these relationships will be evaluated more negatively and therefore have more to lose (Anderson & Fisher, 1991; Powell, 2001). Furthermore, they may better understand and possibly fear that their claims of sexual harassment after a workplace romance has ended will be taken less seriously because of their involvement in the relationship (Pierce et al., 2004).

Social ties at work, including women's friendship and romantic relationships with men, are inevitable. When women experience these as positive, they add immeasurably to the quality of their work and personal lives. Instead of existing solely outside of work and as part of the private sphere, sexuality, romance, intimacy, close relationships, and affectionate bonds are part of the public world—they make up the fabric of work, operate at every level of organizations, and can affect work outcomes in myriad ways. However, the workplace does not operate in isolation from the gender, class, racial/ethnic, and heterosexual hierarchies that exist within the larger culture (Kanter, 1977; Maddock & Parkin, 1994; Salzinger, 2003; Schein, 1994; Williams, 1989). These social and cultural structures and processes make up the context in which women's relationships with men in the workplace occur; thus, more so for women than men, the potential for negative consequences of these relationships is always present. An important first step in changing this social reality is greater research and theory on relational issues in organizations that goes beyond the prevailing, albeit important, emphasis on the standard sexual harassment paradigm, to one that can more fully encompass the contradictory, emergent, and multifaceted reality that these relationships contain for women at work.

REFERENCES

Acker, J. (1990). Hierarchies, jobs, bodies: A theory of gendered organizations. *Gender & Society, 4*, 139–158.

Adams, R. G., & Allan, G. (1998). *Placing friendship in context.* Cambridge, UK: Cambridge University Press.

Adams, R. G., Blieszner, R., & De Vries, B. (2000). Definitions of friendship in the third age: Age, gender, and study location effects. *Journal of Aging Studies, 14*, 117–134.

Abrams, K. (1998). The new jurisprudence of sexual harassment. *Cornell Law Review, 83*, 1205–1213.

American Management Association (2003). American Management Association 2003 Survey. New York: Author.

Anderson, C., & Fisher, C. (1991). Male-female relationships in the workplace: Perceived motivations in office romance. *Sex Roles, 25*, 163–180.

Anderson, C. I., & Hunsaker, P. L. (1985, February). Why there's romancing at the office and why it's everybody's problem. *Personnel, 62*, 57–63.

Andrew, A., & Montague, J. (1998). Women's friendships at work. *Women's Studies International Forum, 21*, 355–361.

Aronson, J. (1998). Lesbians giving and receiving care: Stretching conceptualizations of caring and community. *Women's Studies International Forum, 21*, 505–519.

Badaracco, J. (2002). *Leading quietly: An unorthodox guide to doing the right thing.* Boston, MA: Harvard Business School Press.

Bell, S., & Coleman, S. (1999). *The anthropology of friendship* New York: Berg.

Bennett-Alexander, D., & Hartman, L. (2004). *Employment law for business.* New York: McGraw-Hill.

Berman, E., West, J., & Richter, M. (2002). Workplace relations: Friendship patterns and consequences (according to managers). *Public Administration Review, 62*, 217–230.

Blatt, R., & Camden, C. T. (2007). Positive relationships and cultivating community. In J. E. Dutton & B. R. Ragins (Eds.), *Exploring positive relationships at work: Building a theoretical and research foundation* (pp. 243–264). Mahwah, NJ: Lawrence Erlbaum Associates.

Brass, D. J. (1985). Men's and women's networks: A study of interaction patterns and influence in an organization. *Academy of Management Journal, 28*, 327–343.

Bridge, K., & Baxter, L. A. (1992). Blended relationships: Friends as work associates. *Western Journal of Communication, 56*, 200–225.

Bruni, A. (2006). 'Have you got a boyfriend or are you single?': On the importance of being 'straight' in organizational research. *Gender, Work, and Organization, 13*, 299–316.

Bryson v. Chicago State University, 96 F 3d 912 (1996).

Cancian, F. (1987). *Love in America: Gender and self-development.* Cambridge: Cambridge University Press.

Cannings, K., & Montmarquette, C. (1991). Managerial momentum: A simultaneous model of the career progress of male and female managers. *Industrial and Labor Relations Review, 44*, 212–228.

Castaneda, D. (2006). Romantic relationships in the workplace. In M. F. Karsten (Ed.), *Gender, race, and ethnicity in the workplace: Issues and challenges for today's organizations* (pp. 84–99). Westport, CT: Praeger.

Cheng, G., Chan, D., & Tong, P. (2006). Qualities of online friendships with different gender compositions and durations. *CyberPsychology & Behavior, 9*, 14–21.

Chiaburu, D. S. (2005). The effect of instrumentality on the relationship between goal-orientation and leader-member exchange. *Journal of Social Psychology, 145*, 365–367.

Collins, J. (2001). *Good to great.* New York: Harper Collins.

Cook, C., Bruin, M., & Crull, S. (2000). Manipulating constraints: Women's housing and the "metropolitan context." In K. B. Miranne & A. H. Young (Eds.), *Gendering the city: Women, boundaries, and visions of urban life* (pp. 1893–207). New York: Rowman & Littlefield.

Cox, T., Jr. (1994). *Cultural diversity in organizations: Theory, research, and practice.* San Francisco, CA: Berrett-Koehler.

De Vries, J., Webb, C., & Eveline, J. (2006). Mentoring for gender equality and organisational change. *Employee Relations, 28,* 573–587.

Dillard, J. P. (1987). Close relationships at work: Perceptions of the motives and performance of relational participants. *Journal of Social and Personal Relationships, 4,* 179–193.

Dreher, G. F., & Cox, T. H. (1996). Race, gender, and opportunity: A study of compensation attainment and the establishment of mentoring relationships. *Journal of Applied Psychology, 81,* 297–308.

Duck, S. (2007). Commentary: Finding connections at the individual/dyadic level. In J. E. Dutton & B. R. Ragins (Eds.), *Exploring positive relationships at work: Building a theoretical and research foundation* (pp. 179–186). Mahwah, NJ: Lawrence Erlbaum Associates.

Elesser, K., & Peplau, L. A. (2006). The glass partition: Obstacles to cross-sex friendships at work. *Human Relations, 59,* 1077–1100.

Elfinbein, H. A., & O'Reilly, C. A. (2007). Fitting in: The effects of relational demography and person-culture fit on group process and performance. *Group Organization Management, 32,* 109–142.

Fehr, B. (1996). *Friendship processes.* Thousand Oaks, CA: Sage.

Fehr, B. (2004). Intimacy expectations in same-sex friendships: A prototype interaction-pattern model. *Journal of Personality and Social Psychology, 86,* 265–284.

Festinger, L., Schachter S. S., & Back, K. W. (1950). *Social pressures in informal groups.* Stanford, CA: Stanford University Press.

Fleming, P. (2007). Sexuality, power and resistance in the workplace. *Organization Studies, 28,* 239–256.

Fletcher, J. (1999). *Disappearing acts: Gender, power, and relational practice at work.* Cambridge, MA: MIT Press.

Fletcher, J. (2007). Leadership, power and positive relationships. In J. Dutton & B. Ragins (Eds.), *Exploring positive relationships at work: Building a theoretical and research foundation* (pp. 347–371). Mahwah, NJ: Lawrence Erlbaum Associates.

Gibson, S. K. (2005). Whose best interests are served? The distinction between mentoring and support. *Advances in Developing Human Resources, 7,* 470–488.

Goldner, H., & Strong, M. S. (1987). *Speaking of friendship: Middle-class women and their friends.* New York: Greenwood Press.

Gutek, B. A., Cohen, A. G., & Konrad, A. M. (1990). Predicting social-sexual behavior at work: A contact hypothesis. *Academy of Management Journal, 33,* 560–577.

Harper, Jr., V. B. (2005). Maintaining interpersonal and organizational relations through electronic mail by men and women. *Psychological Reports, 97,* 903–906.

Harrington, P. E., & Lonsway, K. A. (2007). *Investigating sexual harassment in law enforcement and nontraditional fields for women.* Upper Saddle River, NJ: Pearson Prentice Hall.

Harrison, D., Price, K., Gavin, J., & Florey, A. (2002). Time, teams, and task performance: Changing effects of surface- and deep-level diversity on group functioning. *Academy of Management Journal, 45,* 1029–1046.

Hays, R. B. (1985). A longitudinal study of friendship development. *Journal of Personality and Social Psychology, 48,* 909–924.

Hite, L. (2007). Hispanic women managers and professional: Reflections on life and work. *Gender, Work, and Organization, 14,* 20–36.

Hurtado, A. (1996). *The color of privilege: Three blasphemies on race and feminism.* Ann Arbor: University of Michigan Press.

Ibarra, H. (1992). Homophily and differential returns: Sex differences in network structure and access in an advertising firm. *Administrative Science Quarterly, 37,* 422–447.

Ilies, R., Hauserman, N., Schwochau, S., & Stibal, J. (2003). Reported incidence rates of work-related sexual harassment in the United States: Using meta-analysis to explain reported rate disparities. *Personnel Psychology, 56,* 607–631.

Johnson, F., & Aries, E. (1983). The talk of women friends. *Women's Studies International Forum, 6,* 353–361.

Jones, G. (1999). Hierarchical workplace romance: An experimental examination of team member perceptions. *Journal of Organizational Behavior, 20,* 1057–1073.

Kalmijn, M., & Flap, H. (2001). Assortative meeting and mating: Unintended consequences of organized settings for partner choices. *Social Forces, 79,* 1289–1312.

Kanter, R. (1977). *Men and women of the corporation.* New York: Basic Books.

Konrad, A. M., Ritchie, J. E., Jr., Lieb, P., & Corrigall, E. (2000). Sex differences and similarities in job attitude preferences: A meta-analysis. *Psychological Bulletin, 126,* 593–641.

Lafontaine, E., & Tredeau, L. (1986). The frequency, sources, and correlates of sexual harassment among women in traditional male occupations. *Sex Roles, 15,* 433–442.

Lobel, S. A., Quinn, R. E., Warfield, A., & St. Clair, L. (1994). Love without sex. *Organizational Dynamics, 23,* 4–16.

Lu, L., & Argyle, M. (1992). Receiving and giving support: Effects on relationships and well-being. *Counseling Psychology Quarterly, 5,* 123–133.

Luckett Clark, S., & Weismantle, M. (2003, August). Census 2000 Brief. Employment status: 2000. Retrieved on July 18, 2007, from http://www.census.gov/prod/2003pubs/c2kbr-18.pdf.

Maddock, S., & Parkin, D. (1994). Gender cultures: How they affect men and women at work. In M. J. Davidson & R. J. Burke (Eds.), *Women in management: Current research issues* (pp. 29–40). London, UK: Paul Chapman Publishing.

Madsen, S. R., Miller, D., & John, C. R. (2005). Readiness for organizational change: Do organizational commitment and social relationships in the workplace make a difference? *Human Resource Development Quarterly, 16,* 213–233.

Mainiero, L. (1993). Dangerous liaisons? A review of current issues concerning male and female romantic relationships in the workplace. In E. Fagenson (Ed.), *Women in management: Trends, issues, and challenges in managerial diversity, vol. 4.* Newbury Park, CA: Sage Publications.

Mao, H.-Y. (2006). The relationship between organizational level and workplace friendship. *International Journal of Human Resource Management, 17*, 1819–1833.

Markiewicz, D., Devine, I., Kausilas, D. (2000), Friendships of women and men at work: Job satisfaction and resource implications. *Journal of Managerial Psychology, 15*, 161–84.

Martin, J. R. (1994). Methodological essentialism, false difference, and other dangerous traps. *Signs 19*, 630–657.

Mays, V. M. (1985). Black women working together: Diversity in same sex relationships. *Women's Studies International Forum, 8*, 67–71.

McDermott, E. (2006). Surviving in dangerous places: Lesbian identity performances in the workplace, social class and psychological health *Feminism and Psychology, 16*, 193–211.

Miller, J. B. (1976). *Toward a new psychology of women*. Boston: Beacon Press.

Morrison, R. (2004). Informal relationships in the workplace: Associations with job satisfaction, organizational commitment and turnover intentions. *New Zealand Journal of Psychology, 33*, 114–128.

Nielsen, I. K., Jex, S. M., & Adams, G. A. (2000). Development and validation of scores on a two-dimensional workplace friendship scale. *Educational and Psychological Measurement, 60*, 628–643.

Nyamathi, A., Bennett, C., Leake, B., & Chen, S. (1995). Social support among impoverished women. *Nursing Research, 44*, 376–378.

O'Boyle, C., & Thomas, M. (1996). Friendships between lesbian and heterosexual women. In J. Weinstock & R. Rothblum (Eds.), *Lesbian friendships: For ourselves and each other* (pp. 240–250). New York: New York University Press.

Odden, C. M., & Sias, P. M. (1997). Peer communication relationships and psychological climate. *Communications Quarterly, 45*, 153–166.

Ostroff, C., & Rothausen, T. (1997). The moderating effect of tenure in person-environment fit: A field study in educational organizations. *Journal of Occupational and Organizational Psychology, 70*, 173–188.

Padavic, I., & Reskin, B. F. (1990). Men's behavior and women's interest in blue-collar jobs. *Social Problems, 37*, 613–628.

Paludi, M. E. (1990). Sociopsychological and structural factors related to women's vocational development. *Annals of the New York Academy of Sciences, 602*, 157–168.

Parks, M., & Floyd, K. (1996a). Making friends in cyberspace. *Journal of Communications, 46*, 80–97.

Patterson, B., & Bettini, L. (1993). Age, depression, and friendship: Development of a general friendship inventory. *Communication Research Reports, 10*, 161–171.

Pazy, A. (1987). Sex differences in responsiveness to organizational career management. *Human Resources Management, 26*, 243–256.

Pettinger, L. (2005). Friends, relations and colleagues: The blurred boundaries of the workplace. *The Sociological Review, 53*, 37–55.

Pierce, C. (1998). Factors associated with participating in a romantic relationship in a work environment. *Journal of Applied Social Psychology, 28*, 1712–1731.

Pierce, C., & Aguinis, H. (1997). Bridging the gap between romantic relationships in a work environment. *Journal of Applied Social Psychology, 28*, 1712–1730.

Pierce, C., Aguinis, H., & Adams, S. (2000). Effects of a dissolved workplace romance and rater characteristics on responses to a sexual harassment accusation. *Academy of Management Journal, 43,* 869–880.

Pierce, C., Broberg, B., McClure, J., & Aguinis, H. (2004). Responding to sexual harassment complaints: Effects of a dissolved workplace romance on decision-making standards. *Organizational Behavior and Human Decision Processes, 95,* 66–82.

Pierce, C. A., Byrne, D., & Aguinis, H. (1996). Attraction in organizations: A model of workplace romance. *Journal of Organizational Behavior, 17,* 5–32.

Powell, G., & Foley, S. (1998). Something to talk about: Romantic relationships in organizational settings. *Journal of Management, 24,* 421–448.

Powell, G. (2001). Workplace romances between senior-level executives and lower-level employees: An issue of work disruption and gender. *Human Relations, 54,* 1519–1544.

Quick, J. C., Gavin, J. H., Cooper, C. L., & Quick, J. D. (2004). Working together: Balancing head and heart. In R. H. Rozensky, N. G. Johnson, C. D. Goodheart, & W. R. Hammond (Eds.), *Psychology builds a healthy world: Opportunities for research and practice* (pp. 219–232). Washington, DC: American Psychological Association.

Quinn, R. E., (1977). Coping with cupid: The formation, impact, and management of romantic relationships in organizations. *Administrative Science Quarterly, 22,* 30–45.

Ragins, B. R., & Cotton, J. L. (1999). Mentor functions and outcomes: A comparison of men and women in formal and informal mentoring relationships. *Journal of Applied Psychology, 84,* 529–550.

Ragins, B., & Cornwell, J. (2001, April). We are family: The influence of gay family-friendly policies on gay employees. In L. T. Eby and C. L. Noble (Co-Chairs), *New developments in research on family-related HR policies and practice: Beyond Ward and June.* Symposium conducted at the Annual Conference of the Society for Industrial and Organizational Psychology, San Diego, CA.

Ragins, B., Cornwell, J., & Miller, J. (2003). Heterosexism in the workplace: Do race and gender matter? *Group and Organization Management, 28,* 45–74.

Ragins, B. R., Singh, R., & Cornwell, J. M., (2007). Making the invisible visible: Fear and disclosure of sexual orientation at work. *Journal of Applied Psychology, 92,* 1103–1118.

Ragins, B. R., & Dutton, J. E. (2007). Positive relationships at work: An invitation and introduction. In J. E. Dutton & B. R. Ragins (Eds.), *Exploring positive relationships at work: Building a theoretical and research foundation* (pp. 13–25). Mahwah, NJ: Lawrence Erlbaum Associates.

Riach, K., & Wilson, F. (2007). Don't screw the crew: Exploring the rules of engagement in organizational romance. *British Journal of Management, 18,* 79–92.

Randal, A. E., & Ranft, A. L. (2007). Motivations to maintain social ties with coworkers: The moderating role of turnover intentions on information exchange. *Group & Organization Management, 32,* 208–232.

Ray, E. B. (1987). Supportive relationships and occupational stress in the workplace. In T. L. Albrecht & M. B. Adelman (Eds.), *Communicating and social support* (pp. 172–191). Newbury Park, CA: Sage.

Riordan, C. M., & Griffeth, R. W. (1995). The opportunity for friendship in the workplace: An underexplored construct. *Journal of Business and Psychology, 10*, 141–154.

Rose, S. (1995). Women's friendships. In J. Chrisler & A. Hemstreet (Eds.), *Variations on a theme: Diversity and the psychology of women* (pp. 79–105). Albany: State University of New York Press.

Saegert, S., Swap, W., & Zajonc, R. (1973). Exposure context and interpersonal attraction. *Journal of Personality and Social Psychology, 25*, 234–242.

Salzinger, L. (2003) *Genders in production: Making workers in Mexico's global factories*. Berkeley, CA: University of California Press.

Samuels, H. (2003). Sexual harassment in the workplace: A feminist analysis of recent developments in the UK. *Women's Studies International Forum, 26*, 467–482.

Sapadin, L. A. (1988). Friendship and gender: Perspectives of professional women. *Journal of Social and Personal Relationships, 5*, 387–403.

Sayer, L. C. (2005). Gender, time and inequality: Trends in women's and men's paid work, unpaid work and free time. *Social Forces, 84*, 285–303.

Schein, E. H. (1994). *Organizational and managerial culture as a facilitator or inhibitor of organizational learning*. Boston: The Society for Organizational Learning.

Serafica, F., Weng, A., & Kim, H. (2000). Friendships and social networks among Asian American women. In J. Chin (Ed.), *Relationships among Asian American women* (pp. 151–175). Washington, DC: American Psychological Association.

Severance, T. (2005). "You know who you can go to": Cooperation and exchange between incarcerated women. *Prison Journal, 85*, 343–367.

Sias, P. M., & Cahill, D. J. (1998). From coworkers to friends: The development of peer friendships in the workplace. *Western Journal of Communication, 62*, 273–299.

Sias, P. M., & Jablin, F. M. (1995). Differential superior-subordinate relations, perceptions of fairness, and coworker communication. *Human Communications Research, 22*, 5–38.

Stein, C. (1993). Felt obligation in adult family relationships. In S. Duck (Ed.), *Social context and relationships* (pp. 78–99). Newbury Park, CA: Sage.

Stobbe, L. (2006). Doing machismo: Legitimating speech acts as a selection discourse. *Gender, Work, and Organization, 12*, 105–123.

Swim, J. K., Hyers, L. L., Cohen, L. L., Fitzgerald, D. C., & Bylsma, W. H. (2003). African American college students' experiences with everyday racism: Characteristics of and responses to these incidents. *Journal of Black Psychology, 29*, 38–67.

Swiss, D. (1996). *Women breaking through: Overcoming the final 10 obstacles at work*. Princeton, NJ: Pacesetters Books.

Taylor, V., & Raeburn, N. C. (1995). Identity politics as high-risk activism: Career consequences for lesbian, gay, and bisexual sociologists. *Social Problems, 42*, 252–273.

Vault. (2005). Cupid in the cubicle, says new vault survey. Available from http://www.thevault.com/nr/printable.jsp?ch[lowem]id=420&article[lowem]id=235.

Walker, K. (1995). "Always there for me": Friendship patterns and expectations among middle- and working-class men and women. *Sociological Forum, 10*, 273–296.

Williams, C. (1989). Feminity in the marine corp. In C. Williams (Ed.), *Gender differences at work: Women and men in nontraditional work* (pp. 45–87). Berkeley, CA: University of California Press.

Williams, C., Giuffre, P., & Dellinger, K. (1999). Sexuality in the workplace: Organizational control, sexual harassment, and the pursuit of pleasure. *Annual Review of Sociology, 25,* 73–93.

Wilson, S. M., & Ferch, S. R. (2005). Enhancing resilience in the workplace through the practice of caring relationships. *Organization Development Journal, 23,* 45–60.

U.S. Census Bureau (2003, August). Table 1. Selected characteristics of the population 20-64 by employment status: 2000. Census 2000 Brief: Employment status 2000. Retrieved on July 8, 2007, from http://www.census.gov/prod/2003pubs/c2kbr-18.pdf.

Chapter 9

What I See Is What Matters: In My Own Voice

Sharon Butler

What I know means nothing; it is what I see that matters.

As a woman coming of age in the mid-1980s, I have surfed the wave of the "women's movement" at the most exciting time. The women's movement has been a huge public relations success. I know so much about what has kept women from being all that they know and believe they can be. I know of all the conditioning and behaviors that have prevented women from rising above the glass ceilings and taking over the world.

Every man I have encountered both personally and professionally appears to be equally informed. I would say that *"knowing"* the issues has made little impact. By defining our challenges, women have polarized our differences between women and men. I *know* we have come far in identifying the value of women in business, yet . . .

I still see discrimination of women across a number of industries. Earlier in my career it was as simple as being asked to fetch coffee, or worse yet bona fide sexual harassment. But now, often what I see is not men but women keeping women down in the workplace. I have seen women who have established a place for themselves but let other women struggle. It is as if they believe the only reason they have achieved a place of respect among men was solely their gender—any woman would do, therefore all other women are the competition. We are by nature a nurturing gender, yet when defining moments occur, we pretend we are not.

When I reflect on the mentors who have guided me along in my journey as an educated and accomplished woman, I am saddened by the number of women who added baggage to the journeys of other women, all the while claiming that they prefer to work with men. At that moment when mentoring, sharing, and collaborating could occur, power overcomes them and they stand tall among their male colleagues, displaying like armor all of their unwomanly qualities. This phenomenon is one that I have not only witnessed, but experienced firsthand, not once but on three different occasions throughout my career. In all instances, I witnessed women discriminating against women. In interviewing these women that were so significant in my observation, they each defined that the people who gave them opportunity, showed them career paths, or otherwise mentored them were men.

There are so many books, articles, and periodicals about the sisterhood built by women's rights, and I *know* we have all learned so much from reading them and understanding them. The reality is, however, that as women have made a share for themselves in the big offering of business leadership, they have showed that, often, women don't play nicely. That is what I see, and it is in direct conflict with what I know.

Chapter 10

Women in Ethiopia: The Sound of Hope: In My Own Voice

Haimanot Kelbessa

For many years Ethiopians have been praying and struggling against injustice, hoping for a new day to come. The Ethiopian Women Lawyers Association (EWLA) is one of the many positive results of the struggles and prayers that took place in the past. Recently many nongovernmental organizations (NGOs) that are managed by women have been formed, and they are doing an excellent job. Such organizations are mushrooming everywhere in the rural areas as well as in the cities. Their efforts are making a difference, one woman at a time.

In 1996, with her few female colleagues, Meaza Ashenafi, executive director of EWLA, started a legal advocacy group. The main purpose of the organization was to put an end to various discriminatory laws against women in Ethiopia and to bring awareness regarding women's rights. With the help the organization receives from the United Nations Development Fund for Women, the association is able to circulate information about gender equality by teaching women about the law through the paralegal training that they provide, as well as by the counseling services and the media outreach effort they undertake.

Ashenafi was a legal advisor to the Ethiopian Transitional Government Constitution Commission human rights panel. The experience that Ashenafi acquired at the commission while writing position papers regarding women and children was rewarding to her. This experience encouraged Ashenafi to start her own organization, EWLA.

Ashenafi was born in Asossa, a small village in western Ethiopia, near the Sudanese border. She gives a lot of credit to her parents, who instilled in her the importance of education. She appreciates what her mom did for her. Even though her mom was illiterate, she had the insight to raise her five children so that they could go to college. Ashenafi says her mom had a lot of unused potential. In school, Ashenafi was always a hardworking student. Despite the remark that was made by one of her teachers regarding her potential, "you are so smart and have so much potential, it's too bad you are not a boy" (Fidali, 2003, p. 2), she continued her hard work and it paid off. She went on to receive her law degree, from Addis Ababa University.

Her association, EWLA, advances the issue of women's rights in Ethiopia. According to Ashenafi, the fact that women in Ethiopia do not have access to justice is the result of the shortage of women's groups that stand in an organized fashion against unjust laws and practices. Ashenafi explains that several laws affect women directly or indirectly, including family and penal law. She explained that family law gives a right for the husband to discipline his wife. This allows women to be treated as if they were children. The penal law on the other hand gives the right for the criminals who abduct and rape girls to be their husbands.

The EWLA provides women 15 days of basic Ethiopian law training. This provides women the information to know what their rights are under the law and how to assert them. This empowering mechanism has a domino effect that passes from woman to woman by which EWLA hopes to guarantee progress.

With the tireless efforts of the EWLA, the penal law of 1957, which disregarded women's rights, was reformed in July 2004 and enforced in May 2005. The association is not fully content with the law, which still excludes sexual harassment and marital rape. This issue of marital rape is very significant in light of the transmission of HIV/AIDS in African society, where women are mostly voiceless. As a consequence, this disease is killing thousands of women. It is one of the major reasons for so many orphaned children in the country.

One of the cases EWLA fought that attracted worldwide attention involved Aberash Bekele, a 14-year-old girl who was abducted and raped and forced to marry her abductor, like many other young girls in rural Ethiopia. However, Aberash retaliated by killing her abductor, becoming the first woman known in court to stand up against this gender-based violence. The association represented the girl to be not guilty on grounds of self-defense. This exposed the unfair law to Ethiopians and to the outside world.

In another case, EWLA stood in support of an Ethiopian migrant worker in Bahrain for alleged murder of her employer due to abuse. The association initiated a task force to raise money for her legal support and asked for government intervention. This helped the migrant worker obtain a defense lawyer from the Ethiopian government for her appeal. This led to the exposure of the physical and mental abuse, wage denial, and other mistreatment of Ethiopian women working in various Arab countries, because of the lack of legal protection.

One major case that almost resulted in risking EWLA's existence was that of Hermela Wosenyeleh. This woman was harassed and shot by a male perpetrator. The court punished him by sentencing him to only a few months in jail. The association helped this woman to put her story on television, after unsuccessfully attempting to get any results with the law enforcement officials in Ethiopia. Meaza Ashenafi gave the issue even more publicity through an interview she gave with a newspaper.

As a result, EWLA was accused of acting beyond its mandate and its activity was suspended by the Ministry of Justice. With the intervention and lobby of local and international NGOs, the suspension was lifted. The perpetrator was sentenced for 18 years, and the Minister of Justice was removed from his position.

Ethiopian women are hopeful that the new millennium will bring equality, justice, and freedom to all.

Ethiopia celebrated its millennium on September 12, 2007, based on the Coptic Orthodox calendar. This holiday started in the morning with the sound of young girls' voices singing the New Year's celebration song "Abeba-ye-hoy." The girls went from home to home, giving the yellow flowers they collected from the meadow, which marks the season of hope. They looked happy and hopeful.

REFERENCES

Ethiopian Women Lawyers Association: About EWLA. Retrieved on October 9, 2007, from http://www.etwla.org.

Fidali, T. (2003). Ethiopian women of substance: Africa Prize laureate Meaza Ashenafi & EWLA. Retrieved on October 10, 2007, from http://www.tadias.com/v1n5/GRS_2_2003-1.html.

United Nations Development Fund for Women (2000). Ending discriminatory laws against women in Ethiopia. Retrieved on October 9, 2007, from http://www.unifemorg/gender issues/voices from the field/story.php?StoryID=230.

Index

About the Editor and Contributors

Michele A. Paludi, PhD, is the author/editor of 27 college textbooks, and more than 140 scholarly articles and conference presentations on sexual harassment, psychology of women, gender, and sexual harassment and victimization. Her book *Ivory Power: Sexual Harassment on Campus* (1990, SUNY Press) received the 1992 Myers Center Award for Outstanding Book on Human Rights in the United States. Dr. Paludi served as chair of the U.S. Department of Education's Subpanel on the Prevention of Violence, Sexual Harassment, and Alcohol and Other Drug Problems in Higher Education. She was one of six scholars in the United States to be selected for this subpanel. She also was a consultant to and a member of former New York State Governor Mario Cuomo's Task Force on Sexual Harassment. She is the series editor for Praeger's Women's Psychology Series.

Dr. Paludi serves as an expert witness for court proceedings and administrative hearings on sexual harassment. She has had extensive experience in conducting training programs and investigations of sexual harassment and other equal employment opportunity issues for businesses and educational institutions. In addition, Dr. Paludi has held faculty positions at Franklin & Marshall College, Kent State University, Hunter College, Union College, and Union Graduate College, where she directs the human resource management certificate program. She teaches courses in the school of management, such as "Foundations of Human Resource Management," "Managing Human Resources," and "International Human Resource Management."

Erika M. Baron received her BA in psychology from the University of Michigan. She is pursuing her PsyD in school-clinical child psychology at Pace University in New York City. Her research interests include the effects of body image on female adolescent personality development as well as gender issues in a cross-cultural perspective.

Bianca L. Bernstein, PhD, is a professor of counseling psychology, educational leadership & policy studies, and women and gender studies at Arizona State University in Tempe, Arizona. She recently completed a term as director of the Division of Graduate Education at the National Science Foundation, after 8 years as dean of the Graduate College at Arizona State University. Dr. Bernstein specializes in counseling research on stress and cognitive mediation, gender and ethnic issues, and clinical supervision, and in higher education on broadening participation of women and minorities in science and engineering careers, preparing future faculty, and reforming graduate education. Her work has been disseminated through publications in major journals and over 200 presentations at national meetings of scholarly and professional organizations. Dr. Bernstein is the principal investigator of a major research grant from the National Science Foundation to build personal resilience and improve persistence among women in science and engineering PhD programs.

Sharon Butler defines herself as a continuous learner, who is always looking for the next opportunity to mentor or coach someone to the next level of her or his career. Currently serving as a human resource director for a national technology firm, Ms. Butler has set the goal to one day teach and inspire college students. She enjoys a professional career and motherhood and believes each adds value to the other.

Patricia Campbell, DC, resides in a small town in Ontario, Canada, and practiced chiropractic medicine for 16 years before retiring and pursuing other avenues. She teaches chemistry and biology at Georgian College. She received her training at the Canadian Memorial Chiropractic College in Toronto.

Donna Castañeda is an associate professor in the psychology department at San Diego State University–Imperial Valley Campus. She completed her BA in psychology at the University of Washington and her MA and PhD in social psychology at the University of California–Davis. Her research focuses on gender, ethnicity, and their relationship to physical and mental health. She has investigated the impact of close relationship factors in HIV sexual risk behavior, particularly among Latinas/os; the HIV/AIDS prevention needs of women factory workers in Mexico; the close relationship context and how it affects intimate partner violence; and the relationship between marital satisfaction and mental health among wives and husbands.

Breena E. Coates is a professor of management for the department of command, leadership and management at the United States Army War College, Carlisle, Pennsylvania. She has a BA in English from Calcutta University and an MPA and PhD in public policy impacts on organizational behavior from the University of Pittsburgh. Her current research focuses on impacts of public policy on organizational behavior, strategic management, and leadership. A second area of interest is organizational behavior, strategy, and cultural change in the United States military.

Darlene C. DeFour, PhD, is a social psychologist/community psychologist. She is a graduate of Fisk University and received her doctorate from the University of Illinois at Urbana–Champaign. She is currently an associate professor of psychology at Hunter College of the City University of New York. There she teaches classes including "Social Psychology," "Personal Adjustment," "Psychology of Women," "Theories of Ethnic Identity Development," and "Issues in Black Psychology." She is currently a member of the board of directors of the New York Association of Black Psychologists and has served on the board of directors of the national association. She is also active in several divisions of the American Psychological Association. The theme of her current research is the exploration of the various ways that violence in the form of racism and sexism as well as physical violence affects the everyday lives of adolescent and adult Black females.

Florence L. Denmark is an internationally recognized scholar, researcher, and policy maker. She received her PhD from the University of Pennsylvania in social psychology and has five honorary degrees. Denmark is the Robert Scott Pace Distinguished Research Professor of Psychology at Pace University in New York. A past president of the American Psychological Association (APA) and the International Council of Psychologists, Denmark holds fellowship status in the APA. She is also a member of the Society for Experimental Social Psychology and a fellow of the New York Academy of Sciences. She has received numerous national and international awards for her contributions to psychology. She received the 2004 American Psychological Foundation Gold Medal for Lifetime Achievement in the Public Interest. In 2005, she received the Ernest R. Hilgard Award for her career contribution to general psychology. She was the recipient in 2007 of the Raymond Fowler Award for outstanding service to APA. Denmark's most significant research and extensive publications have emphasized women's leadership and leadership styles, the interaction of status and gender, aging women in cross-cultural perspective, and the contributions of women to psychology. Denmark is the main nongovernmental organization (NGO) representative to the United Nations for the International Council of Psychologists and is also the main NGO representative for the APA. She is currently chair of the New York NGO Committee on Aging and a member of APA's Committee on Aging.

Eros R. DeSouza is currently a professor of psychology at Illinois State University. He earned his PhD in community psychology from the University of Missouri at Kansas City. As a community psychologist, he is deeply interested in social justice. He has carried out qualitative and quantitative research on sexuality and gender issues, including sexual harassment from a cross-cultural perspective. As of 2007, he has written several book chapters and more than 40 scholarly articles; he has also co-authored almost 100 papers presented at conferences.

Margaret Gibbs is a professor in the school of psychology at Fairleigh Dickinson University. She received her PhD in clinical psychology from Harvard University. She has addressed women's issues in her research, teaching, and clinical practice.

James Gruber is a professor of sociology at the University of Michigan–Dearborn. He has published extensively on workplace sexual harassment and has presented workshops and expert witness testimony on the topic since the early 1980s. He recently co-edited a book in 2005 with Dr. Phoebe Morgan (*In the Company of Men: Male Dominance and Sexual Harassment*), which offers new directions in theory and research on the topic. Currently, he is conducting research with Dr. Susan Fineran on bullying and sexual harassment in middle and high school. Also, they are studying the impact of sexual harassment on girls who hold jobs while attending high school.

Haimanot Kelbessa was born and raised in Ethiopia. She went to grade and high school in Ethiopia. She came to the United States in 1982. Ms. Kelbessa completed undergraduate studies at the University of Houston, in general studies in 1992. She has worked in a clerical position for the U.S. Army as a civilian in Saudi Arabia. In addition, she has worked in various capacities through the years, primarily in property management. She is currently working toward her human resource management certificate at Union Graduate College.

Maria D. Klara received her BA from Boston College in 1999 and then her MS in counseling psychology from Northeastern University in 2003. She is currently pursuing her PsyD in school-clinical child psychology at Pace University in New York City. Her academic interests include women and gender issues, psychological assessment, and clinical work with adolescents.

Phoebe Morgan holds a PhD in justice studies from Arizona State University and is a professor of criminology and criminal justice at Northern

Arizona University. She teaches courses about women, crime and justice, research methods, and justice policy. Her research specialties include sexual harassment, women's complaint making, and organized claims-making. With James Gruber, she edited *Male Dominance and Sexual Harassment* (Northeastern University Press). Her research also appears in *The Law and Society Review*, the *Journal of Law, Culture and the Humanities*, the *Journal of Criminal Justice Education*, *The Women's Studies Association Journal*, *Affilia Social Work Journal*, the *Sourcebook for Violence Against Women*, *Classic Papers on Violence Against Women*, *Everyday Sexism in the Third Millennium*, *Investigating Difference*, and *The Gendered Economy*. She is currently researching sexual harassment in transnational corporations and the globalization of U.S. sexual harassment policy.

Nancy Felipe Russo is Regents Professor of Psychology and Women and Gender Studies at Arizona State University, where she is the director of the university's new Office for Academic Institutional and Cultural Change and Co-I of the NSF CareerBound project led by Bianca Bernstein. Russo is author or editor of more than 200 publications related to the psychology of women and women's issues, a former editor of the *Psychology of Women Quarterly*, and a member of the editorial board of several other journals. A former president of the American Psychological Association (APA) division of the Psychology of Women, she is the recipient of that group's Centennial Heritage Award for contributions to public policy and Carolyn Wood Sherif Award in recognition of distinguished contributions to research, teaching, mentoring, and service to psychology and society. A former member of the APA Presidential Task Force on Women in Science and Technology, she currently serves on the executive boards of Divisions 1 (General), 35 (Psychology of Women), and 52 (International Psychology) of APA. A former member of the board of directors of the Hispanic Women's Corporation, Russo has been recognized by APA's Board of Ethnic Minority Affairs for contributions to ethnic minority issues, and is the recipient of the APA's Award for Distinguished Contributions to Psychology in the Public Interest.

Marilyn P. Safir is professor emeritus in the department of psychology (specializing in clinical and social psychology). She was the founder and former director (1983–1993) of the University of Haifa women's studies program. She is also a founding member of the executive committee. Safir is a member of numerous professional organizations and a fellow of the American Psychological Association (APA) (Division 35: Psychology of Women; Division 9: Society for the Psychological Study of Social Issues 1; Division 52: International Psychology, of which she is a founding fellow). She is also a charter fellow of the APA. Safir was the first recipient of American Psychological Association's Division for International

Psychology (52) Distinguished Visiting Professorship, August 2005–August 2006. Safir was also the first recipient of the Florence Denmark and Gori Gunvald Award for Research on Women and Gender, International Council of Psychologists, 2002 (Toronto 2003). APA's Committee on Women and Psychology honored her in 1992 with Distinguished Leadership Citation for her professional contributions to the field of psychology of women both nationally and internationally. Safir was also elected member of the International Academy for Sex Research. Safir was cited in The Lexicon of 1000 Israeli Women, 1885–1985. Safir has been listed in *The International Who's Who of Professional and Business Women, 1989; The World's Who's Who of Women, 1987, 9th Ed.; 1989, 10th Ed.; 1991, 11th Ed.; The International Directory of Distinguished Service, 1986, 1st Edition.* She was singled out as one of the *100 Heroines of the World* in Rochester, New York, in recognition of her lifetime achievements in furthering the cause of women's rights, freedom health, and equal opportunities, and for serving as a role model for women and girls around the world.

Janet Sigal is a professor of psychology at Fairleigh Dickinson University. She received her PhD in social psychology from Northwestern University. Her research interests include women's issues, sexual harassment, domestic violence, cross-cultural research, and simulated jury research. Dr. Sigal is a fellow of Divisions 35 and 52 of the American Psychological Association.

Dorothy Wnuk received a BS from Rutgers and an MA from John Jay. She is currently a doctoral student in the clinical psychology doctoral program at Fairleigh Dickinson University.